Christian O. Di

A BOY
IN THE
PENINSULAR
WAR

NAPOLEONIC LIBRARY

Robert Blakeney

A BOY
IN THE
PENINSULAR
WAR

Greenhill Books, London
Presidio Press, California

This edition of *A Boy in the Peninsular War*
first published 1989 by Greenhill Books, Lionel Leventhal Limited,
Park House, 1 Russell Gardens, London NW11 9NN
and
Presidio Press,
31 Pamaron Way, Novato, Ca. 94947, U.S.A.

British Library Cataloguing in Publication Data available
Blakeney, Robert, 1789 - 1858
A Boy in the Peninsular War
(Napoleonic Library 13)
1. Napoleonic Wars. Peninsular campaign.
Army operations during Peninsular campaign of
Napoleonic Wars. Great Britain - Biographies
I. Title II. Series
940.2'7'0924

ISBN 1-85367-029-4

Publishing History
*A Boy in the Peninsular War; The Services, Adventures
and Experiences of* Robert Blakeney, Subaltern in
the 28th Regiment, Edited by Julian Sturgis
was first published in 1899 (John Murray) and is reproduced now
exactly as the original edition, complete and unabridged.

Greenhill Books
welcome readers' suggestions for books that might be
added to this series. Please write to us if there are
titles which you would like to recommend.

Printed by Bookcraft (Bath) Ltd.,
Midsomer Norton, Avon

INTRODUCTION.

OTHELLO, confessing that he cannot grace his cause with studied eloquence, pleads that at the tender age of seven years he gave himself to the grim labours of the tented field. Compared with this dark heroic babe, young Blakeney, joining the 28th Regiment as a boy of fifteen, must seem a hardy veteran. Yet he too pleads, as excuse for lack of style in the Memoirs which he left behind him, that soldiering and fighting began so early in his life as to leave scant time for acquisition of the literary airs and graces. And in the same apologetic vein he says that he wrote his Memoirs in an island where were no libraries and no books of reference in which he might verify the dates and facts of his plain unvarnished tale.

It may be that to some more literary penman the idea of writing memoirs in the Island of Zante, one of those Grecian isles which toward sunset show form so delicate and colour so exquisite that one would think them rather the kingdom of Oberon than the haunt of a retired warrior of the Peninsula—to sit at ease in that enchanted air and summon from the past the gallant deeds of heroes and the kind looks of friends—may seem no despicable recompense for the sad want of all the books of reference.

With groaning shelves and ponderous catalogues in easy reach, conscience makes cowards of us poor followers of

literature ; we are chilled in mid career, and our happy
freedom of statement is checked by intrusive doubt of the
date of this battle or of the name of that general. Even
the irresponsible purveyor of fiction must tramp the
street or fly on the handy bicycle, to make sure that he
has not plunged his hero into the midst of a revolution
two years before it took place, or shown his tender heroine
in tears over the song of an eminent composer ere yet
the moving song-writer was breeched.

How deep was the regret which the author of these
Memoirs felt for the premature end of his lessons and
for the want of invaluable books of reference, I am unable
to say ; but I have ventured to suppress his brief preface
of apology because frankly I claim for him not pardon
nor tolerance, but gratitude and even affection.

As in that island of dreams he recalled his stirring
boyhood, his friendships formed and joyous under the
shadow of death, his zeal and admiration for the great
leaders under whom he served, his personal adventures
and historic battles, his marches, bivouacs and careless
jests, his pen became again like the pen of a boy who
describes his house football match or the exploits of the
favourite hero of the school. Like a boy too, he had
his more important moments—his fine attempts at eloquence, grandiloquence ; he became literary, self-conscious,
innocently pompous, like a boy. The pen in his hand
grew great as he proclaimed the valour of the brave,
the pageant of plumed troops, the pomp of glorious war.
And indeed the pen, grown mightier than the sword,
executed at times cuts and flourishes so intricate that
the modest editor has had to bring it to the scabbard, or,
in his own language of the ink-pot, to contribute once or
twice the necessary fullstop. But these tempestuous

passages, these patches which aim at the purple, are few ;
and it should be said at once that they are never concerned
with the author's own exploits. It is the noble character
of Sir John Moore that starts the rhapsody, or General
Graham, or Paget, or Hill, or the great Wellington himself ;
and, above all, it is the indomitable valour of the British
soldier—of the British soldier who is so often Irish.

There may be some who think that Captain Blakeney
should have apologised for being Irish ; and indeed, though
I protest against any shadow of apology, the Irish nature
of our author, whose ancestors came out of Norfolk, may
be mentioned as an explanation of the frank and flowing
statement of his hopes and fears, his joys and sorrows,
his moving accidents and hairbreadth escapes. Our Anglo-
Saxon ideal of the young soldier becomes more and more
the youth who is a hero and won't mention it. He is a
most engaging person too. Ask him of the deed which
filled the daily papers and the mouths of men, and he
blushes, mutters, and escapes to his club. If you bring
all your power of persuasion to bear upon him in his
most yielding hour, you may draw from him some such
statement as this : " Well, I cut the Johnny down and
I brought the Tommy off. It was all rot, and there was
nothing in it ; any chap would have done it." That is
fine. Perhaps it is the fine flower of a race more eminent
in action than in art. But if we care for memoirs, let
us be thankful for the Frenchman or the Irishman who
will do his deeds of daring and not be ashamed to
describe them for our profit and our pleasure. Nor is it
fair to infer that there is more vanity in the one than
in the other.   In the case of Blakeney, at least, I shall
be disappointed indeed if any reader suspect him of
braggadocio. When he relates his own adventures, his

own acts in battle, his language is simple, direct, vivid ; he states plain facts. When he recalls the exploits of others—of veteran generals, of boys like himself, of private soldiers and especially of his own beloved 28th Regiment, then he cries out a little gloriously perhaps, but with a frankness, a generosity, an honest ardour of admiration which surely may win pardon from the most severe of critics.

In truth it is a gallant and charming young soldier who calls to us from the beginning of the century which is now so near its close. He has waited long for friendly recognition from any but the generals who saw him fight and the young comrades who drank with him at mess and marched with him to battle. The young comrades, like the old generals, have marched the common road ; and it is to a generation who knew not the author that these Memoirs modestly, but with a certain confidence, make their appeal.

The ardent boy joined his regiment in 1804, at the age of fifteen ; and in the next ten years he had had fighting enough to content most men for a lifetime. It is the record of these years which has lain so long in dust, and which I now offer to the reader; and I would ask him to bear in mind, as he reads, the looks and nature of the young soldier whose fortunes he will follow. He was of middle height and lightly made, but active healthy and handsome. He was eager for friendship and for fight, quick and confident in action, observing with keen accurate eyes, and so clever at languages that he picked them up on the march and conversed with the natives of Spain and Portugal and France with equal audacity and success. Perhaps more than all one finds in him that natural gaiety of heart which neither danger nor fatigue could dull, neither the want of wealth and honours nor sight of the appalling horrors of war. His young eyes beheld some deeds done at Badajoz of which the mere description has seemed to me too horrible for print. It will be held by the most bloodthirsty of readers that enough remains.

We are all most warlike now—even the peaceful guardians of the public purse and gentle editors who would not hurt a fly ; and perhaps it is no bad thing to recall the horrors of a captured town, lest we take all war to be but glory and gaiety and something to read about in the papers. Modern governments offer to the people the alarums and excursions of little wars, as the masters of ancient Rome amused their citizens with the grim combats of the circus ; and we read the daily papers in the same spirit in which the Roman crowd followed the fights of favourite gladiators or the young Britons of to-day make holiday in looking on at football matches instead of playing on more modest fields themselves. War is a bad thing at the best. Even our hero, for all his gladness and prowess, was disappointed in the end; nor have many men that abounding gift of gaiety which carried him, one may be sure, through the peaceful years of later life, happy in spite of a recurring sense of injury. If he was neither rich nor famous, he could sing, like the traveller with the empty pockets, in the presence of the robber or of the War Office. And he found pleasure too in the preparation of these Memoirs ; one feels it as one reads. He is in an amiable mood. He expresses the hope that he will hurt the feelings of no man, and all his pages are proof of his sincerity. Except for one or two Spanish generals, whom he cannot endure for the empty pomp and pride which marred the simple valour of their men, he has abundant admiration for friend and foe. He would have you know too, that when he treats of movements and of battles already described, he makes no claim to draw them better. He puts down what he saw with his own eyes, what he heard with his own ears,—that is the value of his work. To me at least he seems to give the very air of the battlefield. He is in the midst of the fight ; he makes us see it from inside, breathe the smoke, and hear the hoarse word of command answered by the groan of the wounded.

It may be of interest to some to know that this young soldier was of the Blakeney family of Abbert in County Galway, where they were granted lands in the time of Queen Elizabeth. They came thither out of Norfolk, where, I am told, there is a Blakeney Harbour, which was called after them.

The Robert Blakeney of these Memoirs was born in Galway in 1789, joined the army in 1804, and left it in 1828. Not long before his resignation he married Maria Giulia Balbi, the last of her ancient family whose name is in the Libro d'Oro of Venice ; for between her birth and that of her brother the Venetian Republic had come to an end. The little Maria was brought by her parents to Corfu. In that most lovely island of the world she grew to womanhood, and there she loved and married Robert Blakeney, whose fighting days were done.

Successive Lords High Commissioners were Blakeney's friends, and found him work to do. Under Lord Nugent he was Inspector of Police in Corfu ; under Sir Howard Douglas he was Inspector of Health in the Island of Zante ; and later, under Lord Seaton, he became Resident of the Island of Paxo. This office he held for twenty-one years, until he died in 1858 in his seventieth year.

So there came to him, when he was still young, a life of peace passed in a land of dreams. But the thoughts of the old soldier turned often to the more misty island of his birth, and to that famous peninsula made sacred to his memory by the blood of gallant comrades. His heart grew warm again as he summoned from the past the battles, sieges, fortunes of his adventurous boyhood, the happy days of youth, of friendship and of war.

JULIAN STURGIS.

CONTENTS.

CONTENTS.

CHAPTER VIII.

CHAPTER IX.

CHAPTER X.

CHAPTER XI.

CHAPTER XII.

CHAPTER XIII.

CHAPTER XIV.

CHAPTER XV.

CHAPTER XVI.

CHAPTER XVII.

CHAPTER XVIII.

CHAPTER XIX.

CHAPTER XX.

CHAPTER XXI.

CHAPTER XXII.

CHAPTER XXIII.

CHAPTER XXIV.

CHAPTER XXV.

CHAPTER XXVI.

CHAPTER XXVII.

CHAPTER XXVIII.

CHAPTER XXIX.

CHAPTER XXX.

CHAPTER XXXI.

ROBERT BLAKENEY.

—◆—

CHAPTER I.

I JOIN THE ARMY AND MAKE ACQUAINTANCE WITH THE PERILS OF THE SEA.

IN the *Gazette* of July 1804 it appeared that Robert Blakeney, gentleman, was appointed to an ensigncy in the 28th Regiment of infantry. Relying on the delusive promise that zeal would meet certain reward, I immediately joined my regiment near Cork, where they lay encamped, forming part of a corps under command of Sir Eyre Coote. On the second day after my joining, the whole of the troops marched to Kinsale, and having taken up a position on some high ground looking down on the bay, the men commenced firing ball with as much anxiety as if the whole French flotilla, filled with ruthless invaders and headed by Napoleon in person, were attempting a landing underneath. Some seagulls were seen to fall, and it was confidently reported that many others were wounded. As soon as the fight was over, the men sat down to dine with all those proud feelings which soldiers are wont to entertain after a victory. Never shall I forget the thrilling emotion which agitated my whole frame at seeing the

1

blood fall from the hand of one of the soldiers, wounded through the clumsy manner in which he fixed his flint. I eyed each precious drop that fell with glowing sensations such as would blaze in the breast of a Napoleon on beholding an old dynasty diadem, or inflame the heart of a Scot in contemplating a new place in the Treasury.

I now became on the effective strength of the 1st Battalion, which I joined the next year. Both battalions of the regiment were removed to Parsonstown, and thence proceeded to the Curragh of Kildare, where twenty thousand men were encamped under the command of Lord Cathcart. Second lieutenants were now given to all first battalion companies, so that immediately on our arrival here the three senior ensigns of the regiment, Robert Johnson Robert Blakeney and Charles Cadell, were promoted ; and thus I again joined the 2nd Battalion in camp. On the breaking up of this encampment, the two battalions of the regiment were separated. The 1st proceeded to Mallow and thence to Monkstown, where they shortly after embarked for Germany in the expedition commanded by the above-mentioned nobleman. The 2nd Battalion, to which I now again belonged, were ordered to do garrison duty in Dublin.

In the December of this year, being ordered to proceed to Exeter on the recruiting service, I embarked on board the mercantile brig *Britannia*, Captain Burrows, bound from Dublin to Bristol ; and a more ignorant drunken lubber never commanded a vessel. The wind, which might be considered a fresh breeze at leaving the port, blew hard as we entered the Bristol Channel, when our ignorant master nearly ran us foul of Lundy Island, which more through good luck than able seamanship we fortunately weathered. As we proceeded the gale became tremendous ;

the billows rolled in majestic, yet horrific, grandeur over our
heads, sweeping everything off deck; and then the master,
far from encouraging the crew and by good example
inspiring them with a due sense of the duty which they had
to perform, added to their terror and dispirited all by
his degrading and worse than useless lamentation, calling
aloud on his wife and children, then in Bristol. An attempt
was made to run the vessel into the small port of Ilfracombe, but this failed through the ignorance and terror
of the master. Still impetuously driven forward, we
approached the small village of Combemartin, when a loud
crash was heard, caused, if I recollect right, by striking
against a sandbank ; and then the captain, in his usual
consolatory language, cried out that all was lost and every
soul on board must perish. A gentleman passenger now
came down to the cabin, and, vainly endeavouring to
restrain his unwilling yet manly tears, embraced his wife
and two young children, who lay helpless in one of the
berths. The innocent little babes clung round his neck,
beseeching him to take their mamma and them on shore.
He endeavoured to soothe their grief ; but that which he
considered it to be his painful duty to impart was most
heartrending. He recommended them and his wife to
remain tranquil in their berths, saying that it was totally
useless to attempt going on deck, for all hope was lost, and
that they should turn all their thoughts to Heaven alone.
The scene was excessively affecting, and acted, I confess,
more powerfully on my feelings than all the dangers with
which we were surrounded ; for although I had lain the
whole time in my berth so overpowered with sea-sickness
as to be incapable of any exertion, I now started up and
hurried on deck just as the brutal drunken skipper was
knocked down by a blow from the tiller whilst trying to

direct it. Urged by the impulse of the moment, I seized the abandoned tiller, and moved it in the direction which I saw the late occupant attempt. At this critical moment we descried a person on horseback making signals. This gentleman, having witnessed our failure to enter Ilfracombe, and foreseeing our inevitable destruction should we be driven past Combemartin, rode at full speed along the shore, waving his hat sometimes in one direction, sometimes in another. Assisted by one of the passengers—I think a Mr. Bunbury (all the sailors were now drunk)—I moved the tiller in conformity with the signals made by the gentleman on shore, and in a short time we succeeded in guiding the vessel through a very intricate and narrow passage between rocks and banks, and finally ran her aground on a shoal of sand. The storm still continuing to blow furiously, the vessel beat violently from side to side against the sandbanks ; but some men having contrived to come off from the village, to which we were now close, and fastening ropes to the mast, bound her fast down on one side, when the whole crew got safe to land. We subsequently learned that eight vessels were that morning wrecked in the Bristol Channel.

It must be allowed that much credit was due to the fishermen of Combemartin for the alacrity they showed in giving us their assistance ; but it must also be confessed that while we remained for a few hours in the village they appeared to be the rudest and most uncouth people I ever met with in Great Britain. Every man in the village claimed to be the first who came to assist us, and as such demanded a suitable reward. Much of our luggage disappeared in being removed from the vessel to the shore, and was heard of no more. The greater part of my own goods, through my own ignorance of voyaging and the carelessness and inattention of the master being left exposed on deck, was washed away during the storm ; but what money I possessed was luckily hoarded up in my trousers pocket ; and in truth my trousers were the only part of my dress I had on during the whole time I was on deck assuming the functions of pilot and captain, the skipper being in a state of torpidity from fright and drunkenness. As soon as we could procure means of transport, which took some hours, we proceeded to Ilfracombe ; for Combemartin was incapable of affording accommodation for so large a party.

Credit was given to me for having saved the crew, but I took none to myself. It was the first time I had ever been on board of any vessel larger than an open fishing-boat, and I was consequently as ignorant of steering a ship as of training an elephant. Any part I took, therefore, was perfectly mechanical, and the inventive and true merit was solely due to the gentleman on shore, by whose directions I was guided. Being subservient to the will of another, I could have as little claim to credit for judgment or plan, principle or reflection, as could a wine-wagged billy-punch or a tail-voter in the House.

Next morning I proceeded to Exeter, but previous to my departure my attention was called to two Dublin ladies, fellow passengers, who, being bound direct for Bristol, were not prepared to meet the expenses of a land journey thither. They appeared much distressed in mind, and declared they would rather die than leave any part of their luggage in pledge. I lent them a few guineas out of my own small stock, upon which they took my address, promising to remit the money as soon as they arrived at Bristol ; but, gaining experience as I advanced, I found that I should have taken their address, for I never after heard of or from them.

After having remained some months in Devonshire on the recruiting service, I was ordered to join the 1st Battalion of the regiment, then quartered at Colchester, after their return from the fruitless expedition into Germany. We did not long remain here. On July 24th of the next year the regiment marched from Colchester to Harwich, and there embarked to join a second expedition, commanded by Lord Cathcart. So profoundly was our destination kept secret, and so ignorant were we all of the object in view, that we could not even conjecture whither we were going, until on August 8th we arrived in the Sound, and anchored late that night close under Elsinore Castle, during the loudest storm of thunder, accompanied by the most brilliant lightning, I ever witnessed. At intervals the immense fleet, consisting of men-of-war, transports and merchantmen, the islands of Zealand, the extent of the Sound, together with the opposite Swedish coast, as if suddenly emerged from darkest chaos, instantly became more visible than if lighted by the noonday sun in all his splendour. These astonishing elemental crashes and dazzling shows were as suddenly succeeded by deathlike silence and darkness so impenetrable that not an individual could be distinguished even by those who stood nearest on deck. Yet, although the ground of the night was perfectly dark, still, guided by the vivid flashes with which it was relieved, every vessel of this apparently unwieldy fleet fell into her proper berth, and, duly measuring the appropriate length of cable, swung securely to her anchor ; and, strange to say, not a single casualty took place through the whole. The scene altogether was excessively grand, and truly presented what in hackneyed poetic phrase is termed sublime. The jarring elements seemed to portend evil to the descendants of Odin, nor were there wanting some with evil eye who foreboded something rotten in the state of Denmark.

CHAPTER II.

FOR some days the most friendly intercourse was maintained between the inhabitants and the British officers. Parties from the fleet landed daily, were hospitably received, and both liberally and cheerfully provided with all such articles as could contribute to their comfort; no suspicion of our hostile intentions was even conjectured by the deluded Danes. At length, the true object of our designs being suspected, a Danish frigate which lay near us slipped her cable on the night of the 13th and contrived to get away in the dark ; but on her escape being discovered at daybreak, the *Comus* sloop of war was sent in pursuit. Since it was a dead calm, she was towed out by the boats of the fleet.

The scene is still fresh in my memory, and I fancy that I see the long line of boats manfully urged forward, our brave jolly tars, after every two or three strokes of the oars, crying out, " Hurrah ! hurrah ! for the Danish black frigate ! " At length the *Comus* came up with her in the Cattegat on her way to Norway, and after a short conflict brought her back a prize into her own port, and this hostile act put an end to all further intercourse on friendly terms. Some English boats which approached the shore next morning were fired at, and none were thenceforward allowed to land.

7

On the 15th we dropped down to Humlebek, a village about seven miles distant from Copenhagen ; and on the following day, covered by seventeen ships of the line, a proportionate number of frigates, gunboats, etc., commanded by Admiral Gambier, the military commanded by Lord Cathcart landed with fire and sword upon ground suddenly considered hostile. No previous intimation of intended hostility was given, as is customary amongst all civilised nations, when real injuries have been suffered, or imaginary ones held forth as a pretext for political aggression.

At this village (Humlebek) it was that a hundred and seven years previous to this our attack the Alexander of the north landed from the *King Charles*, the largest ship then known to the waves and carrying one hundred and twenty guns. Here it was that this extraordinary man heard for the first time the whistling of bullets. Ignorant of the cause, he asked General Stuart by whom he was accompanied ; and the general with characteristic frankness answered, " It is the whistling of bullets fired at your Majesty." " Good," replied the warlike young monarch ; " henceforth it shall be my music."

But how different were the motives which urged the hostile descent in 1700 from those which inspired our attack in 1807—as different as was the beardless Charles, not yet eighteen, in the bloom of youth, with the fiery martial genius which soon made him the terror of Europe, and burning with anger at national aggression and personal insult, from our leader, who was already descending into the vale of years, and who could have felt no greater stimulus than military discipline in strictly obeying orders which he probably disapproved ! Military excitement there was none. On our landing, no whistling bullets greeted the veteran's ear, nor inspired the young soldier to deeds of deathless glory. Laurels there were none to reap, for the defence of the capital depended principally on undisciplined militia and young students at college. To add still further to the contrast, the Swedes landed as open and declared foes, whereas we, coming with no less hostile intent, professed ourselves bosom friends.

On the night of our landing (August 16th) we advanced through a lofty forest. During our march an alarm was given that the foe were approaching. Orders were instantly issued to load with ball and fix bayonets, when many a sleek-chinned boy lost or gained the flush on his cheek. I now forget in which class I ranked, as, with many others present, it was the first time I expected to come in contact with a national foe, for such the Danes were some few hours before declared. The alarm proved false, and we felt grievously disappointed or happily consoled, according to the feelings of the individual.

Next morning we continued our march towards the capital ; but ere we reached the immediate vicinity of Copenhagen our march was interrupted by an occurrence not ordinary in warfare. A dense column of dust proclaimed the advance of some large body, which we naturally considered to be hostile. Horsemen were soon discovered, when we immediately formed in battle array ; but we soon learned that the approaching foe were no other than a civic cavalcade, who escorted the Royal Princesses of Denmark to a place· of safety, having been by special permission allowed to retire from the scene of premeditated slaughter. The royal carriages slowly advanced, accompanied by many of the principal nobility of Denmark, and attended by a small escort of dragoons. The unfortunate Princesses wept bitterly, as did many of the nobles who were with them. In witnessing their grief it was impossible to remain unmoved. The whole appeared a sorrowful funeral procession, although all were living bodies. As the royal mourners passed between our hostile ranks, arms were presented, colours dropped and bands played the National Anthem, " God save the King," thus adding to the poignancy of their woe by vain pageant and heartless courtesy. This distressing ceremony being ended, we pushed forward, and, having arrived before the destined town, each corps took up their proper position.

Our station was near the village of Frederiksborg, in a wheatfield whose golden ears o'ertopped the tallest grenadier ; the stems we trampled down for bedding, giving the grain to our sumpter animals.

This being the first time I ever adventured from the shores of Great Britain, everything was new to me and consequently enjoyed. I saw the first Congreve rockets ever fired against an enemy. They seemed reluctant to add to the conflagration, many of them in the midst of their orbit turning back to whence they were sped. I witnessed the fall of the lofty and majestic steeple, bearing the three crowns, awfully tumbling down among the blazing ruins. The loud and tremendous crash, heard for miles around, was terrific ; and it must have been a heartrending spectacle to the proud and patriotic Danes, who witnessed the destruction of such a noble monument of national grandeur. Immediately after the deafening crash, still growling in the distance, suddenly there arose an immense body of fire, which, detaching itself from the ruins, illumined the whole island, blazing in spiral form towards the heavens, as if to demand retribution. I saw well the splendour of the scene, being that night an outlying piquet with Captain (now Sir Frederick) Stovin. In the meantime the inhabitants were most liberally served with shells, shot and rockets.

While the siege was thus actively carried forward, a report was made that some Danish troops, so called, had occupied in hostile array an eminence in our immediate vicinity. A detachment were immediately sent against them, of which one wing of the 28th Regiment formed a part, and in this wing I was a feather. On our arrival at the base of this eminence we did actually discover a confused multitude congregated on the summit; but upon our preparing to charge they instantly took flight. The affair, although of no consequence, was not unattended with trophies. On the ground occupied by the discomfited Danes were found many old rusty swordblades, and very many pairs of wooden shoes, with which the Danish troops were loosely shod, for, becoming nervous at the threatened charge, they freed themselves from those encumbrances and fled in light marching order, determined, if closely pursued, rather to attempt swimming across the Belt than carry further their cumbrous pontoons. The proud victors returned to the trenches.

For what took place in the interior of the island, since I was not there, I will refer the curious to the despatches written home on the occasion, wherein these skirmishes or manœuvres, if I recollect right, are in glowing language fully detailed. All our batteries—constructed generally in the most beautiful and highly cultivated gardens, belonging to the nobility and wealthy citizens of Copenhagen—opened their fire on September 1st, which with but little intermission continued until the 6th. On the 7th, when about to be stormed, the capital surrendered, after having four hundred houses, several churches, and many other splendid buildings destroyed, and eleven hundred inhabitants of all ages and sexes killed.

As soon as the first paroxysms of furious excitement, wild

despair and just indignation of the unfortunate inhabitants
had somewhat abated, a certain number of officers from each
regiment, with written passports, were permitted to visit
the still smoking city. The spectacle was lamentable and
well calculated to rouse every feeling of sympathy. Many
houses were still smouldering, and in part crumbled to the
ground ; mothers were bewailing the melancholy fate of
their slaughtered children, and there was not one but
deplored the loss of some fondly beloved relative or dearly
valued friend. Yet they received us with dignified, though
cool courtesy, in part suppressing that horror and antipathy
which they must have felt at our presence, though some
indeed exclaimed that their sufferings were the more
aggravated as being inflicted contrary to the laws of all
civilised nations. The unfortunate sufferers seemed not to
reflect that war was will, not law.

In less than six weeks after the fall of Copenhagen
(which time was occupied in rendering the Danish ships
seaworthy, and spoiling its well-stored arsenal to the last
nail and minutest rope-yarn) we departed, carrying away
with us, as prizes, eighteen sail of the line, fifteen frigates,
five brigs, and twenty gunboats.

It would be useless to enter into further detail on
this painful subject. The partial conflagration of the
Danish capital, and the rape of her fleet by her friends
the British, are already too well known throughout
Europe, as well as the reasons adduced in vindication,
namely " precaution "—surely a most unjustifiable policy.
The great Aristides, characteristically called the "just,"
would have spurned the proposal of such ignoble policy,
as may be seen by his celebrated reply to the treacherous
proposition of Themistocles to burn the fleet of their
allies. Aristides, being deputed by the assembly to

ascertain the proposition of Themistocles, who would deliver it only in secret, on his return declared that nothing could tend more to the advantage of Athens than the proposition of Themistocles, nor could anything be more unjust. The high-spirited people of Athens, indignant that a proposition of such nature should be mooted, rejected it with contempt, not deigning even to listen to its import.

The descent on Copenhagen was a flagrant outrage of that divine precept which inculcates that " that which is morally wrong can never be politically right."

CHAPTER III.

EVERYTHING being now in readiness which we could carry away, we departed from the shores of Denmark in the latter end of October, and after a most boisterous passage, in which all the gunboats perished at sea, we arrived in England towards the latter end of November. The 28th Regiment landed at Portsmouth, and a few days later marched for Colchester. Here we occupied our old barracks, in little more than four months from the period of our departure thence for foreign service, but within that short time how wonderfully did we add to the notoriety of Great Britain! It was facetiously said that the British expeditions sent forth at this time were like the drunken Irishman at Donnybrook Fair, intent on fight but devoid of plan, who meets his friend and knocks him down for love.

A few months after my return (it being confidently supposed that the regiment would now remain for some time at home), I procured leave of absence to visit my friends in Ireland ; but shortly after my departure the regiment received orders, in April, to embark at Harwich, and join the expedition under Sir John Moore. I was immediately recalled ; but on my arrival in London I found that the army had sailed already for Sweden. I procured a passage to follow the expedition on board the *Fury Bomb*.

Here I cannot say that I felt comfortable. It was the first time I had the honour of sailing in a man-of-war. There were many ceremonies to be observed of which I was ignorant, and the close observance of these was attended with some annoyance to a novice. As usual I suffered severely from sea-sickness, which at times induced me to sit on a gun or relieve my aching head against the capstan ; and this I was given to understand was a Royal Naval innovation which could not be tolerated. Although Captain Gibson, who commanded, was very polite and frequently entertained me with anecdotes of himself and of a namesake and relative of mine, whom he stated to be his most intimate friend and brother officer, still the only place I could procure to sleep on was a trunk immediately under the purser's hammock. Even this luxury I was denied in daytime, for everything being cleared away at an early hour, I was compelled to quit my roost at cock-crow in the morning. It not unfrequently happened, too, that, running up on deck, urged by a sick stomach, I forgot the ceremony of saluting the quarter-deck, and the omission was always followed by reproof. Although a strict observance of these regulations was rather teasing to me in my irritated state of mind and body, yet I feel perfectly aware of its expediency on board a man-of-war.

Having at length anchored in Gottenborg harbour, I descended from the noble punctilious man-of-war, and was lowered into the humble transport, where I found *ad libitum* sea-sickness a luxury compared to the restraint which I had lately undergone.

I now doubly enjoyed the society of my old comrades. By these I was informed that on the arrival of the expedition at Gottenborg, which took place a few days previously, the troops were refused permission to land. About this period, although the British troops were sent to all parts as friends, yet unfortunately they were everywhere viewed with distrust, and a strict watch kept on all their movements. The prohibition to land his troops being totally contrary to the expectations of Sir John Moore, he immediately proceeded to Stockholm to demand explanation of this extraordinary conduct on the part of Sweden and also to seek instructions, having, as it would appear, received none at home.

In an interview with his Swedish Majesty the British general declined to accept some extraordinary propositions matured in the quixotic brain of that inconsistent monarch. The first was, that Sir John Moore, with his ten thousand British troops, should conquer the kingdom of Denmark ; the second, that a similar attempt should be made with like means on the Russian empire. Finally, as Sir John Moore peremptorily refused to shut up the British army in the fortress of Stralsund (then about to be invested by an overwhelming French army), he was placed under arrest by the king.

In the meantime we were actively employed in practising landings from the flat-bottomed boats, as if in the face of an enemy, and scampering over the rocks to keep the men in exercise. This salubrious mode of warfare continued without intermission until Sir John Moore contrived to have secret information conveyed to the army, when we immediately dropped down out of reach of the Swedish batteries ; and shortly afterwards, having eluded the vigilance of Gustavus, to the great joy of all, on June 29th our gallant chief arrived safe on board the fleet.

Setting sail for England on July 2nd, we arrived off Yarmouth about the middle of the month. Here taking

in water and fresh provisions, we continued our course for
Spithead ; and thence we took our second departure from
England, this time for Portugal, the more delighted since
we left our tails behind us. To the great joy of the whole
army an order arrived from the Horse Guards, while we
lay at Spithead, to cut off the men's queues. These, from
their shape, and being generally soaped for effect, were
called pigtails ; thenceforth the custom of plastering the
men's heads with soap was abolished in the British Army.

Sailing from St. Helen's on July 31st, 1808, August
19th brought us close off the coast of Portugal. Next
morning we commenced landing at Figueira, close to
the mouth of the Mondego. A large part of the army
were already on shore, and some of the troops had commenced moving forward when Sir John Moore received
a despatch informing him that Sir Arthur Wellesley
had fought and defeated the enemy at Rolica, and' hourly
expected a second engagement. The disembarkation was
instantly countermanded ; the troops on march were
recalled, and put on board as quickly as the high surf
and rapidity of the current would permit. Everything
again in sailing order, and every heart elate, we continued
our course southward, now steering direct for the theatre
of actual war ; and the true martial spirit glowed in the
breast of every true soldier.

Imagine, then, what must have been our feelings on
the following morning (August 21st) when in almost a
dead calm we moved slowly along, apparently rendered
more slow by our plainly hearing the heavy booming of
cannon, at that moment pouring forth their fury from
the heights of Vimieiro. But they alone who have been
in battle and cordially mingled in fight, can sympathise
with the feelings which thrill through every nerve and

agitate the frame of those who, all but in reach of the field, yet are withheld from participating in its glory. Intense excitement painfully marked the veteran's contracted brow, while fiery impatience flashed in the eyes of the young soldiers.

Creeping along the scarcely ruffled surface of the waters like wounded snakes or Alexandrine verse, we, seemingly in so many years, arrived in three days in the unquiet bay or roadstead of Peniche. Here, although the distant sea continued calm, still the surf so dashed against the shore that we found much difficulty in landing. When this at last was done, we immediately proceeded to unite with Sir Arthur Wellesley's troops, whom we found still upon the ground, so late the theatre of their gallant exploits. This, our first march, although but of three leagues, was severely felt, since with the exception of a scramble over the rocks in the vicinity of Gottenborg harbour, we had been for upward of four months cooped up in miserable little transports. The men had scarcely the use of their limbs ; and being so long unaccustomed to carry their packs, to which were now added three days' provisions and sixty rounds of ball-cartridge, in this their first march, with the thermometer between ninety and a hundred, many were left behind and slowly followed after. The 4th or King's Own Regiment, with whom we were then brigaded, from its seniority of number, marched in front. Although at the time perhaps the finest looking body of men in the Army, the select of three battalions, yet, being generally rather advanced in age as soldiers and heavy-bodied, they were on this day continually falling out of the ranks and flanking the road. This afforded an opportunity to one of our light hardy Irishmen (a class of which the 28th Regiment was then chiefly composed) to remark : " Faith ! this is a very deceiving march; the royal milestones are so close to each other."

Nor did the officers suffer less than the men. Being mostly very young, and with the exception of those who were at Copenhagen, where little or no marching took place, never having seen a shot fired, they were totally ignorant of the nature of a campaign. Means of transport being always very difficult to procure in Portugal and Spain, we all overloaded ourselves, carrying a boat-cloak, in itself heavy, in which was rolled a partial change of dress. Our haversacks contained, as did the men's, three days' provisions, to which was added an extra pair of boots or shoes ; and every gentleman carried a stout charge of rum on service, when so fortunate as to be able to procure it. Each young warrior too hampered himself with a case of pistols and a liberal quantity of ball-cartridge, and generally a heavy spyglass. Thus heavily equipped, many of us commenced our first day's march in the Peninsula, in the month of August, with thermometer at ninety-five. However, before we proceeded much further in the campaign, a light cart was allowed to each regiment for the convenience of the officers, which by diminishing our loads wonderfully increased our comfort.

We now fully expected to move rapidly forward against the foe ; but slow and solemn marches were substituted. Nor could we account for this extraordinary inaction, although rumour was abroad that this our first campaign in Portugal was in honourable progress through the medium of foolscap and sheepskin. Still we plodded forward, until we arrived at the plains of Queluz, about five miles distant from Lisbon, where we halted, and where our late sluggish movements were accounted for, when we heard of the

celebrated Convention of Cintra. By this the Muscovite
fleet, which by all the laws of war we considered securely
our own, were allowed triumphantly to depart from out the
Tagus with their national colours flying ; and Junot also,
with his troops and all their plunder, sacrilegiously carried
off from holy temples or wrung from the helpless orphan
or widow,—and this ill-gotten freight was conveyed in
British ships to the shores of our most inveterate foes.

The three Commanders-in-chief, with whom the more than
anxious care of the ministry contemporaneously furnished
the small army in Portugal, were recalled to England to
account for their conduct, or misconduct—one for having
offended some part of the ministry by gaining a splendid
victory, another for having offended his country by blasting
the fruits of that victory, and the third for having done
nothing but ratify a degrading convention, odious to all.
It is scarcely necessary here to state that these high
personages were (beginning with the junior) Sir Arthur
Wellesley, Sir Harry Burrard, and Sir Hugh Dalrymple.

A fourth commanding general was now appointed in the
person of Sir John Moore, destined to lead the greater part
of the British forces in Portugal against the emney.
Immediately upon this appointment the greatest activity
prevailed throughout every branch of the service. The
new Commander of the forces, although anxiously employed
in forming magazines and depôts and organising the whole
material of the army, yet appeared to be continually riding
through our ranks or inspecting the different regiments.
I recollect that the 28th Regiment were inspected the day
following the one originally appointed, in consequence of
the general not being able to attend. We stood one thousand and ninety-nine bayonets, officers and sergeants not
included. Had we been inspected the previous day, we

should have stood exactly eleven hundred bayonets, but one man was sent to hospital the night previous. After the inspection was over, Sir John Moore called the captains and officers commanding companies together, whom he thus addressed : " Gentlemen, what I have to say to you is pleasant. I have never seen a body of men in finer order than your regiment ; they appear more like the picture of a battalion than actual men bearing arms." Then addressing Captain (now Colonel Sir Frederick) Stovin, he said : " The fame of your Grenadier company has gone through the army ; but, much as I expected from report, I am more pleased at its appearance than I could have anticipated."

CHAPTER IV.

A LL arrangements being now in a state of forwardness, the army broke up the camp of Queluz about the middle of October and, following different routes and moving by regiments in succession, marched for Spain ; and an army in better heart, finer condition, or more gallantly commanded were never produced by any nation upon earth. We, the 28th Regiment, marched on the 14th. I recollect the date well, being on that day appointed to the light company.

To attempt to give a daily account of our march to Salamanca is beyond the scope of my memory ; and even though I should be capable of so doing, it would be attended with little more interest than mentioning the names of the different towns and villages through which we passed or describing the houses in which we were lodged at night. We marched with the headquarters. On the route through Guarda one battery of artillery accompanied us, whom Captain Wilmot commanded. They consisted of six light six-pounders ; and even these we had the greatest difficulty in getting through the pass of Villavelha. The first gun conveyed across had two drag-ropes attached, and to resist its rapidity while being trailed downhill these ropes were held by as many soldiers as the short and frequent turning of this zigzag descent would permit ; yet their resistance was scarcely sufficient to preserve the guns from rolling over the precipice. This in a great measure arose from Captain Wilmot having opposed locking any of the wheels, alleging that by so doing the carriages would suffer materially, and consequently become unserviceable much sooner.

Trailing the guns down in this manner was excessively laborious to the soldiers, and not unattended with danger. Several men who could not get clear of the ropes on suddenly coming to the sharp turns were absolutely dragged through the walls which flanked the road. The resistance necessary to check the velocity of even these light guns must have been very great, for I can attest that there was not one soldier of the 28th Light Company who had heels to his shoes after the drag.   They were a good deal shaken and much dissatisfied, considering it a great hardship to have a pair of shoes destroyed in one day without being allowed any remuneration.

Captain Wilmot, having witnessed the danger in which the first gun frequently was of being precipitated over the flanking wall and consequently lost, as well as the great risk to which the men were exposed, and being still unwilling to lock the wheels, determined to try the bed of the Tagus. In pursuance of this project he had the horses of two or three guns harnessed to one gun at a time, and in this manner passed the remainder of the guns in succession across the stream, cheered by the whole of the men during the entire operation, which lasted a considerable time, and was of course attended with much fatigue and exertion. The guns during their passage were accompanied by a part of the soldiers to give what assistance lay in their power, in case of meeting obstacles in the bed of the river. The horses were immersed above their bellies and the men up to their middles ; yet Captain

Wilmot never quitted the stream, crossing and re-crossing until all the guns were safely landed. The principal difficulty arose in drawing them up the opposite bank, but this being an affair of mere physical force all obstacles were soon overcome. After this, our first check, we moved on cheerily, as is usual with soldiers, who never dwell upon hardships a moment longer than their continuance.

Our next great annoyance, and I may add suffering, was caused by the inclemency of the weather. On the day upon which we marched into Guarda the 5th Regiment lost five men and the 28th Regiment two men, who actually perished on the road in consequence of heavy rain which incessantly fell during the whole day. A person who has never been out of England can scarcely imagine its violence. Let him fancy himself placed under a shower-bath with the perforations unusually large, the water not propelled divergingly with a light sprinkling, but large globular drops pouring down vertically and descending in such rapid succession as to give the appearance rather of a torrent than a shower; he may then form an idea of the rainy season which drenches Portugal during the autumnal months. Exposed to such rain, we marched many miles to gain the top of the hill upon which stands Guarda. Having at length performed this harassing march, the regiments (I think three in number) were lodged in large convents situated in the immediate suburbs, which had been prepared for our reception. Immense fires were soon lit, and the men commenced first wringing and then drying their clothing. Rations were delivered as soon as possible, and the glad tidings of a double allowance of rum loudly rang throughout the holy aisles.

The soldiers now began to forget what they had suffered during the day. The business of cooking went on cheer-

fully, but from the blazing fires which illumined the
convent much precaution was necessary to preserve the
building from being burned. The men being made as
comfortable as circumstances would permit, and there
being no accommodation for the officers in the convent,
they were as usual billeted upon private houses in the
town, each regiment leaving an officer in the convent to
preserve good order, for after hardship, as after victory,
soldiers are prone to commit excesses.

In walking through the town next day but one (we
halted there two days), I met the Commander of the forces,
accompanied by two of his staff and one orderly dragoon.
He rode to and fro in the street several times, evidently
in search of something. As I stood still, as if to ask
if I could be of any use, Sir John Moore rode up and
asked me if the men's clothes and appointments were
yet dry. I replied that they were not perfectly so, but
would be in the course of the day. He expressed his
satisfaction, adding : " You must march to-morrow at
all events. I shall not ask about your arms or ammunition ;
the 28th know their value too well to neglect them." He
then said that his horse had just lost a shoe, for which he
was in search. I also searched for a moment, but to no
purpose. The general then remarking that no doubt he
should find some place along the road to have his horse
shod, rode away. I mention this trifling circumstance,
otherwise uninteresting, because it illustrates Sir John
Moore's constant habit of speaking to every officer of his
army whom he met, whatever his rank, asking such
questions as tended to elicit useful information, and in the
most good-humoured and courteous manner making such
remarks as indirectly called forth the most strenuous
endeavours of all to a full discharge of their duties. But

when he considered a more direct interference requisite, he was prompt in showing it without partiality and regardless of persons. An instance of this took place a few days previous to our breaking up the camp at Queluz. On meeting an old officer, with whom he was long acquainted and who was his countryman, he asked him familiarly how he did. The officer answered, in the manner which men in good health usually do, that he was perfectly well, and he added : " I am totally at your Excellency's service. I have nothing to do." He hinted perhaps that a staff employment would not be unacceptable nor injurious to the service. Sir John Moore politely bowed. Next day commanding officers were called upon to use every exertion necessary to bring their regiments fully equipped into the field with as little delay as possible, and to see that every officer under their respective commands was employed with equal diligence as themselves, which he feared was not the case, for no later than the day before a major of a regiment told him that he had nothing to do. He therefore held commanding officers responsible that the particular duties of every officer should be clearly and distinctly pointed out ; and he added that this would forward the service and prevent discontent from want of employment. I was acquainted with the individual alluded to, a gallant officer who has since met the fate of a soldier in the field of glory.

After two days' halt at Guarda we continued our march without any other interruption than the falling waters, and having traversed Portugal, we on November 10th marched into Fuentes de Oñoro. This was the first Spanish town we entered, and here we halted for the night.

Villa Formosa, distant about two miles from Fuentes de Oñoro, is the nearest frontier town to Spain on that

road. The two nations are here divided by a rivulet so
inconsiderable that upon its being pointed out, many of
us stood over it with one foot in Portugal and the other in
Spain. But even if this national boundary had not been
pointed out, we should have immediately discovered upon
entering the town that we were no longer in Portugal.
The difference was very striking and perceptible even in
the first Spanish glance which we encountered. During
our march through Portugal we mixed with people who in
a manner looked up to us and showed rather a grovelling
deference. We now encountered a nation whose inhabitants
never regarded others as in any way superior to themselves.
Their greatest condescension in meeting any other people
was to consider them as equals ; superiority they denied
to all. The Portuguese showed us the greatest hospitality
and in the civilest manner ; yet their hospitality appeared
the result of some obligation or constraint, not unmixed
with gratitude. The Spaniards, though equally generous,
were proudly hospitable. There hospitality was sincere,
and not marked or rendered cold by ostentation ; it
appeared to be spontaneously offered, as mere matter of
course, unconnected with other sentiments, disdaining any
consideration beyond the act itself. The Portuguese, in
his conversation, studied more the smooth arrangement
of his specious words than the laudable sentiments by
which they should be dictated. He endeavoured by many
a ludicrous gesture and grotesque posture to add that
force to his subject which was wanting in matter ; and
whatever might be the result he always retired fawningly.
The Spaniard, invariably polite in his language and
dignified in attitude, solely depended on the soundness
of his argument, and talking looked you full in the face.
His words clearly expressed his thoughts, and he felt

hurt if obliged to repeat ; and he concluded his discourse with a graceful inclination of his person. The Portuguese are not so fine or so handsome a race as the Spaniards, and in figure they are far inferior. The females have all black eyes (lampblack, if you please), but dim and dusky when compared to the brilliant black eyes of the Spanish fair.

We passed the night at Fuentes de Oñoro with mingled feelings of annoyance and pleasure, annoyed at not being able to join the inhabitants in conversation, which in some degree we could do in Portugal. I felt quite in the background, for from what little of the Portuguese language I was enabled to pick up during the march, I had acted as a kind of regimental interpreter. Pleasure we experienced at the wonderful contrast between the people whom we had just quitted and our present hosts, entirely in favour of the latter; and although we did not understand their language, yet it fell so melodiously on the ear that I for one could never after suffer the Portuguese dialect. I remembered how Charles V. said, or was reputed to have said, that whenever he wished to address his God he always did so in the Spanish language.

Next day we marched to Ciudad Rodrigo, or the city of Don Roderick, the last of the Visigoth monarchs who reigned in Spain. Here I was billeted at the house of an hidalgo or nobleman, who treated me most hospitably, and ordered my baggage-pony to be put into his private stable. But the hatred which existed between the Spaniards and Portuguese seemed to prevail even among their animals, for my unfortunate horse was so kicked and maltreated that, after endeavouring to carry my baggage to S. Martin del Rio, where we halted for the night, the poor animal dropped down dead. Besides the in-

convenience which his loss caused me, I regretted his
death very much.   I purchased him at Queluz, near
Lisbon, and he always followed me through the camp,
keeping up with my pace like a dog.

On our next day's march we again had some work with
the artillery.   The bridge over the Huelva was too narrow
for the guns ; it was considered that too much time
would be occupied in marching over it ; therefore in
courtesy it was left for the baggage animals.   As we had
becbme partly amphibious by our aquatic march through
Portugal, and being now drenched by the incessant fall
of rain, we forded the river, immersed up to our hips
and exposed at the same time to a heavy shower.   This
operation performed, we pushed forward at a hasty pace
to the town not far distant from the bridge.   Having here
piled our arms, we returned to the stream to aid the
artillery, and hauled the guns safely across, notwithstanding the depth and rapidity of the current, now literally
a torrent.   Under the circumstances this duty was excessively fatiguing and harassing ; but the indefatigable
zeal and anxiety which Captain Wilmot showed during
the whole of the march to bring his guns and horses
perfect into action, induced every individual willingly to
come forward and put his shoulder to the wheel.

The next day's march brought us to the celebrated city
of Salamanca.   Our entrance into this city was attended
with great excitement.   It was the goal for which we
started from Queluz camp, and whenever any unpleasant
circumstance occurred during the march, Salamanca was
loudly vociferated by every lip to cheer us on.   Here it
was that we expected to join the main body of our
cavalry and artillery, who, in consequence of the im-
practicability of moving them by any other road, were,

with four regiments of infantry, the whole amounting to about six thousand men, marched through Alemtejo and Spanish Estremadura under the command of Sir John Hope.

In this place we were in the immediate neighbourhood of foes, with whom we so ardently desired to measure swords. The ardour was equal on either side. The French, flushed with recent victories obtained in Italy Germany and Spain, felt anxious to display their vaunted prowess, national flexibility in manœuvre, and tactical experience gained by all, enabling each individual to act independently when deemed necessary. The British, on the other hand, with full confidence in the result whenever they came in contact with their old foes, were desirous to prove that though partially broken they never would bend; and, proud of their ignorance of trifling detail and spurning individual self-sufficiency, were always determined to fight to the last on the ground where they stood. They restrained even their natural tendency to rush forward from a full confidence in the judgment of their general, who would move them at the right moment.

At length Sir John Hope arrived at Alba de Tormes, within a few leagues of us, on December 5th.

CHAPTER V.

WE were now in active preparation for a march, but whether to be led back to Portugal or forward to Valladolid not a soul in the army could tell. All our movements depended on the information received from the Spaniards, which to a tittle always proved to be false ; and if we had been guided by it, although it frequently passed through official English authorities, the British forces in Spain must have been lost.

The army now underwent a partial remodelling. A corps of reserve were formed, composed of select troops. They consisted of the 20th, 28th, 52nd, 91st, and 95th (Rifles) Regiments. The 20th and 52nd Regiments formed the 1st Brigade, commanded by General Anstruther ; the 2nd Brigade consisted of the 28th, 91st, and 95th Regiments, commanded by General Disney ; the whole were under the orders of General Paget.

All being prepared for a move, the British army commenced their advance from Salamanca on December 11th, with intention of marching direct to Valladolid ; but on the arrival at headquarters at Alaejos, on the 13th, an intercepted despatch from the Prince of Neufchâtel to the Duke of Dalmatia was brought to the general. These despatches were of such a nature as to induce our general to deviate somewhat from the route intended. Leaving

Valladolid more to our right, our headquarters were removed to Toro.

On the night of the 14th General Charles Stuart, with a detachment of the 18th Dragoons, surprised a detachment of the enemy, consisting of fifty infantry and thirty cavalry, cutting down or taking prisoners almost all of them. One dragoon who escaped carried the report of the destruction of the detachment, and was scarcely credited by General Franceschi, who commanded about four hundred cavalry at Valladolid ; for previous to this surprise the French were fortunately in total ignorance of our vicinity, reasonably concluding that by all the rules of war we were in full retreat towards Portugal.

The reserve, in the meantime, arrived at Toro, where the advanced guard of General Baird's corps, consisting of the cavalry under the command of Lord Paget, joined Sir John Moore's army.

It now being evident that after the surprise of their outpost at Rueda the enemy could no longer be ignorant of our advanced movements, Sir John Moore pushed on his columns as fast as the severity of the weather would permit. On the 16th the reserve were at Puebla, on the 17th at Villapando. On the 18th headquarters were at Castro Nuevo. On the 19th the reserve continued their march, and on the 20th reached Santarbas. On this day the whole of the army were united, and so far concentrated as shelter and deep snow would permit. The weather was excessively severe, and the flat bleak country could furnish but little fuel.

Lord Paget, being informed that General Debelle, with from six to seven hundred dragoons, was in the town of Sahagun, marched on the night of the 20th, with the 10th and 15th Hussars, from the different small villages where they were posted in front of the army at Mayorga. The 10th marched directly for the town, and the 15th led by Lord Paget endeavoured to turn it by the right and thus cut off the enemy's retreat; but his advance was unfortunately discovered by a patrol, and the French had time to form on the outside of the town before the 15th could get round. When therefore his lordship arrived at the rear of the town about daybreak, with four hundred of the 15th (the 10th not being as yet come up), he discovered a line of six hundred cavalry in a field close to the town and prepared to oppose him. They were drawn up in rear of a ravine which protected their front from being charged. But in those days the superior numbers or strength of position of the French cavalry had very little influence over our dragoons. After manœuvring a very short time, each party endeavouring to gain the flank of their opponent, Lord Paget charged with his wonted vigour, broke the enemy's line, and chased them off the field. The result of this gallant affair was a loss on the enemy's side of twenty men killed, two lieutenant-colonels, eleven other officers, and one hundred and fifty troopers prisoners; while the loss on our side amounted only to six men killed and from fifteen to twenty wounded.

Continuing our advance, headquarters were established at Sahagun on the 21st, and on the same day the reserve marched to Grajal del Campo. In our present cantonments the British army were within a day's march of the enemy posted at Saldaña and along the Carrion. Such close neighbourhood braced every nerve for deeds of arms. Our thoughts, which heretofore dwelt upon the sparkling eyes, beautiful faces and splendid figures of the Spanish fair, were now totally engrossed by the veteran soldiers of Napoleon. Love yielded to war; yet the flame which animated our breasts remained, its ardour ever increasing as the object in view became more glorious.

On the 22nd the whole army halted to refresh the troops, to put the guns in proper order, and, what was of still greater consequence, to repair the men's shoes, which were seriously damaged during our eleven days' march over rugged roads covered with frost and snow. Our reserve supplies had not yet come up. These preparations were diligently carried on during the day and early part of the ensuing night, it being intended that on the next day we should march against the enemy. The Commander of the forces, however, calculated that by commencing his march in the morning we should approach the enemy early enough to be discovered, but too late to attack ; and that consequently we should be compelled to halt in the snow until daybreak enabled us to see what we had to do. A night attack may perhaps succeed ; but the exact position of the party to be assaulted must be thoroughly ascertained previous to making the attack. We possessed no such information ; no two reports ever agreed as to the enemy's position or strength. For these reasons the march of the troops was deferred until the evening. Marching during the night, however severe the weather, was far preferable to a freezing halt in the snow, and the men would be in much better plight to attack the enemy at daybreak on the morning of the 24th ; and, in fact, no time would be lost, for had we marched on the morning of the 23rd instead of the evening, still the attack could not have taken place before the morning of the 24th.

In pursuance of this plan, orders were received at Grajal del Campo early on the morning of the 23rd directing that the reserve should march that evening on the road towards the Carrion, indicating the point of junction with the rest of the army, and there halt until the headquarters should arrive. On receipt of these instructions, General Paget used every endeavour to induce the men to lie down and take repose, exhorting the officers to keep the soldiers as much as possible in their billets, but, without issuing any orders on the subject, to tell them that the general's anxiety arose in consequence of a long march which was to take place that night. We (the reserve) therefore moved forward that evening about four o'clock from Grajal del Campo in light marching order, on our way towards the Carrion.

After proceeding some hours, we halted not long after dark. The whole country was deeply covered with snow, and the sprightly national carols customary on the approach of Christmas were changed for a cold and silent night march to meet our national foes ; yet no hearts ever beat lighter in the social enjoyment of the former than ours did at what we confidently anticipated would be the result of the latter. But cruel necessity required that we should be grievously disappointed. After our halt, which took place at the point destined for our junction with the other column, had continued for two hours, conjecture became various as to the cause of their delay. We were first told that it was to give the artillery, which rolled heavily over the snow, time to come up ; subsequently we were informed that the Marquis of Romana either mistook or wilfully failed in his engagements to co-operate, and that the attack must consequently be postponed. Thenceforward a hatred and contempt of the Spaniards in arms filled the breast of every British soldier. This feeling was renewed at Talavera and confirmed at Barossa, and for similar causes was kept alive so long as a British soldier remained in the Peninsula.

The report relative to Romana was not, however, in this instance strictly a fact ; for he actually did move forward from Leon to Mancilla with six or seven thousand half-starved and half-naked, wretched troops, having previously left his artillery in the rear. The true cause of our halt and subsequent retreat was Sir John Moore having received information from Romana, as well as from others in whose accuracy he placed more reliance, that two hundred thousand enemies were put in motion against him. The British general that night commanded twenty-three thousand men ; Soult, within a day's march of his front, commanded twenty thousand men ; Napoleon, with fifty thousand of the Imperial Guards marching or rather flying from Madrid, was fast closing upon him and making rapid strides to cut off his only line of retreat : thus he was placed in the immediate vicinity of seventy thousand hardy veterans—more than triple his numbers. In this statement Ney's corps are not included, although within two marches of Soult, with orders to press forward. Under such circumstances there could be no hesitation how to act. A movement on Corunna was decided upon.

The information just mentioned relative to the movements of the enemy against the British army was received at headquarters (Sahagun) about six o'clock in the evening of the 23rd, in time to enable the Commander of the forces to countermand the forward march of the troops stationed there ; but as it was too late to prevent the forward march of the reserve, orders were sent to the place intended as the point of rendezvous directing their return to Grajal del Campo, where we arrived on the morning of the 24th. There we halted the remainder of that day to get ready our heavy baggage (for we had moved in light marching order the previous night) and to give a day's start to the leading columns, Sir David Baird's and General Hope's divisions which had marched that morning; the former for Valencia, the latter towards Benevente.

On the 25th the reserve, accompanied by the light brigade, and covered by the cavalry, marched under the immediate orders of Sir John Moore, and, following the track of Hope's division, crossed the Esla by the bridge of Castro Gonzolo on the 27th. Thence we moved on to Benevente, distant about four miles. After passing Mayorga on the 26th, Lord Paget, with two squadrons of the 10th Hussars, charged a large detachment of the enemy's dragoons, strongly posted on a rising ground, and, notwithstanding the strength of their position and great superiority of numbers, he killed twenty and took a hundred prisoners.

The destruction of the bridge having commenced, and to favour this arduous undertaking, as well as to cover the passage of the cavalry, who had not as yet come up, General Robert Craufurd, with the 2nd Light Brigade and two guns, took up a position on the left bank, which from its boldness commanded the bridge and both banks, being thus from necessity left on the enemy's side of the stream, the right bank flat and low offering no vantage ground. The cavalry having crossed on the afternoon of the 27th, the destruction of the bridge commenced, which occupied half the light brigade until late on the night of the 28th, the other half being in constant skirmish with the advancing enemy. The bridge being constructed of such solid material, the greatest exertions were required to penetrate the masonry ; and from the hurried manner and sudden necessity of the march from Sahagun, there had been no time to send an engineer forward to prepare for the undertaking. These circumstances much retarded the work, and an incessant fall of heavy rain and sleet rendered the whole operation excessively laborious and fatiguing. To add to this, Napoleon, having been informed of our movement towards Valladolid, was determined to crush us for daring to advance ; while Soult, now aware of our retiring, was resolved to punish us, elate at our not having previously punished him, which we most certainly should have done on Christmas eve had it not been for the astounding information received by Sir John Moore late on the evening of the 23rd, to the effect that his little army were then the focus upon which two hundred thousand French troops were directing their hasty strides. Those two consummate generals, Napoleon and Soult, pushed on their advanced guards with such celerity that Soult's light troops and the chasseurs of the Imperial Guard came in sight whilst our rearguard were crossing the Esla.

During the evening of the 27th and the whole of the 28th continued skirmishes took place in the vicinity of the bridge, and the enemy kept up a desultory fire along the banks. The Imperial chasseurs, flushed with the capture of a few women and stragglers, whom they picked up in the plain, had the hardihood more than once to gallop up close to the bridge, with the intention no doubt of disturbing the men employed there ; but they always retired with increased celerity, leaving not a few behind to serve as a warning-off to others.

On the night of the 28th, the preparations at the bridge being completed, the troops retired. Fortunately it was dark rainy and tempestuous ; and so the light brigade passed unobserved over the bridge to the friendly side in profound silence, except for the roaring of the waters and the tempest, and without the slightest opposition. Immediately on our gaining the right bank the mine was sprung with fullest effect, blowing up two arches, together with the buttress by which they had been supported, and awakening the French to a sense of their shameful want of vigilance and enterprise. Had they kept a strict watch, and risked an assault during the passage, which they would have been fully borne out in doing from the number of their troops already in the plain, and which were hourly increasing, the light division would have been perilously situated; for Craufurd had passed over the guns some time previously, and had immediately after cut one of the arches completely through, so that the men were obliged to cross over a narrow strip formed of planks not very firmly laid, while the impetuous torrent, now swollen above its banks from the constant heavy rain and snow, roaring rather through than beneath the bridge, threatened to carry away both men and planks. All being thus happily terminated, the troops moved into Benevente; but Craufurd's brigade were so excessively fatigued, having worked incessantly and laboured severely for nearly two days and two nights, their clothes drenched through the whole time, that they could scarcely keep their eyes open.

CHAPTER VI.

WITH THE REARGUARD OF THE RETREATING ARMY.

THERE was now a large force suddenly collected in Benevente, which under any circumstances causes much confusion, but more particularly at that moment, when our chief employment was the destruction of stores. Nevertheless the duty was performed with extraordinary forbearance on the part of the men, particularly when it is considered that the Spanish authorities, either from disinclination to serve the British or from a dread of the enemy, who, as they knew, must occupy the town in a very short time, took no care whatever to supply our troops regularly with provisions, or indeed with anything which we required. The same feelings pervaded all ranks of the inhabitants ; and although with payment in our hands we sought for bread, wine, and animals to convey our baggage, yet nothing could be procured. The magistrates either hid themselves or retired ; the inhabitants denied everything of which we stood most in need, and whilst all the shops were open in Madrid and in all other towns through which the French army passed or which they held, every door was shut against the British army. It seldom fell to the lot of the reserve to sleep in a house during the movement to Corunna, but in those which we passed whilst marching along every article of food was hid with which the enemy were subsequently supplied in abundance ; and in no part of Spain was this want of good feeling towards the British more apparent than in Benevente, a specimen of which will be seen in the following anecdote :—

After the destruction of Gonzolo bridge, when the 52nd Regiment marched into Benevente, though benumbed with wet and cold, yet they could not procure a single pint of wine for the men, either for love or money, or for mere humanity which under such circumstances would have moved the breast of most men to an act of charitable generosity. During the anxious pleading to the feelings and the dogged denial, a sergeant of his company came to Lieutenant Love, of the above-mentioned regiment, informing him that in an outhouse belonging to the convent in which they were billeted he discovered a wall recently built up, by which he conjectured that some wine might have been concealed. Love instantly waited on the friars, whom he entreated to let the men have some wine, at the same time offering prompt payment. The holy fat father abbot constantly declared, by a long catalogue of saints, that there was not a drop in the convent. Love, although a very young man at the time, was not easily imposed upon. Reconnoitring the premises, he had a rope tied round his body, and in this manner got himself lowered through a sort of skylight down into the outhouse, where the sergeant had discovered the fresh masonry through a crevice in the strongly barricaded door. After his landing, the rope was drawn up, and two men of the company followed in the same manner. They fortunately found a log of wood, which, aided by the ropes, they converted into a battering ram, and four or five strong percussions well directed breached the newly built wall. Now rushing through the breach, they found the inner chamber to be the very sanctum sanctorum of Bacchus. Wine sufficient was found to give every man in the company a generous allowance. The racy juice was contained in a large vat, and while they were issuing it out in perfect order to the drenched and shivering soldiers, the fat prior suddenly made his appearance through a trap-door, and laughingly requested that at least he might have one drink before all was consumed. Upon this one of the men remarked, " By Jove! when the wine was *his*, he was damned stingy about it ; but now that it is *ours*, we will show him what British hospitality is, and give him his fill." So saying, he seized the holy fat man, and chucked him head foremost into the vat ; and had it not been for Love and some other officers, who by this time had found their way into the cellar, the Franciscan worshipper of Bacchus would most probably have shared the fate of George Duke of Clarence, except that the wine was not Malmsey.

This anecdote was told to me at the time by some officers of the 52nd. Then it was I had the pleasure of first making the acquaintance of Lieutenant Calvert of that regiment, long since lieutenant-colonel. This acquaintance was afterwards renewed under no ordinary circumstances at the battle of Barossa. The anecdote was many years later confirmed by Love himself in the Island of Zante, where in 1836 he was quartered with the 73rd Regiment, of which he was lieutenant-colonel at the time when I was writing these Memoirs. I read him the whole of these Memoirs, and found his recollection of the campaign very interesting. The dates of his commissions and mine in the respective ranks of ensign, lieutenant, and captain were within a few months of each other; but he became lieutenant-colonel long before I retired from the service still as captain. Yet he was an old soldier at the time ;

and if gallant conduct on all occasions which offered during
a long career, devoted attachment to his profession and
ardent zeal to promote its honour and glory can give a
claim to advancement, by none was it better merited. The
only extraordinary circumstance attending his promotion
was that he obtained it through personal merit.

On the 28th the divisions of Generals Hope and Fraser
moved out of Benevente for Astorga; the reserve and light
brigade remained until the 29th. On that morning the
enemy's cavalry, commanded by Napoleon's favourite
General, Lefèbre Desnouettes, forded the Esla, and as
they were taken for the advance of a large force, the reserve
and light brigades were ordered instantly to retire on the
road leading to Astorga. Although General Stuart, who
took command of our cavalry piquets, gallantly resisted
Lefèbre, and every step was met with a blow, yet the
French general sternly moved forward along the plain
which skirted Benevente. Lord Paget, who viewed from
a distance what passed at the extremity of the plain, in
courtesy allowed the French general to advance until it
became too dangerous for his troops to proceed farther;
then, at the head of the 10th Hussars, whom he had
previously formed under cover of some houses, he
rode furiously at the enemy, who, wheeling round, were
pursued into the very bed of the Esla, where "many a
deadly blow was dealt," and it was shown once again that
British steel was not to be resisted when wielded by British
soldiers determined to vindicate the superiority of their
national productions.

On gaining the opposite bank of the river the enemy
immediately formed on rising ground which overlooked
the stream, and displayed symptoms of returning to the
fight; but our artillery having interfered with some well-

directed shrapnel shots, the foe retired in disgust and pride, leaving their gallant and accomplished general behind to refine our manners, if not our steel. On his arrival in England he was sent to Bath, where he showed with what facility a Frenchman can insinuate himself into society as a man of spirit and gallantry.

Whilst our guns continued to fire upon the retreating enemy, the rearguard of the reserve were evacuating Benevente. During our march we were passed on the road by seventy or eighty dragoons of the Imperial Guard, together with their leader General Lefèbre, who were made prisoners in the affair of the morning. The general looked fierce and bloody, from a wound which he received across the forehead while gallantly defending himself in the stream wherein he was taken. In this affair our dragoons suffered a loss of fifty men killed and wounded. The French left fifty-five killed and wounded on the field, and seventy officers and men prisoners, together with their general. It cannot be said that there was any disparity of force, for although in the commencement of the affair the French were far more numerous, yet towards the close the reverse was the case.

We arrived at Labaneza that night, and next day marched into Astorga. Here we were crossed by the ragged, half-starved corps of Spaniards under the partial control of the Marquis of Romana, which circumstance not a little astonished us, as the marquis repeatedly promised Sir John Moore that he would retire into the Asturias. This un-expected interruption to our march was attended with the most serious consequences to our army, and from it may be dated the straggling which soon commenced. The Spaniards, shivering from partial nakedness and voracious from continued hunger, committed the greatest disorders

in search of food and raiment. Their bad example was
eagerly followed by the British soldiers in their insatiable thirst for wine; and all the exertions, even of the
Commander of the forces personally, were not of much
avail. We could not destroy the stores, which had to be
abandoned. The civil authorities rather impeded than
assisted us in procuring the means of transport ; nor could
rations be regularly served out to the men sufficient for a
two days' march. The troops of the two nations seemed
envious of each other, lest the depredations of one should
give it what they in their blind excesses considered an
advantage over the other. They prowled about the town
the greater part of the night, and when they attempted
to take repose there arose a contention for choice of
quarters ; so that our march was commenced next morning
without the men having taken useful nourishment or
necessary repose.

It was on that night which we passed at Astorga that
I discovered a circumstance of which I had not been
previously aware—namely, that in the light company of
the 28th Regiment there was a complete and well-organised
band of ventriloquists who could imitate any species of
bird or animal so perfectly that it was scarcely possible
to discover the difference between the imitation and the
natural tone of the animal imitated. Soon after we contrived to get into some kind of a quarter, the men being
in the same apartment with the officers owing to the crowd
and confusion, a soldier named Savage, immediately on
entering the room, began to crow like a cock, and then
placed his ear close to the keyhole of a door leading into
another apartment, which was locked. After remaining
in this attentive position for some moments, he removed
to another part of the room and repeated his crowing.

I began to think that the man was drunk or insane, never before having perceived in him the slightest want of proper respect for his superiors. Upon my asking him what he meant by such extraordinary conduct in the presence of his officers, he with a smile replied, " I believe we have them, sir." This seemingly unconnected reply confirmed me in the opinion I had formed of his mental derangement, the more particularly as his incoherent reply was instantly followed by another crow ; this was answered apparently in the same voice, but somewhat fainter. Savage then jumped up, crying out, " Here they are ! " and insisted upon having the door opened ; and when this was reluctantly done by the inhabitants of the house, a fine cock followed by many hens came strutting into the room with all the pomp of a sultan attended by his many queens. The head of the polygamist, together with those of his superfluous wives, was soon severed from his body, notwithstanding the loud remonstrances of the former owners, who, failing in their entreaties that the harem should be spared, demanded remuneration ; but whether the men paid for what they had taken like grovelling citizens, or offered political reasons as an apology like great monarchs, I now cannot call to mind. But however the affair may have been arranged, the act was venial, for had the fowls been spared by our men they must have fallen into the stomachs of our enemies next day; and it is not one of the least important duties of a retreating army to carry away or destroy anything which may be useful to their pursuers, however severely the inhabitants may suffer.

During the night I was awakened by the ventriloquists, who, with appropriate harmony, were loudly bleating, cackling, crowing, cooing, lowing—in fact, imitating every

species of animal ; so that at the moment I awoke I fancied
myself in an extensive menagerie.   Indeed, the powerful
effect of their music on many occasions during the retreat
came to my knowledge ; and so judiciously did they exert
their talents that animals of all descriptions came frisking
to their feet, offering a practical elucidation of the powers
attributed to Orpheus when round him danced the brutes.

On the last day of 1808 we marched from Astorga with
more headaches than full stomachs ; and the light brigade
having moved on the route to Vigo, the rearguard fell
exclusively to the reserve during the remainder of the
retreat.   The distance we had to move on that day being
short, we continued until late to destroy stores and such
field equipments as, for want of animals, could not be carried
away ; and after eight or nine miles' march we arrived in
the evening at a small village called Cambarros.   At
this place our evil genius, the Spaniards, again crossed us,
and the scenes at Astorga were partially renewed ; but
as only the sick and stragglers of the Spanish army were
there, the contention was but little—in fact, their miserable
and forlorn condition called forth compassion rather than
other sentiments.   Two or three cartloads of them being
put down at an outhouse where I was on piquet with the
light company, we took them in.   Such misery I never
beheld, half-naked, half-starved, and deprived of both
medicine and medical attendance.   We administered a
little of our general cordial—rum ; yet three or four of
these wretches expired that night close to a large fire
which we lit in the middle of the floor.

Our stay at Cambarros was but short, for scarcely had
the men laid down to repose, which was much wanted in
consequence of the manner in which they had passed the
previous night, when some of our cavalry came galloping

in, reporting that the enemy were advancing in force. We were immediately ordered to get under arms, and hurried to form outside the town on that part facing Bembibre. While we were forming a dragoon rode up, and an officer who being ill was in one of the light carts which attended the reserve, cried out, " Dragoon, what news ? " " News, sir ? The only news I have for you is that unless you step out like soldiers, and don't wait to pick your steps like bucks in Bond Street of a Sunday with shoes and silk stockings, damn it ! you'll be all taken prisoners." " Pray, who the devil are you ? " came from the cart. " I am Lord Paget," said the dragoon ; " and pray, sir, may I ask who you are ? " " I am Captain D——n, of the 28th Regiment, my lord." " Come out of that cart directly," said his lordship ; " march with your men, sir, and keep up their spirits by showing them a good example." The captain scrambled out of the cart rear, face foremost, and from slipping along the side of the cart and off the wheels, and from the sudden jerks which he made to regain his equilibrium, displayed all the ridiculous motions of a galvanised frog. Although he had previously suffered a good deal from both fatigue and illness, yet the circumstance altogether caused the effect desired by his lordship, for the whole regiment were highly diverted by the scene until we arrived at Bembibre, and it caused many a hearty laugh during the remainder of the retreat.

We arrived within a league of Bembibre at daybreak on the morning of January 1st, 1809, and were there halted at a difficult pass in the mountains to cut the road. It appeared that some of the leading divisions had already commenced this work ; spades, pickaxes, and such tools were found on the spot. We had not continued long at this employment when we were ordered to desist, since

Bembibre was turned by the Foncevadon road, which joined that on which we were, not far from Calcabellos, and so the work was considered useless. This order was received with the greatest joy ; indeed, there was no duty which we would not more willingly perform than that of handling the pickaxe, and that too during a severe frost and after a long night march. We therefore joyfully moved on to Bembibre.

On approaching this village, we discovered Sir David Baird's division, who had just left, and were proceeding on the road to Villa Franca. We now fully anticipated some repose, to which we thought ourselves entitled by our laborious occupation of destroying stores at Astorga the whole time we were there, and the long and severe night march which we had just terminated ; but we were sadly disappointed. The leading columns, well aware of the value and necessity of vigilance, although it was shamefully neglected by themselves, left sufficient matter behind to prevent the reserve from sleeping too much ; and when we entered the town of Bembibre and expected to stretch our wearied limbs, we were ordered to pile arms and clear all the houses of the stragglers left behind.

The scenes here presented can only be faintly imagined from the most faithful description which even the ablest writer could pen ; but little therefore can be expected from any attempt of mine to paint the scandal here presented by the British troops or the degrading scenes exhibited through their debauchery. Bembibre exhibited all the appearance of a place lately stormed and pillaged. Every door and window was broken, every lock and fastening forced. Rivers of wine ran through the houses and into the streets, where lay fantastic groups of soldiers (many of them with their firelocks broken), women, children, runaway

Spaniards and muleteers, all apparently inanimate, except
when here and there a leg or arm was seen to move, while
the wine oozing from their lips and nostrils seemed the
effect of gunshot wounds. Every floor contained the
worshippers of Bacchus in all their different stages of
devotion ; some lay senseless, others staggered ; there were
those who prepared the libation by boring holes with their
bayonets into the large wine vats, regardless of the quantity
which flowed through the cellars and was consequently
destroyed. The music was perfectly in character : savage
roars announcing present hilarity were mingled with groans
issuing from fevered lips disgorging the wine of yesterday ;
obscenity was public sport. But these scenes are too
disgusting to be dwelt upon. We were employed the
greatest part of the day (January 1st, 1809,) in turning
or dragging the drunken stragglers out of the houses into
the streets and sending as many forward as could be moved.
Our occupation next morning was the same ; yet little
could be effected with men incapable of standing, much less
of marching forward. At length the cavalry reporting the
near approach of the enemy, and Sir John Moore dreading
lest Napoleon's columns should intersect our line of march
by pushing along the Foncevadon road, which joined our
road not many miles in front of us, the reserve were ordered
forward, preceded by the cavalry, and the stragglers were
left to their fate. Here I must say that our division,
imbibing a good deal of the bad example and of the wine
left behind by the preceding columns, did not march out
of Bembibre so strong as when they entered it.

We had proceeded but a short distance when the enemy's
horsemen nearly approached the place ; and then it was
that the apparently lifeless stragglers, whom no exertion
of ours was sufficient to rouse from their torpor, startled at

the immediate approach of danger, found the partial use
of their limbs. The road instantly became thronged by
them ; they reeled, staggered, and screaming threw down
their arms. Frantic women held forth their babies, suing
for mercy by the cries of defenceless innocence ; but all
to no purpose. The dragoons of the polite and civilised
nation advanced, and cut right and left, regardless of
intoxication, age or sex. Drunkards, women and children
were indiscriminately hewn down—a dastardly revenge for
their defeat at Benevente ; but they dearly paid for their
wanton cruelty when encountered next day at Calcabellos.
The foe, rendered presumptuous by their easy victory gained
over the defenceless stragglers, rode so close to our columns
that that distinguished officer, Colonel Ross with his
gallant 20th Regiment was halted and placed in an ambush,
formed by the winding of the road round the slope of a
hill which concealed them until nearly approached. The
remainder of the reserve marched on and halted at a
considerable distance. But the French were over cautious,
and after a lapse of more than an hour, during which time
many wounded stragglers joined the main body of the
division, Colonel Ross was recalled, much disappointed by
the enemy's declining to advance. He reluctantly joined
the main body of the reserve, who immediately moved
forward. Thus every means was used compatible with
prudence to cover and protect the unworthy stragglers from
Bembibre ; and great risk was run, for we did not feel
ourselves secure until we passed the junction of the roads
mentioned, not knowing what force might be pushing
forward along the Foncevadon line.

Continuing our march at a rather accelerated pace
until we passed the junction, we arrived at Calcabellos
about an hour before dark.

CHAPTER VII.

THE Commander of the forces, with the main body of the cavalry, had marched in the morning from Bembibre, and immediately on his arrival at Villa Franca used every endeavour to remedy and quell the disorders committed there. The disgraceful conduct which took place at Astorga and Bembibre was here perpetrated by the preceding divisions. All the doors and windows were broken open, the stores robbed, and the commissaries so intimidated as to be prevented from making any careful distribution of the provisions. One of the stragglers left behind had the hardihood, although knowing that the Commander of the forces was present, to break open and plunder a magazine in broad daylight ; but being taken in the act, he was ordered to be executed, and was shot in the market-place.

After using every exertion to restore order and discipline, the general returned to Calcabellos, and met us just as we halted. We were immediately formed in contiguous close columns in a field by the road, when the Commander of the forces rode up and addressed us in the most forcible and pathetic manner. After dwelling on the outrageous disorders and want of discipline in the army, he concluded by saying : " And if the enemy are in possession of Bembibre, which I believe, they have got a rare prize.

52

They have taken or cut to pieces many hundred drunken British cowards—for none but unprincipled cowards would get drunk in presence, nay, in the very sight of the enemies of their country ; and sooner than survive the disgrace of such infamous misconduct, I hope that the first cannon-ball fired by the enemy may take me in the head." Then turning to us, he added : "And you, 28th, are not what you used to be. You are not the regiment who to a man fought by my side in Egypt. If you were, no earthly temptation could even for an instant seduce one of you away from your colours." He then rode off and returned to Villa Franca. This feeling and pungent address made a deep impression on every individual present, as well officers as men ; but the feeling of remorse was but of short duration—future temptations brought on future disorders.

Immediately on the departure of the General-in-chief General Paget placed the reserve in position, giving us to understand that our not being lodged in the village arose not from any necessity strictly military, but that it was entirely owing to our own misconduct. After the disgraceful scenes presented at Bembibre, it was not considered safe to lodge the men in houses, more particularly as we could not tell at what hour, day or night the enemy's advancing columns might be upon us. A detachment of from three hundred to four hundred cavalry (the only ones left behind), together with about the same number of the 95th Regiment, were pushed forward about two miles upon the road leading to Bembibre, to watch any enemy coming thence or from Foncevadon. Late on this evening General Paget issued an order strongly censuring our past conduct, and stating that, although we committed fewer excesses and were guilty of fewer disorders than any other division of the army, and consequently had fewer stragglers, yet we were unworthy the proud situation which we held, and had forfeited the high honour conferred upon us when we were selected to lead into action and to cover the army when required. He added that every instance of drunkenness in the troops under present circumstances was compromising the honour of their country ; but that drunkenness in the reserve was wilfully betraying the lives of their comrades in arms and endangering the safety of the whole army. The reserve must be exemplary in their good conduct ; every soldier of which it is composed must consider himself at all times a sentinel at the post of danger, consequently at the post of honour. Orders were issued that no man was on any pretence whatever to enter the town without being accompanied by a non-commissioned officer, who was held strictly responsible for the due return of those committed to his charge. Parties were ordered frequently to patrol the town during the night, and make prisoners of any stragglers they should meet.

Notwithstanding these orders, the moving appeal of General Paget, and the severe reproof so deservedly called forth from the Commander of the forces against the whole army, scarcely had darkness prevailed when stragglers from our position, with many who had escaped from Bembibre, continued their disorders and depredations, principally against the wine vats. Many were taken during the night breaking open doors and plundering cellars ; and two men were seized in the act of committing a more serious crime, that of robbing the person of an inhabitant.

Early on the morning of the 3rd the reserve marched up towards the crown of a low hill, in front of Calcabellos

on the Bembibre side. Here we halted, leaving so much of
it above us as served to screen us from the view of an
approaching foe. No enemy having as yet advanced, the
general of division ordered a hollow square to be formed,
facing inwards. A drumhead court-martial sat in rear of
every regiment, and within the square were placed the
triangles. The culprits seized in the town, as soon as tried
and sentenced, were tied up, and a general punishment
took place along the four faces of the square ; and this
continued for several hours. During this time our vedettes
came in frequently to report to the general that the enemy
were advancing. His only reply was, " Very well." The
punishment went on. The two culprits whom I have
mentioned as having been seized in the act of committing
a robbery stood with ropes round their necks. Being conducted to an angle of the square, the ropes were fastened
to the branches of a tree which stood there, and at the
same time the delinquents were lifted up and held on the
shoulders of persons attached to the provost-marshal. In
this situation they remained awaiting the awful signal for
execution, which would instantly be carried into effect by
a mere movement from the tree of the men upon whose
shoulders they were supported. At this time (between
twelve and one o'clock, as well as I can remember) a cavalry
officer of high regimental rank galloped into the square
and reported to General Paget that the piquets were
engaged and retiring. " I am sorry for it, sir," said the
general ; " but this information is of a nature which would
induce me to expect a report rather by a private dragoon
than from you. You had better go back to your fighting
piquets, sir, and animate your men to a full discharge of
their duty." General Paget was then silent for a few
moments, and apparently suffering under great excitement.

He at length addressed the square by saying : " My God !
is it not lamentable to think that, instead of preparing the
troops confided to my command to receive the enemies of
their country, I am preparing to hang two robbers ? But
though *that* angle of the square should be attacked I shall
execute these villains in *this* angle." The general again
became silent for a moment, and our piquets were heard
retiring up the opposite side of the hill and along the road
which flanked it on our left. After a moment's pause he
addressed the men a second time in these words : " If I
spare the lives of these two men, will you promise to
reform ? " Not the slightest sound, not even breathing,
was heard within the square. The question was repeated :
" If I spare the lives of these men, will you give me your
word of honour as soldiers that you will reform ? " The
same awful silence continued until some of the officers
whispered to the men to say " Yes," when that word
loudly and rapidly flew through the square. The culprits
were then hastily taken away from the fatal tree, by a
suspension from which they but a moment before expected
to have terminated their existence. The triangles were
now ordered to be taken down. and carried away. Indeed, the whole affair had all the appearance of stage
management, for even as the men gave the cheers
customary when condemned criminals are reprieved, our
piquets appeared on the summit of the hill above us, intermixed with the enemy's advanced guard. The square was
immediately reduced, formed into columns at quarter distance and retired, preceded by the 52nd Regiment, who
started forward at double quick time, and, crossing the
River Guia, lined its opposite bank. The division coming
up passed over the bridge, with the exception of the
28th Light Company, who were left behind with orders to

remain there until the whole of the reserve should have crossed, and then to follow.

General Paget now moved forward and took up a strong position on the side of a sloping hill immediately in front of Calcabellos. His extreme right somewhat outflanked the town, his left rested on the road leading to Villa Franca. The whole line was protected by a chain of hedges and stone walls which ran close in front. Our battery of six guns was pushed some way down the road leading to the bridge, to take advantage of a small bay by which they were protected and concealed from the enemy. The light company of the 28th, as soon as they retired from the bridge, were to be posted immediately under the guns, which were to fire over our heads, the declivity of the road allowing that arrangement. The left wing of the 28th Regiment were pushed forward immediately in rear of the guns and for their protection. The right wing of the 28th Regiment now formed the extreme left of the direct line. Further in advance, and extended to the left along the bank of the stream, their right close to the bridge, the 52nd were placed.

The Guia, an insignificant stream, but at this season rising in its bed, runs along the base of the sloping hill upon which Calcabellos is situated, at the distance of from four to five hundred yards, and passing under the narrow stone bridge, winds round the vineyards in which the 52nd Regiment were posted. At this bridge the light company, as has been said, were posted until everything belonging to the reserve should pass over ; and, before this was entirely accomplished, our cavalry (at first preceded by the 95th, whom they passed through) came galloping down to the bridge, followed closely by the enemy's dragoons. The enemy's advance being seen from the high ground in our rear, the battalion bugles sounded our recall; but it was impossible to obey, for at that moment our cavalry and the rifles completely choked up the bridge.

The situation of the light company was now very embarrassing—in danger of being trampled by our own cavalry, who rode over everything which came in their way, and crowded by the 95th and liable to be shot by them, for in their confusion they were firing in every direction. Some of them were a little the worse for liquor—a staggering complaint at that time very prevalent in our army; and we were so mixed up with them and our own cavalry that we could offer no formation to receive the enemy, who threatened to cut us down. At length, the crowd dissipating, we were plainly seen by the French, who, probably taking us for the head of an infantry column, retired. We sent them a few shots.

As soon as the 95th, who had lost between thirty and forty prisoners on the occasion, had crossed over and lined the hedges on the opposite side, and our cavalry, taking retrograde precedence more through horse-play than military etiquette, had cleared the bridge, the light company followed. It was mortifying to reflect that after such an uninterrupted series of brilliant achievements, their farewell encounter with their opponents should thus terminate, even although they may have been somewhat outnumbered; but neither of their two gallant leaders were present.

The light company now occupied their destined post under the guns, and accounted for not having obeyed the battalion bugles, which had continued to sound the recall during the whole time of our absence. The cavalry rode on without a halt to join the main body, then on march for Lugo.

Shortly after we had gained our position, either supposing that the bridge was abandoned by the retirement of the light company, or because their courage was wound up to proper fighting pitch, the French cavalry advanced at a quick trot down the hill. Our guns instantly wheeled out upon the road, and played upon their column until they became screened from their fire by the dip in the road as they approached the bridge. Here they were warmly received by the 52nd Regiment, now freed from our own dragoons, and the 95th ; and upon this they made a most furious charge at full speed over the bridge and up the road towards our position. During this onset they were severely galled by the 95th, who by this time had lined the hedges on either side of the road within a few yards of their flanks, and by the light company immediately in their front, whom it was evidently their intention to break through, as they rode close to our bayonets. But their ranks being much thinned by the destructive flanking fire of the rifles and of the standing ranks of the light company, their charge was vain, and, their gallant leader having fallen close under our bayonets, they wheeled about and underwent the same ordeal in retiring, so that but few survived to tell the tragic tale. The road was absolutely choked with their dead. One alone among the slain was sincerely regretted, their gallant leader, General Colbert ; his martial appearance, noble figure, manly gesture, and above all his daring bravery called forth the admiration of all. I say that one only was regretted, for the wanton cruelties committed against the women and children on the previous day were too recent to be either forgotten or forgiven.

This attack of the French cavalry was most ill advised, ill judged, and seemingly without any final object in view.

It is true that their bravery was too obvious to be doubted ; but they rushed on reckless of all opposition, whether apparent or probable, and had they succeeded in cutting through the light company, which they would have found some difficulty in doing, and although they would then have escaped much of the cross-fire of the 95th, yet they would have been in a worse position than before. When they had passed beyond the light company a hundred yards they would have encountered the left wing of the 28th Regiment, supported, if necessary, by the right wing directly on their flank, although a little in the rear ; and had their number, which was but from four to five hundred men, been quadrupled, every man must have been shot, bayoneted or taken prisoner. In fact, there is no calculating what amount of cavalry would be sufficient to force an infantry regiment formed in column on a road flanked with a high hedge on either side. I speak of British infantry, among whom no swerving takes place, each individual being well aware that his greatest safety depends on his manfully facing and strenuously opposing the foe.

At this time the Commander of the forces arrived, having left Villa Franca as soon as he heard the report of the first gun fired. He immediately withdrew the 52nd Regiment, who, as I have stated, were a good way in front of our left, and placed them on the high ground towards the centre of our position. Sir John Moore did not at all differ from General Paget as to the strength of the position, but their intentions differed. Paget took up the best possible position which the nature of the ground offered to maintain a battle, however prolonged ; Sir John Moore perceived that both flanks of the 52nd were liable to be turned, especially after the light company had retired from the bridge, which would more than probably bring on a general action of the whole reserve. This he studiously avoided, and for the best possible reasons. He was ignorant as to the amount of force with which the enemy were advancing against our position, but from all accounts he was led to believe that it was very great ; and at that time our nearest division, that of Sir David Baird, was at Nogales, distant nearly forty miles.

Not long after the failure of the charge headed by General Colbert, some French dragoons together with their light troops crossed the Guia under the high ground occupied by our right and centre. They were opposed by the 95th, who moved from the hedges which flanked the road to meet them, and a severe skirmish ensued. The enemy's cavalry, who on this occasion mixed with their skirmishers, were fast gaining ground on the right of the rifles ; the bugles from the position sounded the retreat, but were very imperfectly obeyed. Some of the 52nd Regiment, who could no longer restrain their feelings at seeing the critical situation in which their old friends were placed, darted forward from their position above to their assistance ; and the 28th Light Company, making a partial extension along the hedge which flanked the road upon which they were stationed, sent many an effectual shot in their aid.

The fight now became confused, and the enemy's numbers increased every instant. Cavalry, tirailleurs, voltigeurs, 95th, and those of the 52nd Regiment who flew to the aid of their friends, now formed one indiscriminate mass ; and the light company on the road could no longer fire except at the dragoons' heads, some few of whom were lowered. It stung us to the heart to see our gallant comrades so maltreated with aid so near ; for had we of the light company crossed the hedge under which we were drawn up, and advanced a short way in regular order so as to form a *point d'appui*, all would have been put to rights. But we durst not move an inch, being posted close to our guns for their protection, and every moment expecting to encounter another charge of cavalry.

At this time General Merle's division appeared on the hills in front of our position, and moved forward. The reserve now showed themselves, probably with a view of inducing the enemy to delay their attack until the morning. A heavy column of the enemy were pushed forward towards the left of our position, in front of where the 52nd Regiment had been posted. Their intention was evidently to cross the stream ; but their column soon becoming unveiled, our guns again wheeled out on to the road, and opened such a destructive fire that, although close to the Guia, they hastily retired, after having sustained considerable loss. Had the 52nd remained as first posted, the carnage in the column must have been immense ; but it is probable that the enemy were aware of that regiment having shifted ground, for they sent no skirmishers in front of their column. The skirmish, hitherto sharply maintained by the 95th and 52nd against their opponents, now slackened and shortly ceased. The French tirailleurs and cavalry, perceiving the failure of their infantry attack on our left, and that they were fast retiring, retired also down to the banks of the Guia.

It being now quite dark, our guns were withdrawn up to the main body of the reserve, and were followed by the light company. The 95th also fell back on to the main body ; and, leaving strong piquets along the line, the whole force moved on towards Villa Franca. Everything was now quiet, with the exception of a few shots fired from the bank of the stream in answer to some few of the 95th, who still remained behind, and, although without any cause, persisted in continuing to fire, exposing themselves by the flashes. Indeed, it was more difficult to withdraw our men from the fight than to loose the hold of a high-bred mastiff.

I have told already how during the hottest part of the skirmish the bugles from the position sounded the retreat, which was not at all, or at most but imperfectly obeyed. At this period of the retreat the reserve were always closely pursued and harassed by the enemy without their having an opportunity of revenge ; and this, from their being unaccustomed to campaigning, wrought them up to a pitch of excitement amounting to frenzy. They suffered privations, and were at the same time exposed to temptations which to British soldiers not habituated to the presence of an enemy were irresistible ; wine lay in their way and in abundance, forsaken too by its owners. Thus it was that, when on this day the French infantry first came in close contact with ours, when bayonets were crossed and blood was profusely drawn, our men were so wild and hot for the fray that it was hard to drag them from the field.

That Britons will fight to the last—that is, while they can stand—is well known ; and it was this determination that caused Napoleon at the battle of Waterloo to say that the English were beaten according to every rule of war, but did not know it. Long may they remain in this species of ignorance, and, whether feasted flushed or fasting, continue to maintain their true national character, a specimen of which was given at Calcabellos ! Some there were who fought with stomachs full, many more with stomachs empty, and some there were who, if true men, gave proof of their veracity in wine.

Thus terminated the first encounter which took place between the reserve and the foremost columns of the French infantry. It was conjectured that upwards of five hundred men must have fallen, killed and wounded, in both armies. The loss sustained by General Merle's division could not be ascertained. Calculating, however, from the depth of the column, the fitness of the range for the practice of our guns, and the celerity with which they retired, it must have been severe ; but the greatest loss was in their cavalry—a just retribution for their wanton cruelty at Bembibre.

Gratified by this preface to our future work, our morals improved by the justly merited punishment which we received that morning, refreshed by the clean sheets of driven snow upon which we had reposed, and our frames more braced than benumbed by the cold to which our own irregularities had doomed us, we pressed forward like soldiers upon whom the light of conviction had flashed and to whom physical powers were not wanting, and so marched that night to Herrerias, a distance of eighteen miles, and, if I mistake not, without leaving a single straggler of our division behind. The reserve again became disciplined soldiers, determined to prove themselves such. They gave their word of honour as soldiers to their general that they would reform, and this too while the enemy were pressing forward to bear testimony to this pledge, by the fulfilment of which they were to become the principal sufferers.

It was at this time currently reported that the cause of our sudden night march from Cambarros to Bembibre was a false alarm given to our cavalry, stating that Napoleon had entered Astorga that evening (December 31st) and was pushing forward his columns ; this of course rendered it necessary for the reserve immediately to retire, Cambarros being scarcely two leagues from Astorga. The groundlessness of this alarm became apparent through more certain information and succeeding events ; it was fully ascertained that Napoleon did not enter Astorga until the afternoon of next day (January 1st). False alarms must be expected in all campaigns, but more particularly in such a campaign as ours. In this instance the alarm proved very injurious to us. The night march of the reserve pushed on unnecessarily, harassed them a good deal, which, added to the manner in which they were employed next day in rousing the stragglers, caused them to leave many men behind in Bembibre ; and had Sir David Baird's division not been started up long before daybreak to make way for the reserve, but allowed to take some few hours more repose to give the men time to sleep away the fumes of the wine swallowed during the previous evening, some hundreds of stragglers would have been saved to the army.

CHAPTER VIII.

THE RETREAT CONTINUED.

ON leaving Calcabellos three or four miles behind, we approached Villa Franca. The whole town seemed on fire. This conflagration was caused by the destruction of stores and provisions ; and so tenacious were the commissariat in preserving everything for the flames that they had guards posted around even the biscuits and salt meat to prevent the men as they passed from taking anything away. A commissary or one of his satellites stood close to each sacrifice, who exhorted the officers as they passed to use every exertion in preventing any diminution of the sumptuous repast prepared for the hungry flames and grudged to the hungry soldiers. But notwithstanding these precautions and strict orders and the chastisement received in the morning, many of the men had the hardihood as they passed to stick their bayonets, and sergeants their pikes, into the salt pork which was actually being set fire to. Several junks were thus taken away, and many of the officers who cut and slashed at the men to prevent such sacrilege against the commissariat *auto da fe*, were very thankful that night at Herrerias to get a small portion of the salt meat thus carried off.

At this place we arrived about a couple of hours before

66

daybreak on the morning of the 4th. Being a good deal
fatigued, we halted to take some rest ; but as soon as
the genial light of morning diffused its renovating influence
over wearied mortals, we pressed forward for Nogales,
distant from eighteen to twenty miles. During this day's
march the misery and suffering attendant on wanton
disorders and reckless debauchery among the men were
awfully manifested ; some were lying dead along the
road, and many apparently fast approaching a similar fate.
Cavalry horses too were continually being shot. One
circumstance I shall mention which roused every feeling
both of humanity and indignation. About seven or eight
miles from Herrerias, seeing a group of soldiers lying in
the snow, I immediately went forward to rouse them up
and send them on to join their regiments. The group
lay close to the roadside. On my coming up, a sad
spectacle presented itself. Through exhaustion, depravity,
or a mixture of both, three men, a woman and a child
all lay dead, forming a kind of circle, their heads inwards.
In the centre were still the remains of a pool of rum,
made by the breaking of a cask of that spirit. The
unfortunate people must have sucked more of the liquor
than their constitutions could support. Intoxication was
followed by sleep, from which they awoke no more ; they
were frozen to death. This was one of the closing scenes,
brought on by the disgraceful drunkenness and debaucheries
committed at Villa Franca during the previous two or
three days. Being marked with peculiar circumstances,
the scene is still fresh before me.

Whilst I was contemplating the miseries and depravities
of human nature, and paying no heed to the frequent
discharge of pistols by our dragoons, I was aroused by
hearing my name, and recognised an old acquaintance,

Captain Bennet, of the 95th. He rode slowly and was much bent over his saddle-bow, suffering severely from a wound received the previous evening at Calcabellos. He bore up stoutly, notwithstanding his sufferings, which were manifold. His mind was afflicted with thoughts of his family ; he dreaded falling into the hands of the advancing foe, and the bodily pain which he was suffering may be imagined, as he had ridden upwards of five-and-twenty miles with a musket-ball in his groin, during a freezing night through a country covered with snow. Poor Bennet ! the only assistance which I could then afford was to give him a silk pocket-handkerchief, which I placed between his wounded side and the saddle ; yet little as this assistance was, it added to his ease, which he more gratefully acknowledged than the trifling incident merited.

The slaughter of the horses continued throughout the day. They were led to the last by the dragoons, who then, whilst unable to restrain their manly tears, became the unwilling executioners of these noble animals, which had so lately and so powerfully contributed to their heroic deeds, and with a martial spirit equal to that of the gallant riders whom they bore irresistibly against the foe. Upon my enquiring of the men how it was that horses in apparently tolerable condition were incapable of at least proceeding quietly along, the invariable answer which I received was, that from the roughness of the road, hardened by continued frost, they cast their shoes, and that they had not a nail to fasten on those picked up, nor a shoe to replace those lost ; and they added that there was not a spare nail or shoe in any of the forge carts, which retired with the cavalry. This appeared the more strange as the cavalry were the previous day at Herrerias—the " Forges," so-called from the number of blacksmiths' work-

shops there found ; in fact, the greater part of the town
consisted of forges. In one of these some of us were
quartered during the few hours we halted on the preceding night, and there we partook of our sumptuous repast,
consisting of a little salt pork and biscuit served upon
a massive plate, a blacksmith's anvil, and in place of a
superfluous nut-cracker there was a sledge-hammer to
smash the flinty biscuit.

This day's march was much retarded through our endeavours to rouse the stragglers forward, who were very
numerous, all left behind by the leading divisions. Added
to this, we were compelled to await the 95th Regiment,
whom we had left when we retired from our position at
Calcabellos late on the previous evening. Piquets of the
95th were left to occupy all the approaches leading to
the position, and the regiment halted some way in their
rear for support. The piquets were repeatedly attacked
during the early part of the night by strong patrols ;
although they lost some men, killed and wounded, they
firmly maintained their posts, always beating back the
enemy, who invariably retired in total ignorance as to
whether the reserve had evacuated or still maintained their
position. Towards the end of the night the piquets,
according to orders previously received, fell back on their
regiment, who now followed the track of the division.
As far as Herrerias all was safe for them, as well from
the darkness of the night as the start they had of a few
hours before the enemy discovered their retirement.

After Herrerias precautions became necessary. The
95th were a rifle regiment. Rifles and swords were not
so efficient as muskets and bayonets to resist an attack
of cavalry ; and our last cavalry guard had passed to
the rear early on the preceding evening. We were there-

fore obliged to make occasional halts to allow the rifles nearer approach to efficient support.

During these halts the men lay down in martial wedlock, each folding to his breast his better half—his musket—and thus enjoyed more repose than they would have done in triple the time if regularly marched into quarters ; for when soldiers come into a town they become curious travellers, and search very minutely for desirable objects— not that I rank them as antiquarian virtuosi, since soldiers care rather for the new and fresh than that rendered venerable by old age, and for quantity more than quality. A bucketful of common black-strap even would by them be preferred to a lesser portion, though it should be of the true old Falernian ; and a new polished dollar more highly estimated than a dusky old medal or coin, although its antiquity should bear date even as far back as the days of the first Darius.

In the evening, as dusk approached, and within two or three miles of Nogales, we fell in with some Spanish clothing, shoes and arms.   The carts which contained these articles were totally abandoned ; there were neither mules, mule- teers, nor guards.   Our men immediately commenced an inspection of necessaries ; and the officers (I know not why) repeated the same opposition as at Villa Franca.   But in this instance the soldiers, many of whom were severely suffering from want of shoes, were not so easily deceived, and carried away many pairs of these absolutely necessary articles, and also several pairs of trousers and other clothing.

At length we arrived at Nogales, long after dark.   By this forced march we made amends for the day we halted at Calcabellos to cover Villa Franca during the destruction of such stores as could not be removed, as well as to push forward the numerous stragglers. It also enabled us to regain our proper echelon distance from the leading columns. In this place we were very reluctantly received by the inhabitants ; so much so that in most instances we were compelled to break open the doors to get under shelter, for the owners had either fled or concealed themselves to the last moment. This latter was the case at the house upon which I, with the light company of the 28th, was billeted.

To force a Spanish door is not easy. They have large nails driven through the panels at small intervals ; these nails, or rivets, have heads on the outer side of the doors nearly the size of a halfcrown piece. And the doors are very massive—made of hard wood, generally oak ; so that striking against them with the butt ends of the muskets was totally useless. On this occasion, after knocking for some time to no purpose, we took a large stone, and, putting it into a sergeant's sash, four men stood close to the door supporting the sash, which formed a kind of sling ; others pulled away the stone as far as the length of the sash permitted, and then, adding all their force to its return, sent it with a tremendous bump bang against the door. After we (for I acted engineer on the occasion) had repeated this mode of rapping five or six times, the door became uneasy on its hinges, and the master of the house put his head out of a window, as if just awakened, and began to remonstrate loudly against the outrage ; upon which some of the men, in their desperation, threatened to shoot him at the window, and I believe that, had his remonstrances continued much longer, I should have found it difficult to prevent their carrying the threat into execution. However, it could not have been held malice prepense, since the muskets were always loaded ; and as to manslaughter or justifiable homicide, they were practising it every hour. The door being at length wheeled back on its tottering hinges, we hurried into the house ; and so uncouth were we under such circumstances—fatigued, fasting and freezing—that before we enquired after the master's health, the welfare of his wife and family, or whether he had any such, he was closely interrogated as to the state of his larder and cellar. It is lucky that we were even so far courteous, as it was the last house we entered during the retreat. By "we" I mean the reserve, always considering ourselves distinct from the *clodhoppers*— a term given by our men to the leading divisions, who were always from one to three days' march ahead, as we advanced to the rear.

Soon after we entered our billets we all became on the best terms with the landlord, who treated us very liberally ; but notwithstanding our not getting under cover until a late hour, being excessively fatigued and feeling certain that we should be engaged with the enemy as soon as the morning dawned, yet the men, except for their uniforms, resembled more a party of sportsmen after a long day's pleasant hunt than soldiers after a long and harassing march.

The officers being obliged to lie down in the same apartment with the men, we were condemned to listen to their rough jokes and loud repartees, which under the circumstances were excessively unseasonable and annoying.

"Gentleman" Roach, a title given to him from his continually boasting of a long line of ancestors, was on this night more than usually facetious. He certainly had received an education far above his present station ; but he did not rank among the best soldiers of the light company, not being a stout marcher, rather inclined to be a lawyer, and fighting his battles more poignantly with his tongue than with his bayonet. His incessant chatter annoyed the whole company, who, being anxious to enjoy a little repose, upbraided him for his loquacity.

Being no longer able to bear with his noise and vanity, which always bent towards pride of ancestry, one of the men interrupted him by crying out : " Bad luck to you and all your ancisthors put together ! I wish you'd hould your jaw, and let us lie quiet a little bit before the day comes, for we can hardly hould up our heads with the sleep."

The " gentleman," always put on his mettle at the mention of his ancestors, with indignant voice exclaimed : " Wretch ! you personify all the disproportions of a vulgar cabbage-plant, the dense foliage of whose plebeian head is too ponderous for its ignoble crouching stem to support."

" Faith, then," replied the plebeian, " I wish we had a good hid o' cabbage to ate now, and we'd give you the shrinking part,—that's like yourself, good-for-nothing and not able to stand when wanted ; and, damn your sowl, what are you like, always talking about your rotten ould ancisthors ?   Sure, if you were any good yourself, you wouldn't be always calling thim to take your part. Be Jabers ! you're like a praty, for all your worth in the world is what's down in the ground."

" Contemptible creature ! " replied the " gentleman," " if even the least of my noble line of ancestors were to rise from the grave, he would display such mighty feats of arms as would astound you and all the vulgar herd of which you appear to be the appropriate leader."

The conclusion of this contemptuous speech, being accompanied with a revolving glance, and his right arm

put into semicircular motion, including all the men as it
passed through its orbit, brought him many adversaries.

One of his new antagonists bellowed out with a loud
laugh : " Bury him, bury him ! Since all the bravery
that belongs to him is with his ould dads in the ground,
maybe, if we buried him a little while to make an ould
ancisthor of him too and then dug him up again, he might
be a good soldier himself."

" Arrah ! sure it's no use," cried out another, " to be
loosing your talk with a dancing-masther like him. Wasn't
he squeezed up behind a tree, like the back of an ould
Cramona fiddle, while I was bothering three Johnny Craps,
when they were running down screaming like pelebeens
to charge the bridge ? And, after all that, I'll engage
with his rotten ould ancisthors that when we goes home
he'll have a bether pinshun than me, or be made a sergeant
by some fine curnil that always stays at home and knows
nothing at all about a good soldier."

At this period of the noisy orgies, the night being far
advanced, with no chance of repose owing to the loud
laughter, a man of the company, who was always looked
upon as a kind of mentor, at length interposed, and by
some admirable and personal arguments put an end to the
noisy revels.

How little the minds of soldiers on service are occupied
with thoughts of the enemy from the moment they are
separated from them may plainly be seen by the merriment
which they enjoyed during the greater part of this night ;
and how reckless they are of the manner in which they
will be employed next day, and how completely their hardships and fatigues are forgotten as soon as terminated, was
also made clear on that same night : for although we had
been for the previous four days and nights either marching

or fighting or outlying piquets in the snow, yet some of the
light company returned back nearly three miles to where
the carts containing the Spanish clothing were abandoned,
in the hope of procuring more shoes, thus voluntarily adding a night march of six miles to the most fatiguing march
which took place during the whole campaign. The shoes
thus procured, as well as those carried away previous to
our entering the town, were regularly distributed among
the company, which enabled the men to march stoutly next
day. They who carried off some three, four or five pairs of
shoes supplied those who were so unfortunate as not to
have been enabled to carry away any. But the shoes were
not given as presents ; they were sold at high prices on
promise of payment at Corunna or on arriving in England.
Some of those promissory notes became post-obits next
evening along the road to Constantino, and many more
shared the same fate before and at the battle of Corunna.

Having been somewhat refreshed by our short repose at
Nogales, we commenced our march on the morning of the
5th about daybreak ; but scarcely was darkness succeeded
by light when the fight again commenced, and continued
until darkness again returned. For as soon as the enemy
discovered on the morning of the 4th that the reserve had
retired during the previous night from the position which
they occupied at Calcabellos, they had pushed forward
and by a forced march arrived at Nogales before daybreak
on the 5th. Our skirmish with their cavalry, who all
carried long carbines, was rather sharp during the morning ; but at a few miles' distance from Nogales, as we
approached a beautiful bridge, the skirmish became much
more lively. This bridge, the name of which I do not
recollect, presented a most romantic appearance. It was
situated close to the foot of a hill. The stream immediately

after passing through the bridge suddenly winding round the
base of the high ground on the opposite bank, was entirely
screened from our view as we approached the bridge, thus
giving its numerous arches the appearance of so many
entrances to subterranean caverns beneath the mountains,
into which the current rushed. On the opposite bank and
not far from the bridge, the road assumed a zigzag course ;
and to have allowed the enemy, who were fast increasing
in numbers, to come too near would have subjected our
men to a destructive fire while ascending this meandering
road. To avoid this General Paget marched us quickly
across, and having surmounted the zigzag road, halted us
just beyond range of musket-shot from the opposite bank ;
he then ordered the guns to be unlimbered and the horses
removed to the rear ; and the division then moved on,
leaving the guns apparently abandoned. At this bridge
we found a party of engineers endeavouring to destroy it,
but as the stream was fordable on either side, the party
were sent to the rear to practise their art elsewhere.

We remained at our post beyond the bridge for about an
hour, during which, although the firing continued, it became more slack. The enemy held back, evidently awaiting
reinforcements ; yet they were continually pushing small
parties across the fords. General Paget, who sat the whole
time on a slope where the light company were posted in
sight of the bridge, anxiously awaiting any attack which
might be made to capture the guns, and seeing the passage
at the fords, addressed me, saying, "You are a younger
man than I am ; run up that hill " (rather on our flank, and
round it the stream ran), "and see what force the enemy
have collected on the other side." I instantly started off,
and returning as quickly as possible, reported that the
enemy on this bank were from two to three hundred men,

infantry and cavalry, but that they were collecting in
greater force on the opposite side.   The general merely
remarked, " It is no matter," and ordered the guns to be
horsed, saying, " These fellows don't seem inclined to add
to their artillery."   Had they indeed taken the guns, which
I believe it was the intention of the general to permit, they
could never have been more warmly received, and they
would have paid most dearly for their momentarily held
prize.   The light company were posted behind a low hedge
immediately on the flank of the guns ; the grenadiers
were drawn up about a hundred yards in their rear ; the
remainder of the regiment (28th) were posted at an
appropriate distance in rear of their grenadiers, ready to
push forward, and our gallant general was present to
animate and direct.

The guns being horsed were immediately sent forward
to join the main body of the reserve, who by this time
had got a start of four or five miles, to gain which
advantage was the principal object of our halt.   But
General Paget, perceiving the great number of the enemy
coming upon him, and his flank partly turned, judged
it prudent to delay no longer, the more especially as
he had but one regiment with him in the rear.   We
therefore lost no time in following the guns.

The general, observing our disappointment at the reluctance of the enemy to come forward to attack us, took
a pinch of snuff out of his buff-leather waistcoat pocket,
and said, " 28th, if you don't get fighting enough, it is
not my fault."

Scarcely had we moved when a column of the enemy
crossed the bridge in perfect order.   Their light troops,
together with those who forded in the morning, were
soon close to our rear, when the skirmish resumed its

lively character, which was incessant during several miles'
march. Hurrying our pace about noon and thus gaining
a mile or two ahead of our pursuers, we halted on the
road (we of the light company only), at a place where
we could only be attacked in front, and that by a strong
force ; we therefore threw out no flankers. The mountain
on our left, as we turned round to face the enemy, was
stupendous, covered with snow, and rose nearly perpendicularly from where we stood. On our right the precipice
was very deep, its steepness bearing proportion to the
sudden rise of the mountain above.

The enemy, seeing it impossible to force us in front
until their heavy columns should come up, sent their
voltigeurs and some cavalry into the valley low down
on our right to turn that flank—an operation attended
with many difficulties. The country being deeply covered
with snow, the inequalities of the ground were undis-
coverable to the eye ; and it afforded us much amusement
to see men and horses tumbling head over heels as they
advanced through the valley.

It was during this short halt that an officer wearing
a blue coat rode up from our rear (we faced the enemy),
and on his enquiring for General Paget, some men of the
company sent him forward to me for an answer.

Upon his coming up he addressed me by saying, " Pray,
sir, where is General Paget ? "

As the general was not five yards distant, leaning
against the wall of the road, and heard the demand as
plainly as I did, I considered it would be indecorous in
me to make any reply. The officer with the blue coat
repeated his question rather hastily, and for the reason
already mentioned I remained silent.

The general then stood up, and putting on his hat

said, "I am General Paget, sir; pray, what are your commands?"

By a partial closing of one of the general's eyes I discovered a small shadow under the inner corner of its lower lid, which, although it did not prophesy a raging monsoon, yet clearly indicated severe weather not far distant.

"Oh, beg pardon, sir," said the blue-coat officer; "I am paymaster-general, and——"

Here he was interrupted by the general, who, advancing one or two paces towards him, said in a voice not to be mistaken, "Alight, sir!"

The gentleman complied, yet apparently as if he did not see the absolute necessity of so doing. Then, repeating that he was a—or *the*—paymaster-general, I forget which, continued by saying: "The treasure of the army, sir, is close in the rear, and the bullocks being jaded are unable to proceed; I therefore want fresh animals to draw it forward."

"Pray, sir," said the general, "do you take me for a bullock-driver or a muleteer, or, knowing who I am, have you the presence of mind coolly to tell me that through a total neglect or ignorance of your duty you are about to lose the treasure of the army committed to your charge, which, according to your account, must shortly fall into the hands of that enemy?" (And he pointed to the French advanced guard, who were closing upon us.) "Had you, sir, the slightest conception of your duty, you would have known that you ought to be a day's march ahead of the whole army, instead of hanging back with your foundered bullocks and carts upon the rearmost company of the rearguard, and making your report too at the very moment when that company is absolutely

engaged with the advancing enemy. What, sir! to come
to me and impede my march with your carts, and ask
me to look for bullocks when I should be free from all
encumbrances and my mind occupied by no other care
than that of disposing my troops to the best advantage
in resisting the approaching enemy! It is doubtful, sir,
whether your conduct can be attributed to ignorance and
neglect alone."

There were other expressions equally strong which are
now in part forgotten; yet the words, "ought to be
hanged!" have been hanging on my memory for many
years.

While the sterling and the pound-sterling generals were
thus giving and getting, the enemy were creeping round
our right flank. Soult's heavy columns were closely
approaching in front, and their balls coming amongst us
obliged us to retire. I thought at the time that the
general prolonged his discourse to give the man of money
an opportunity of witnessing how the rearguard were
generally occupied, and to show him the different use of
silver and lead during a campaign.

We now retired and soon came up to the treasure, contained in two carts lugged by foundered bullocks, moving
so slowly as to render motion scarcely visible even in the
wheels. The light company were now ordered to the
rear in double quick time, to a village called, I think,
Gallegos, about two miles distant, there to refresh and
halt until called for. This order, although we had been
fighting since daybreak, rather astonished and mortified
us; but General Paget formed a pretty correct idea as to
how we were to be employed during the remainder of the
day. As the light company passed to the rear the
regiment were drawn up close to the carts, and preparation

commenced for the fall of the dollars. As they rolled
down the precipice, their silvery notes were accompanied
by a noble bass, for two guns were thundering forth their
applause into Soult's dark brown column as they gallantly
pressed forward.

After the money had been thus disposed of, and the
enemy's column for a short time checked, the regiment
and the guard of the treasure, consisting of a subaltern's
party of the 4th or King's Own, passed to the rear. The
light company by this time had had a halt of upwards
of an hour, during which time we had some little repose,
and sparingly partook of our frugal fare ; but our modera-
tion arose more from economy than care of health, of which
there was no necessity, for scarcely had the regiment and
guard of the 4th Regiment got clear through the village
when our old friends came up and liberally supplied us
with their pale blue digesting pills. We were instantly
under arms ; and the fight proceeded, and was well
maintained on either side during several miles without
the slightest intermission, until we came to a low hill
within little more than musket-shot of the village of
Constantino.

CHAPTER IX.

THE RETREAT CONTINUED.

ON this hill the artillery attached to the reserve were embattled ; the 95th Regiment were drawn up in line on either side, and one company advanced in loose order to cover the front. The road itself was now occupied by the 28th Light Company, close to the guns, being the only bayonets present. From this position the road descended suddenly in semicircular direction down to the bridge which separated us from Constantino, a village built on the slope of another hill beyond the stream. To arrive at this further hill the road from the bridge assumed a winding, zigzag course. Against our position on this side of the stream the enemy's light troops continued to advance, and became warmly engaged with the company of the 95th thrown forward. But on their heavy column coming up and gaining a full view of our position, they came to a halt, which continued for some time—a most fortunate circumstance, for at this juncture the main body of the reserve were passing over the bridge and wending their way up the zigzag road leading to the summit of the hill on the opposite bank, on which, as soon as gained, they were placed in position by Sir John Moore himself. Had the enemy's heavy column, who were close behind their skirmishers, pushed gallantly forward, which they would have been fully borne out in doing from their numbers, they must have forced our guns and the 95th down to the bridge, and by occupying the near bank of the stream, which was very high, they would have been enabled to fire within pistol-shot into the retiring columns, and this must have caused the greatest confusion and loss.

Having at length gained confidence from increasing numbers or feeling ashamed to delay their attack, the column, doubling its skirmishers, moved forward at the very moment when, the reserve having gained the opposite bank, our guns were withdrawn and passed us in a sharp trot down towards the bridge. The 95th and the light company now began also to withdraw, but scarcely had we left the position which we held when the French cavalry occupied it. Their numbers were every moment increasing, but, knowing that our guns had not as yet gained the opposite ridge, we retired with measured step. During our movement towards the bridge the cavalry frequently evinced an inclination to charge the light company on the road; but seeing the beautiful manner in which the 95th retired, close on either flank of the road, through thickly planted vineyards, amongst which a horse could scarcely move, and knowing the murderous fire which that gallant corps would have poured forth had the cavalry attacked the light company, who with stern aspect were prepared to receive them, the horsemen declined to give us the honour of a charge.

We now approached the bridge; and the 95th, closing from the flanks, came on to the road, which here narrowed and wound so suddenly towards the bridge and so close, that, the bank being much above its level, it lay concealed until approached within a few yards. The light company now halted, and forming across the road as deep as our

strength permitted, faced the cavalry. They also halted ;
and the 95th, favoured by the sudden turn, wheeled round
and quickly crossed the bridge unperceived. We now fully
expected that the affair would terminate in a trial of
bayonets and sabres ; but although the cavalry seemed
preparing for a charge, yet, doubtful as to our true position
and not knowing what had become of our guns or of the
95th, and dreading an ambuscade such as was prepared
for them in the morning, they hesitated and remained firm.
The light company now wheeled round, and with a quick
but orderly pace crossed the bridge unmolested. By this
time the reserve had occupied their new position. The
bank, which we had just gained, was lined down to the
water's edge by the 95th and other light troops, the end of
the bridge strongly defended, and our guns admirably posted.

All this preparation was closely seen by the enemy, and
yet it was only now that they came forward in force and
resolute in attack ; in fact, the warfare at the bridge
seemed a revival of that courteous chivalry renowned in
olden times, when the advancing army delayed their attack
until their opponents should be prepared to resist the
assault. As their dense column, preceded by the sharpshooters and cavalry, pushed forward to assail the bridge,
they suffered severely from our guns, which being advan-
tageously posted above them had open play and beautiful
practise at the column ; and the sharpshooters and cavalry
who mounted the bridge were instantly shot, which caused
all their attacks to fail.

On this day the whole reserve presented a rather curious
appearance, in consequence of their being partially clad
with the raiment which they had snatched from the Spanish
carts the previous night. I recollect that Lieutenant
Cadell, of the 28th Regiment (now lieutenant-colonel), cut

a hole in a blanket, through which he thrust his head, and thus marched the whole day. Being a tall man, a grenadier, his appearance was afterwards called to mind when we saw the shepherds clad in sheepskins crossing the Pyrenean mountains on stilts. But the light company of the 28th Regiment, being better supplied, in consequence of their nocturnal visit to the carts from Nogales, appeared more diversified in their dress than any others. Gray trousers, blue trousers, and white breeches were promiscuously seen. Some wore black shoes, some white; and many there were who wore shoes of both colours. This being the company whom the enemy had in view almost the whole day, they may have been led to imagine that we were all mixed up with the stragglers from Romana's army. But their variety of dress affected neither the resolution nor discipline of the reserve; and after three successive rushes which the enemy vainly made, cavalry and infantry uniting to force their way over the bridge, they returned each time under a thorough conviction that they had been received by British troops alone—British to a nerve.

The fighting at the bridge continued. About dusk the main body of the reserve retired, leaving piquets and a strong supporting party to defend the passage. The piquets maintained an incessant fire with the enemy on the opposite end of the bridge so long as either party could distinguish the other; darkness intervening, the firing ceased. After remaining quiet for some time and lighting our fires, and no movement being perceived on the opposite bank, the piquets and supports were silently withdrawn about half-past eleven o'clock and followed the track of the main body, whom we joined about dawn on march to Lugo.

This morning's march was heavy; for the enemy's cavalry alone having come up and keeping rather distant, the men complained of not having an enlivening shot to break the dreary monotony. However, we were soon gratified by seeing the whole British army in position about three miles in front of Lugo.

We marched through the brigade of guards, who were for the most part in their shirts and trousers, and in the act of cooking. All their appointments swung airily from the branches of trees. As we passed, some of the officers asked Major Browne if we had heard anything of the French. "I'll tell you what, my honest lads," replied Browne, "you had better take down your pipeclayed belts from those trees, put them on, and eat your dinners, if you have any, as quick as you can; otherwise you may not have an opportunity of finishing them." The guards laughed with an air of incredulity. We marched on, but had not proceeded half a mile when we heard our guns, which were placed in the position mentioned, open on the advancing enemy. We now laughed in our turn at the guards, and continued our march to Lugo, where we arrived about two o'clock in the afternoon.

We were instantly ordered to commence pipeclaying our belts, and to polish or clean every part of our appointments. This was considered useless hardship ; for grumbling at any orders, even supposed to come from the Commander of the forces, was the order of the day, and few considered that this very pipeclaying and polishing most powerfully tended to restore that discipline throughout the army which was so shamefully neglected during the march.

On the morning of the 7th we turned out at daybreak, although it rained heavily, as clean as if we had just come out of our barrack-room in Colchester, and marched as orderly into position in front of Lugo as if crossing parade-ground in England. Here we remained the whole of the 7th and 8th to no purpose : for although Soult came up on the morning of the former day, he merely made one or two demonstrations to feel our strength and find out whether the whole British army were there or not ; and although he received a loudly affirmative answer wherever he moved, yet from the morning until the night of the 8th the French army slept. For, however active Soult was on the 7th in feeling his way along our position, by which he sacrificed nearly four hundred men, on the 8th not a shot was fired ; and thus Sir John Moore evidently perceived that it was not the French marshal's intention to attack until he should be joined by an overwhelming force, which he knew was fast approaching.

Nothing remained then for the British general but to retire. To attack Soult commanding a stronger force than his own, and holding a stronger position, would be preposterous ; the most favourable result which could occur would be to gain a victory, which, with a second stronger force close by, would be worse than useless, as it would increase the delay and consequently the peril. We had no hospitals, no transports for sick or wounded, no magazines, no provisions, not even spare ammunition, and not the shadow of an ally to support us.

Whatever Sir John Moore's wishes as to fighting a battle at that period of the campaign might have been, it is certain that he considered a halt necessary to restore order and good conduct in the army. To this effect the general issued a pungent order, censuring the want of discipline among the men, and the neglect of those whose principal duty it was to preserve it.

Having fully succeeded in restoring discipline, and in a

great measure remedying the immediate wants of the army, he determined without further delay to continue his march to Corunna. The army therefore retired from Lugo at half-past nine o'clock on the night of the 8th ; and had we had twelve hours of tolerably clement weather or even half that time, our march would have been comparatively prosperous. But fortune seldom favoured us ; storms of sleet rain and wind immediately assailed us on quitting our ground.

The reserve arrived without fail on the road leading to Corunna, as was previously ordered, and was the only division, as well as I recollect, who did arrive at the time appointed. The other divisions, having missed their way, wandered about the greater part of the night before they gained the road ; therefore the reserve (the proper rearguard) moved forward, but slowly, making frequent halts to await the arrival of the misled divisions. Frequent halts and slow marching between—always very detrimental to marching—was on this occasion doubly harassing to the reserve. We felt all the fatigue and anxiety of a rearguard, with most of our own troops behind us. On the approach of any number of persons we were immediately on the alert, not knowing whether to receive friends or resist foes. The night being pitch dark and rainy, this continual halting and turning round was excessively tormenting ; and the men, from whom the true cause was kept concealed, grumbled much at what they termed this cockney kind of marching, to which they were not accustomed. Add to this that General Paget gave a most positive order that no man should on any account whatever quit the ranks or get off the road, not even during any of our halts. This may appear harsh, but if the strictest discipline had not been maintained in the reserve, the army, would have been exposed to imminent danger. Had the disgraceful scenes which occurred at Bembibre taken place now in the reserve, with a veteran army close at our heels and commanded by such an officer as Soult, the result must have been too evident to require comment.

On the morning of the 9th the wandering divisions having come up, the whole army halted for some hours in the rain, after which to our great joy the main body, with the cavalry in their front, moved on, and the reserve fell into its proper place, the rearguard. We allowed them to get as far ahead as possible, and then again felt, as we had done all through the retreat, a different corps and differently organised from the other divisions; nor did we feel the same confidence in them, except when drawn up before the enemy, when the general character of British soldiers caused all distinctions to cease.

But one of our greatest plagues was still to come. Some of the divisions in front, instead of keeping together on the road during a halt, which took place on the approach of the night of the 9th, were permitted to separate and go into buildings; and on their divisions marching off, immense numbers were left behind, so that when the reserve came up we were halted to rouse up the stragglers. In many instances we succeeded, but generally failed; we kicked, thumped, struck with the butt ends of the fire-locks, pricked with swords and bayonets, but to little purpose. There were three or four detached buildings in which some wine was found, and which also contained a large quantity of hay; and between the effects of the wine and the inviting warmth of the hay it was totally impossible to move the men. And here I must confess that some even of the reserve, absolutely exhausted from the exertions they used in arousing the slothful of other divisions to a sense of their duty, and not having seen anything so luxurious as this hay since the night of December 22nd (the one previous to our march from Grajal del Campo), could not resist the temptation ; and in the partial absence of the officers, who were rousing up other stragglers, sat and from that sunk down probably with the intention of taking only a few minutes' repose ; yet they too remained behind.

The division at this time were excessively harassed and fatigued. We had formed an outlying piquet for the whole army on the night of the 7th at Lugo, all the other troops being put under cover. Our occupation on the night of the 8th and the following day and night was still more harassing ; and here I must say that all our losses (those fallen in action excepted) arose from our contiguity to the main body.

After having used every exertion to stimulate the stragglers to move forward, we continued our march for about a mile and a half, and then took up a position, thus affording support to the stragglers and covering the army, who had previously marched into Betanzos, about three miles distant.

During this disastrous march from Lugo to Betanzos more men had fallen away from the ranks than during the whole previous part of the campaign. The destruction of several bridges was attempted, but a failure was the invariable result.

On the 10th the whole army halted. The main body remained in the town of Betanzos ; the reserve maintained its position in bivouac.

Directing our attention towards the stragglers as soon as day dawned, we discovered them formed in tolerably good order, resisting the French cavalry and retiring up the road to where we were in position. General Paget saw the whole affair, and perceiving that they were capable of defending themselves, deemed it unnecessary to send them any support ; but he declared in presence of the men, who from a natural impulse wished to move down against the cavalry, that his reason for withholding support was that he would not sacrifice the life of one good soldier who had stuck to his colours to save the whole horde of those drunken marauders who by their disgraceful conduct placed themselves at the mercy of their enemies.

The stragglers by this time became formidable ; and the enemy's cavalry having lost some men, and seeing the reserve strongly posted, declined to follow further this newly formed levy *en masse*, who, true to their system, straggled up the hill to our bivouac.

This affair between the stragglers and the cavalry was termed by the men the battle of the Panniers, from the following circumstance. A soldier of the 28th Regiment, really a good man, who had the mule of Doctor Dacres, to whom he was batman, having fallen in the rear because the animal which carried the surgeon's panniers was unable to keep up with the regiment, stopped at the houses mentioned ; and, getting up before day-break to follow the regiment he was the first to discover the enemy as they advanced rather cautiously, no doubt taking the stragglers for our proper rearguard. The doctor's man shouted to the stragglers to get up and defend themselves against the French cavalry ; but before they could unite into anything like a compact body, some were sabred or taken. He then gallantly took command of all those who, roused to a sense of danger, contrived a formation, until, to use his own words, he was superseded by a senior officer, a sergeant, who then assumed supreme command ; upon which General Panniers, with his mule, retired up the hill to where the reserve were posted. I understand that the sergeant got a commission for his good conduct among the stragglers ; but the poor batman was neglected—a not unusual instance of " Sic vos non vobis " in the British army.

On the stragglers perceiving that they were no longer pursued by the dragoons, they showed strong inclination to straggle anew and keep aloof; but a strong piquet was now sent to meet them, not for their assistance, but to prick them forward and compel them to close upon the division. A guard was thrown across the road at the entrance to our position, through which all the stragglers must pass. Each man as he came up had his pack and haversack taken off and closely searched ; and all the money found upon them which it was fully ascertained could have been acquired by robbery only was collected in a heap and distributed among the men who never swerved from their colours, thus rewarding the meritorious and well disciplined to the mortification of those who disgraced their profession. The sum thus collected amounted to a great deal ; for many plunderers abandoned their ranks at an early period of the retreat, contriving to keep between the reserve and the other divisions, or keeping between the contending armies or on their flanks. But it is totally impossible to enumerate the different articles of plunder which they contrived to cram into their packs and haversacks. Brass candlesticks bent double, bundles of common knives, copper saucepans hammered into masses, every sort of domestic utensil which could be forced into their packs, were found upon them without any regard as to value or weight ; and the

greater number carried double the weight imposed by
military regulations or necessity. On this day upwards
of fifteen hundred robust marauders, heavily laden with
plunder, passed through the rearguard of the reserve.
Those belonging to the division were of course halted ;
but the great body were sent under escort to Betanzos,
there to be dealt with by their different corps.

CHAPTER X.

THIS night we passed in feasting, supplies of provision having been sent out from Corunna; and the commissary gave our mess a canteen full of rum, some biscuits, and an extra piece of salt pork in exchange for a wax candle, which enabled him to serve out the rations and saved him from error in securing his own slight portion. We were excessively happy at the exchange, as it enabled us to entertain some friends that night ; and we felt proud at furnishing the candle, which was not the less appreciated for being in the first instance sacrilegiously plundered from a church by the stragglers, then violently wrested from them by the light company, and finally returning to the purpose for which it was originally intended, and religiously expiring in throwing light on the works of the commissary.

After two nights' uninterrupted repose in comfortable quarters, the main body of the army, under the immediate command of the General-in-chief, marched from Betanzos on the morning of the 11th, followed by the reserve from their bivouac at due distance, and the reserve, as usual, closely attended by Soult's advanced guard, headed by Franceschi's light cavalry. On this day they were not very pressing until after we had crossed the bridge of Betanzos. Close to this bridge the 28th Regiment were

94

halted to protect the engineer officer and party employed to blow it up, all the necessary preparations having, it was supposed, taken place the day previously. The desired explosion now took place by which it was confidently expected that for a short time at least we should be separated from our teasing pursuers, and thus be enabled to arrive in good order before Corunna. Our expectations were, however, blasted by the explosion itself; for as soon as the rubbish had fallen down and the smoke cleared away, to our great surprise and annoyance we perceived that one half of one arch only had been destroyed, the other half and one of the battlements remaining firm.

On witnessing the abortive result of all this labour and fuss, General Paget, who was close by, exclaimed in astonishment, " What, another abortion ! And pray, sir, how do you account for this failure ? "

The engineer officer replied that he could account for it in no other way than that the barrel of powder which effected the partial destruction had in its explosion either choked or shaken from its direction the train leading to the second barrel, which consequently still remained whole in the undemolished part of the arch.

Upon this the general demanded to know within what period of time the disaster could be remedied.

" In less than twenty minutes, sir," was the engineer's reply.

" Very well, sir," said General Paget ; and then, turning to me, he said, " Go over the bridge."

I considered this order to be addressed to me individually, for the purpose of reconnoitring, a service in which the general had frequently employed me during the march ; and, taking a rapid view of the probable conse-

quences of passing over the smouldering embers of the
half-choked train, which might still revive and creep its
way to the second barrel, however flattered at being
selected, yet I confess I did not relish the affair. But
whatever my sensations, they were my own private
property ; my person, I felt fully aware, belonged to my
king and country.

Immediately moving forward to the bridge, I found
that the order to cross it was intended not for me alone ;
the whole light company and the grenadiers were ordered
to cross over. The main road led directly forward
through the town of Betanzos ; but close to the end of
the bridge which we now approached a branch road
turned off at a right angle, winding round the base of
the hill upon which Betanzos stands. At this angle and
on the side of the road next the bridge was a large
house, which intercepted the view between the bridge
and the turn of the branch road ; and so we got on to
the wrong road by mistake.

Captain Gomm, General Disney's major of brigade, was
sent to recall us, when we of course turned round, followed
by the French cavalry at a short distance, within which
they could easily keep, in consequence of the winding nature
of the road.

As soon as the grenadiers, who now led, turned the
angle of the road above mentioned they were immediately
on the bridge, and, never forgetting the barrel of powder,
they, followed by the light company, moved in double
quick time over the narrow part of the bridge—by the men
called the Devil's Neck.

The enemy, perceiving us in such a hurry, no doubt
attributed the haste to timidity (and it may be remarked
in all contending animals that as courage oozes out of

one it appears to be imbibed by its adversary); for
scarcely had the light company passed twenty yards beyond
the Devil's Neck when the cavalry gave a loud cheer—
sure indication of a charge. I instantly gave the word,
" Right about turn, forward ! " and, being now in front
of the men, in my anxiety to gain the narrowed part of
the bridge—the Devil's Neck—I happened to shoot five
or six yards ahead, when, the dragoons advancing close,
the front ranks of the company behind me came down
on the knee. I had not time to turn round, for at that
moment a French officer, darting in front rode full tilt
at me. I cut at him, but my sword approached no nearer
perhaps than his horse's nose ; in fact my little light
infantry sabre was a useless weapon opposed to an immense
mounted dragoon, covered, horse and all, with a large green
cloak, which in itself formed a sufficient shield. After
the failure of my attack I held my sword horizontally
over my head, awaiting the dragoon's blow, for it was
far more dangerous to turn round than to stand firm.
At this very critical moment a man of the company, named
Oats, cried out, " Mr. Blakeney, we've spun him ! " and at
the same instant the dragoon fell dead at my feet. I flew
with a bound to the rear, and regained the five or six paces
incautiously advanced. The cavalry were now up to our
bayonets, covering the whole pontine isthmus.

This affair, trifling in itself, yet to me very interesting,
did not occupy as much time as I have taken in its
narration. Along the other side of the bridge the dragoons
charged forward, until they came to the edge of the chasm
formed by the explosion, when they were of course arrested ;
and on the opposite side of the chasm the grenadiers were
drawn up, standing, being protected from a charge by the
opening. The dragoons in the rear, not knowing the cause

of the check, rode furiously forward, and, crowding their
front ranks, who were pulling up or wheeling round, and
exposed to the fire of the grenadiers, the greatest confusion
ensued ; while those at our side, finding all attempts at
breaking through the light company fruitless, and being
severely galled by the fire of the rear rank as well as a
flanking fire from some of the grenadiers, all wheeled round
and galloped off at full speed. Arriving at the house near
the end of the bridge, their leading squadrons wheeled
short round ; but the suddenness of the turn, made too
whilst in full speed, checked the whole column, and the
light company, now free to act on their feet, poured a
wicked well-directed fire into their ranks. So hot was the
peppering, and so anxious were the rear squadrons to get
away, that they refused the turn, and, increasing their
speed, rode direct into the town of Betanzos. Here we had
beautiful practice, for the road was straight ; and to enter
the town they must pass through an archway, which caused
a second check, when many were lowered from their horses.

All having at length retired, I stepped forward the
nearly fatal five paces and took possession of my late
fierce antagonist's green cloak, which from the inclemency
of the weather was extremely useful. I long kept it as
a boyish trophy, although to Oats alone belonged any merit
attending the fall of its late gallant owner. Oats, seeing
the dangerous predicament in which I was placed, was
the only man in the front rank of the company who did
not come on his knee ; he was immediately behind me,
and remained firm on his feet to enable him to fire over
my head, and, waiting the proper moment and taking steady
aim, sent his ball through the dragoon's head just as his
sabre was about to descend upon mine.

It now appeared that during the time when the two

flank companies of the regiment moved forward to check
the cavalry, by which they ran such risk of being blown
up or cut off, no progress had been made in the destruction
of the standing half of the injured arch ; and now the
enemy, possessing themselves of the building at the end of
the bridge, fired upon us from the windows. From this
house they could not be driven, our guns having moved
forward.

Although all expectation of destroying the bridge was
now relinquished, still it was absolutely necessary to
prolong our halt. The whole British army were on
march from Betanzos to Corunna ; and to have allowed the
enemy to approach before the main body had crossed the
bridge of El-Burgo, eight or ten miles farther on, must
have caused serious loss.

During our halt the French dark brown infantry
columns were seen pouring into Betanzos, which they soon
occupied in considerable force. They threw out some
skirmishers, and showed frequent symptoms of rushing
forward *en masse* to force the bridge ; but to our great
disappointment they never attempted carrying their menacing threats into execution, brought to their senses by
the severe chastisement which their cavalry had received
shortly before in their vain attempt to cross the bridge.

A retiring army has seldom an opportunity of ascertaining the losses sustained by their pursuers ; however, in this
instance they must have suffered severely, and had it not
been for a drizzling rain, which continued the whole morning and caused many of the musket locks to refuse fire,
few, if any, of the dragoons who charged at the bridge
would have returned. We had but a few men wounded
either by pistol or carbine shots, but not a man cut down.

Here I must express my astonishment that, notwithstanding the impetuosity with which the dragoons rushed forward, neither man nor horse was precipitated into the stream, although closely pressed by their own ranks in the rear, and being suddenly compelled to rein up whilst in full speed on the very edge of the chasm. They of course had heard the explosion, but being at some distance were ignorant of the effect which it produced ; and, seeing us after it had taken place cross and recross the bridge, they most probably considered the attempt to destroy it a total failure, as all other similar attempts had been ; and the chasm, from the rubbish and the convexity of the bridge, lay concealed till they were on the brink.

The enemy seemed to be philosophically calculating their strength, whether of nerves or what, and of the resistance to be overcome by advancing. It would indeed be difficult to decide on the force necessary to win the bridge. The rifles with sure and steady aim incessantly poured their fire from the rising ground and hedges which our bank of the stream offered. The light company (28th) kept up a deadly fire upon all who trod the bridge, immediately supported by the grenadiers. The 28th Regiment formed a barrier of steel in rear of its flank companies. The 20th, 52nd, and 91st Regiments, boiling with eagerness to mingle in the fight, were scarcely restrained in their position not far above us, ready, in the event of the enemy forcing their way over the dead bodies of the 28th Regiment, to hurl to destruction all those who dared to pass the fatal bridge. General Paget was amongst us. Sir John Moore with anxious looks watched from the position above each individual movement. This we knew, and, knowing it, had the hero of Lodi and Arcola himself headed the opposite host, he must have been content with his own end of the bridge or have surely perished at ours.

General Paget, having considered that the main body of the army had by this time got sufficiently ahead, followed with the reserve, leaving the bridge without having destroyed even one arch; and scarcely had we retired ten minutes when the enemy's advanced guard passed over in polite attendance, maintaining their courteous distance, which was this day increased. Not having seen our guns at Betanzos, it is not improbable that they suspected an ambush such as had been tried at the romantic bridge.

This, our last day's march, was the first time, since Sir John Moore became Commander of the forces, that the whole British army marched together; consequently it was the most regular. Sir John Moore directed in person; every commanding officer headed his regiment, and every captain and subaltern flanked his regularly formed section; not a man was allowed to leave the ranks until a regular halt took place for that purpose. But the evil attending irregular marching was past and irreparable; unfortunately this soldier-like manner of marching was resorted to too late to be of much effect.

We, the reserve, arrived that evening at El-Burgo, a small village within four miles of Corunna. Extraordinary measures seemed to have been taken for the destruction of the bridge which there crossed the Mero. The preparations being terminated, the 28th Light Company, who still formed the rearguard, crossing over the bridge were drawn up close in its rear. Many remonstrated against our nearness, but were sneeringly assured of being more than safe: thus high-bred scientific theory scorned the vulgarity of common sense. The explosion at length took place, and completely destroyed two arches; large blocks of masonry whizzed awfully over our heads, and caused what the whole of Soult's cavalry could not effect during the retreat. The light company of the 28th and Captain Cameron's company of the 95th broke their ranks and ran like turkeys, and regardless of their bodies crammed their heads into any hole which promised security. The upshot masonic masses continuing their parabolic courses passed far to our rear, and, becoming independent of the impetus by which they had been disturbed, descended and were deeply buried in the earth. One man of the 28th was killed, and four others severely wounded were sent that night into Corunna. This was the only bridge destroyed during the whole retreat, except that of Castro Gonzolo, although many were attempted.

Headquarters were this night at Corunna, and the whole of the troops under cover. Even the 28th Light Company, although on guard over that wonder, the blown-up bridge, were sheltered. We occupied a house quite close to the end of the bridge. Nearly opposite to us, on the other side of the street, a company of the 95th were stationed, also in a house; and each company threw out small detached parties and sentinels along the bank of the river.

The French infantry did not come up that evening; but next morning, as day broke, we discovered the opposite bank lined by their light troops; and a small village not far distant was held in force. But a few shots from our guns obliged the enemy to abandon the post; and a sentry from the 95th was pushed forward to the verge of the broken arch, screened by stones and rubbish. Our opponents took up a similar post on their side during the night, so that, the British troops having now turned round to face the enemy, the advanced posts of the contending armies were only the breadth of two arches of a bridge asunder. In this situation we continued for two days, keeping up an incessant fire, so long as we could discover objects to fire at. This continued blaze was to our advantage, as it obliged the enemy to answer us. We were plentifully supplied with fresh ammunition from Corunna, whereas the expenditure on the part of our foes was not so easily remedied ; this they afterwards felt at the battle of Corunna.

The light company were very critically situated. On one side our windows were exposed to a flanking fire ; at the end of the house they were directly open to the enemy ; and both were exposed to fire from the opposite bank, which was hotly maintained, so that it was impossible to cross the room we occupied except by creeping on our hands and knees. But in one angle we were as secure as in a coffee-house in London. We could have been altogether out of danger in a magazine underneath, but from there we could not see what the enemy were about ; and every moment it was expected they would attempt to repair the bridge, or in some way endeavour to cross the river, which was found to be fordable at low water. We therefore placed a large table—the only one found in the house—in the safety corner. A magazine was discovered filled with potatoes, the only ones we saw since leaving Salamanca ; and some fowls, detected in an outhouse, were cackled forth from their hiding-places by the melodious, though perfidious, notes of the ventriloquists in their search for game.

Having a sumptuous dinner on this day, we invited Captain Cameron, commanding the Highland company of the 95th, who were on piquet in the house opposite, to come over and dine with us. Cameron was an excellent fellow and a gallant and determined soldier ; he willingly accepted the invitation, but hesitated as to crossing the street, not thinking himself justified in risking his life for a dinner when employed upon duty so important. But I told him that if he would wait until three shots had been fired at the window from which I was speaking (but standing at a respectful distance from it), he would be safe in running across the street. I then put my cap upon the point of my sword, pushing it gradually out of the window, at the same time cautiously, as it were, moving forward a musket. The three shots were soon fired at the cap. Cameron then bolted across the street; but just as he was entering the door a fourth shot was fired, which I did not expect, and, as well as I can remember, passed through the skirts of his greatcoat without doing any other injury. The danger was not here finished, for as soon as he arrived within three steps of the top of the stairs he was obliged to crawl on all fours, and continue that grovelling movement until he arrived within the sanctum sanctorum. The servant who brought in dinner was obliged to conform to the same quadruped movement, pushing the dishes on before him. On that day also, Lieutenant Hill of our regiment came to visit us, passing along the rear of the houses.

We were now rather numerous in the safe corner, being four in number—Cameron, Hill, Taylor, and myself. Hill, who came in late, was warned to keep within due bounds; yet in a moment of forgetfulness he placed his glass outside the safety line, and, as luck would have it, just as he withdrew his hand the glass was shattered to pieces by a musket-shot. A loud laugh arose at his expense; there was no other glass to be found, and each being unwilling to lend his, he drank sometimes out of one and sometimes out of another. The scene was truly ridiculous; and the manner also in which we discovered wine is not unworthy of being noticed. A man of the

company, named Savage, came running to say that he
had discovered wine, and conducted me to a house close
by, in which General Disney, who commanded our brigade,
was quartered. Looking through a crevice pointed out
by Savage, for whose continued laughter I could not
account, as soon as my eye became familiar with the dim
light within I discovered the general and his aide-de-camp,
Captain D'Oyly, of the guards, filling their canteens with
wine. Rather at a loss and not thinking it decorous to
interrupt the general whilst officially employed for the
good of the service, I went round to the door, which I
discovered whilst peeping through the microscopic fissure ;
here I waited until they came out, not badly provisioned
with not bad wine. Just as they were about to lock the
door I sprang forward, saying that I had discovered wine
to be in the house, and came to inform him. The general
thanked me very politely, saying that he intended acquaint-
ing me privately, but that great caution must be observed
to keep it a profound secret from the men. This was
the good of the service alluded to. The general then gave
me the key. We sent for our canteens, which for several
days had hung uselessly over the men's shoulders ; our mess
was plentifully stocked, and we gave every man a bottle
of wine half at a time. Shortly afterwards D'Oyly came
with the general's compliments, to ask if I could lend him
a piece of salt pork, which he promised to repay at Corunna.
Our mess had none to give, but I procured a four-pound
piece from the company, which I must say he has never
recollected to repay, so that should he ever meet the
28th Light Company he will have an opportunity of
fulfilling his obligations.

On the evening of the 13th the reserve received an order
to evacuate El-Burgo immediately. It stated that no

regular formation whatever was to take place, neither
regiments, companies, nor sections ; every man was to move
out independently, and as soon as possible, in the direction
of Corunna. The light company of the 28th were directed
to retire in the same manner as soon as the place should
be evacuated by the whole of the reserve. Such an order
coming from General Paget astonished us all. But our
speculations ceased when we reflected upon the source
whence the order emanated ; for such was the high
estimation entertained of General Paget, and such the
confidence reposed in him by every officer and man in
the reserve, that any orders coming from him were always
received as the result of cool determination and mature
judgment. When that officer gave an order there was
something so peculiar in his glance, so impressive in his
tone of voice, and so decisive in his manner, that no
ône held commune, even with himself, as to its pro-
priety or final object. The order was clear ; the execution
must be prompt.

In obedience to this order the reserve commenced
moving out of the town, directing their steps towards
Corunna in the manner indicated. The light company
perceiving the village evacuated by all except themselves,
prepared to follow the example by moving out of the
hothouse which they had occupied for two days, when all
of a sudden we were not a little startled by a tremendous
crash ; a cannon-shot, followed by another and another,
passed through the roof, shattering tiles beams and every
article that opposed. Our sanctum sanctorum, or safety
corner, now became no longer such ; we hurried downstairs,
not delaying to assume our accustomed quadruped position.

This was the first time the enemy brought artillery
to bear on the rearguard, although their guns were in

position at Lugo. The previous unaccountable order was now fully explained. General Paget had discovered a partially masked battery in forwardness on the summit of a hill, and the whole village was entirely exposed to its fire ; into this battery the enemy were dragging their guns, while the reserve were evacuating El-Burgo. The general, perceiving the place no longer tenable, fortunately ordered it to be abandoned in the manner mentioned. Had he waited to make regular formations, the loss of men on our part must have been considerable ; for as the light company passed through, the whole village was under cannonade and the streets raked by musketry from the bridge. Thus the reserve bade adieu to the advanced guard of Marshal Soult's army as an advanced guard. They insulted us at parting by firing while we were withdrawing our advanced sentries, pressing necessity preventing us from resenting the affront ; but we warned them to beware, should we meet again.

CHAPTER XI.

AT THE BATTLE OF CORUNNA.

AND now, before I join the army at Corunna, I beg to make a few remarks about the light company, 28th Regiment, during the retreat which ended at El-Burgo. It must, I imagine, appear evident from the narrative that this company fully participated in all the fatigues, hardships and privations which occurred throughout the campaign in question; that they, in common with the reserve, traversed eighty miles of ground in two marches, passed several nights under arms among the snow-covered mountains, covered the army as a piquet at Lugo, Betanzos, and Corunna, at which the reserve were for two days in continual fire; that scarcely a shot was fired during the campaign at which the company were not present, nor a skirmish in which they did not bear a part. And it must be clear, from the nature of light troops' duty and movements, that they took as much exercise and passed over as much ground, as the most actively employed part of the army. From their being exclusively charged twice by the enemy's cavalry at Calcabellos, once furiously charged at the bridge of Betanzos, and as the rearmost company of the rearguard, on January 5th, engaged from morning until night along the road from Nogales to Constantino, it is but reasonable to suppose that they must have suffered at least as many casualties as any company of the army ; and finally, they marched, the last company of the whole army, through the village of El-Burgo under a heavy cannonade and a sharp fire of musketry. Yet it now fell in as strong, if not the strongest company present, and as efficient, willing, and ready for fight as any which the army could produce ; and were I to give my testimony in presence of the most solemn tribunal, I could not say, so far as my memory serves, that a single individual of that company fell out of the ranks, or was left behind, in consequence of intolerable fatigue. The captain of the company (Bradby) was left behind, sick, at Lisbon ; and the senior lieutenant (English) was sent in the sick-carts from Benevente to Corunna on December 27th, 1808, suffering from dysentery ; but no man fell out on the march.

This short statement is not given with a motive of extolling the service of the company or of proclaiming their strict discipline, though that would only be performing an act of justice towards the distinguished corps of which the company formed a part. I mention it rather as forming in my humble opinion a strong feature in the character of the whole retreat.

In bringing the 28th Light Company so frequently into contact with the enemy, on which occasions the regiment were always at hand, I will not assert that some little predilection may not have been entertained by General Paget. I use the term predilection rather than confidence lest such term might be considered unpleasing to the other gallant corps who formed the reserve ; but whatever be the term used, the inclination was most natural. General Paget had commanded the 28th Regiment, and had left it but a few years previous to the campaign now under notice ; consequently he knew many of the men, and was acquainted with all the old officers. He commanded the regiment too in a situation which put nerve and discipline to the severest trial which has ever been recorded. He it was who, when in command of the 28th Regiment in Egypt, and attacked front and rear at the same moment, ordered the rear rank to face about, and in this situation, novel in warfare, received the double charge, which the men firmly resisted and victoriously repulsed; thus he put to flight that chosen body who, previous to this extraordinary circumstance, were termed the " French Invincibles."

It cannot then be wondered at (nor can any other regiment feel jealous) that General Paget wished in the hour of trial to have his old corps near his person—not for his protection, but because wherever the enemy made their boldest attacks in the vain hope of reviving their claim to invincibility, there was he to be found triumphantly disputing such claim, confident of success when at the head of the same corps with whom he had destroyed their original title—a title which after many a gallant effort made in its support expired on March 21st, 1801, on the bayonets of the "Old Slashers."

On the evening of the 13th the reserve fell into position with the army at Corunna; but still there was no appearance of the transports. On this night the enemy by indefatigable labour put the bridge of El-Burgo in a passable state; and early on the morning of the 14th they crossed over two divisions of infantry and one of cavalry. As it was impossible to prevent this movement, it was feebly opposed, with the object of economising our strength for a more serious event. However some gunshots were exchanged.

On this morning a large quantity of powder sent for

the use of the Spaniards was destroyed, to prevent its
falling into the hands of the enemy. The casks were
piled up in a large and lesser magazine, built together
upon a hill about three miles from the town. The smaller
one blew up with a terrible noise, which startled us all ;
but scarcely had we attempted to account for the occurrence,
when, the train igniting the larger one, the crash was
dreadful. A panic seized all ; the earth was agitated for
miles, and almost every window in Corunna was shattered.
This was the largest explosion of powder which had ever
taken place in Europe—four thousand barrels.

On this evening the long-expected transports hove in
sight, and soon entered the harbour of Corunna. Preparations
for embarkation immediately commenced ; and during the
night the sick, the best horses and upwards of fifty pieces
of artillery were put on board ready for a start—but eight
or ten Spanish guns were kept on shore ready for a fight.

On the 15th Laborde's division arrived—a formidable
reinforcement—and immediately fell into position on the
extreme right of the enemy's line.

The despondency which seized the minds of many at
the long delay of the transports, and the accumulating
strength of the enemy which increased the danger of
embarkation, induced several general officers to recommend
to the Commander of the forces that he should ask the
French marshal for terms under which he might retire
to his transports without molestation. Few men of sound
reflection could imagine that, even should the Commander
of the forces crouch to this humiliating proposition, it would
be acceded to by the haughty French marshal. Besides,
there was no necessity for the degrading step : the enemy,
it is true, had upwards of twenty thousand men in a strong
position, and we had about fourteen thousand men in an

inferior position—the only one left us to occupy. But the inhabitants of Corunna were determined to stand by us to the last, and in a great measure cover our embarkation ; and once embarked we were not in very great danger, for all the batteries on the sea face had been dismantled. Another great advantage was that every English soldier was furnished with a new firelock and his pouch filled with fresh ammunition, ready to be replenished from Corunna when required. These advantages compensated for more than half the difference in our numerical strength. Above all Sir John Moore was not a man who would recommend a British soldier to petition on his knees to an enemy, or to lower his national high bearing ; the high-spirited Moore was the last general in His Majesty's service who would submissively lead a gallant British force, however small, through the Caudine Forks. He rejected the ignoble proposition with feelings such as it deserved.

The conduct of the inhabitants of Corunna was doubly honourable, as they knew that in a very few days their town must fall into the hands of the enemy, whom they were now so strenuously opposing.

On the evening of the 15th a smart skirmish took place between our piquets on the left and a party sent forward on the French right, in the neighbourhood of Palavia Abaxo. Laborde sent forward two guns to strengthen his party. Lieutenant-Colonel M'Kenzie, of the 5th, with some companies rushed forward, endeavouring to seize the battery ; but a strong line of infantry who lay concealed behind some walls started up and poured in such a sharp fire that the piquets were driven back, carrying their lieutenant-colonel mortally wounded.

During the night of the 15th Soult completed his

arrangements. His right rested close to the Mero ; and prolonging his line over rocky and woody ground, he placed his left close to a rocky eminence, upon which he planted his principal battery, consisting of eleven guns, posting several other guns as vantage-ground offered along his line. To the left, and in advance of this big battery, their cavalry were drawn up. Franceschi's dragoons on their extreme left were nearly a mile in rear of General Baird's division, in a diagonal direction. The rocky eminence which sustained the great French battery stood at the edge of a valley which lay on Baird's right, extending in a semicircular direction by his rear and not far distant from the harbour of Corunna.

On our side, General Hope's division formed the left of the line, resting their left flank on the slimy banks of the Mero, extending his right so as to join Baird's division towards the centre of our line. From this, Baird prolonged his division to the right, in front of the enemy's left, and was outflanked by the great battery, which in an oblique direction was situated in his front. Our left wing and the right of the enemy were much further asunder than the contending wings on the other flank. This materially weakened our position ; but it could not be avoided, owing to the conformation of the slopes upon which alone we could be drawn up. These slopes gradually retired from our right to our left, and consequently the great French battery raked the whole of our line. General Fraser's division were drawn up close to Corunna, to watch the coast road, and to be in readiness to proceed to any part where needed most.

On the morning of the 16th all the incumbrances of the army which had not been embarked the previous night were put on board, and then everything prepared

8

for a battle or retreat. It was intended to embark the army that night as soon as darkness should screen their retirement. The reserve, whose post was not so open to the observation of the enemy, were to go on board in the afternoon. We were told that in consequence of general good conduct during the retreat, and having covered the army at Corunna for two whole days, we should be the first division to embark, and thus have time to make ourselves comfortable. All our baggage and such sea-stock as we could procure was shipped, and after the men had dined we marched towards the transports. Our minds were now occupied by thoughts of home ; but we had not proceeded above a hundred yards when we heard the firing of guns. The division halted to a man, as if by word of command ; each looked with anxious enquiry. But we were not kept long in suspense. An aide-de-camp came galloping at full speed to arrest our progress, telling us that an extraordinary movement was taking place throughout the enemy's line ; the three guns fired were a signal to give notice. We instantly countermarched, and passed through the village of Los Ayres, where but twenty minutes before we had bidden adieu to Spain, and considered ourselves on the way to England. But many there were who in a few hours were prevented from ever beholding their native shore ; they paid the last tribute to their country, surrendering their lives in maintaining the sacred cause of liberty and national independence.

Immediately on passing through this village we halted. The enemy's dark columns were seen advancing from three different points, and with rapid pace literally coming down upon us, cheered by their guns, which sent their shot over their heads but plunged into our line, which at the same time was raked from right to left by their great battery.

During these primary operations we became the reserve in reality, but continued so only until the Commander of the forces should ascertain to a certainty where the enemy intended making their fiercest attack ; and as to the point where this was to take place, Sir John Moore was not mistaken. He knew that he was opposed to the ablest marshal of France, and he therefore prepared to resist the attack at that point where he himself would have made it had the order of battle been reversed. Firm in his opinion, he shortly after our arrival at Los Ayres ordered the 95th Regiment to be detached from the reserve. Their duty was to keep the heavy dragoons of Lorge and Franceschi's light cavalry in play. Between the rifles and the right of Baird's division the 52nd formed a loose chain across the valley. He then rode off, leaving orders with General Paget that at the opportune moment he was to move into the valley, turn the French left, and capture their heavy battery, sending at the same time orders to General Fraser to support the reserve.

In the meantime the battle kindled along the whole line. Laborde's division on their right pressed hard upon Hope, and took possession of Palavia Abaxo. This was retaken and maintained by Colonel Nichols, who gallantly charged the enemy through the village at the head of a part of the 14th Regiment. On our right two heavy columns descended against Baird's division. One passed through Elvina, a village about midway between the two lines; this place was held by our piquets, who were driven back in confusion, but was subsequently retaken. This column made direct for Baird's right, obliging the 4th Regiment to retire their right wing, and then advanced into the valley. The other column attacked the whole front of Baird's division.

On Sir John Moore's seeing the advance of the column through the valley, he cast a glance to the rear, and, perceiving that Paget had commenced his movement, he felt confident that all would go well in that quarter. He then rode up to the right of Baird's line, and told Colonel Wench, of the 4th Regiment, that his throwing back the right of his regiment was just what he wished. He then moved off towards the village of Elvina, where, after remaining for some time directing the active operations, he fell mortally wounded ; but this, when known, served rather to increase than damp the ardour of the men, now more than ever excited to vengeance.

Before this melancholy event the enemy's column, who passed by Baird's right, flushed with the idea of having turned the right of the British army (since the 4th Regiment had retired their right wing), moved sternly forward, certain, as they thought, to come in rear of our troops. But as they advanced, they met the reserve coming on, with aspect stern and determined as their own ; they now discovered the true right of the British army. The advanced troops of Soult's army during the march now formed his left ; we recognised each other, and the warning at El-Burgo was recollected. A thousand passions boiled in every breast. Our opponents, madly jealous at having their military fame tarnished by the many defeats which they sustained during the march, determined to regain those laurels to them for ever lost. We, on the other hand, of the reserve had many causes to rouse our hatred and revenge. We painfully recollected the wanton carnage committed on the defenceless stragglers of all ages and sexes at Bembibre, and the many bitter cold nights we passed in the mountains of Galicia, when frost and snow alone formed the couches on which we tried to snatch a few hours of repose. The haughty and taunting insults too of our gasconading pursuers were fresh in our memory. One sentiment alone was opposed to our anger; the time was come when it gave us pleasure to think of our past misfortunes, for they who caused them resolutely stood before us, foaming with impatience to wipe away the stain of former defeats. They were no longer inclined to keep aloof.

Thus urged forward by mutual hate, wrought up to the highest pitch by twelve days' previous fighting, and knowing the approaching conflict to be our last farewell, we joined in fight

> " With all the fervour hate bestows
> Upon the last embrace of foes."

Our foes stood firm.. But the time occupied in firing was but short; we soon came to the charge, and shortly the opposing column was dissipated. Their cavalry now thought it prudent to retire to and behind their great battery; the 95th, freed from their presence, joined us; and the 52nd, who had slowly retired as the enemy's column first advanced through the valley, also united with their division; and now the reserve were again all united.

We now pushed on all together, and turned the French left, and were preparing to charge and carry the great French battery. Had Fraser's fresh division, who had not fired a shot, come up now and joined the reserve according to the Commander of the forces' orders, the whole British line could have made an advance echelon movement to the left, and Soult's army had been lost. Their cavalry had retreated behind their great battery, when they became useless from the rocky nature of the ground; the battery itself was all but in our possession, and only required the short time necessary to march into it. Elvina, on our right, the great point of contention throughout the day, was in our possession, as was the village of Palavia Abaxo on our left. Our whole line had considerably advanced, and the enemy falling back in confusion fired more slackly, not so much owing to the casualties they sustained as to the scarcity and damaged state of their ammunition. Their muskets were bent and battered, while our fire was strong and rapid, our ammunition fresh and abundant, our muskets new and the nerves which spanned them tense. The only retreat the enemy had was over the patched-up bridge of El-Burgo, and this, after the 14th Regiment had taken Palavia Abaxo, was nearly, if not quite, as close to our left as to the French right. The Mero in full tide ran deep broad and rapid in their rear; and if Napoleon the Great himself had been there, his escape would have been impossible. But the excited troops were drawn away from decisive and continued victory.

As darkness approached, our piquets as usual lit large fires; and the British army retired to Corunna, and embarked that night without the slightest confusion, so completely had everything been previously arranged.

On the morning of the 17th, the piquets being withdrawn, the wounded were collected and with the exception of very few put on board, covered by a brigade still left on shore for that purpose. About noon on this day Soult managed to bring up some guns to the village of S. Lucia, which played upon the shipping in the harbour, some of which were struck. This causing some disorder amongst the transports, several masters cut their cables, and four vessels ran ashore; but the soldiers and crews being immediately rescued by the men-of-war's boats, and their vessels burned, the fleet got out of harbour. The Spaniards nobly redeemed their pledge to keep the enemy at bay and cover the embarkation to the very last. The few wounded who still remained ashore, together with the rearguard, were put on board early on the morning of the 18th without the loss of a single individual ; and the whole sailed for England.

Without the remotest intention of depreciating the merits of his gallant successor, Sir John Hope, whose valour and military talents are renowned through the army, there is but little doubt that if Sir John Moore had not fallen the battle, though glorious to his successor and to the British army, would have terminated more decisively. Sir John Moore felt the keenest in the whole army. He, like the lion long baited and fretted by distant darts, had turned at last, and finding his pursuers within his reach would have been content with nothing less than their total destruction.

That the battle of Corunna, under the peculiar circumstances which attended it, was one of the most glorious which has been fought in modern times will not be denied ; it was that which furnished the most unequivocal proof of British firmness. The army could not have occupied a worse position, as Sir John Moore declared ; but it could not be remedied. Our troops were not sufficiently numerous to occupy a more advanced post, which was therefore left for the enemy. The British soldiers had been harassed by a long and fatiguing retreat in the severest season of the year and during peculiarly inclement weather. Their route had been through mountains covered with snow ; they had been irregularly fed, and the clothing partly worn off their backs. The enemy were far superior both in position and numbers ; and the English army fought without either cavalry or artillery. But however glorious was the result of the battle to England, yet it was cause of national rejoicing to the enemy, although conquered; for Sir John Moore no longer guided a British force to rouse the jealousy and mar the plans of two hundred and fifty thousand French veterans accustomed to victory. He lay down on the land for whose freedom he bled, and slept on Iberia's breast for ever.

Sir John Moore's first appearance produced sentiments in the beholder not remote from reverence. His tall, manly and perfect form attracted general admiration, while his brilliant and penetrating eye denoted profound observation, and proclaimed the determined soldier and able general. His words, voice and bearing realised all you had ever imagined of a perfect and highly polished gentleman endowed with every talent necessary to form the statesman or warrior. His features were formed to command the attention of man and make the deepest impression on the female heart. His memory, as I have been told by old officers who knew him well, was extraordinary, yet amiably defective; and what was once said of a great warrior might be justly applied to him—that he recollected everything save the injuries done to himself. Few have ever been gifted with more personal or mental charms than Sir John Moore; yet the perfection with which he was sent forth was far outshone by the glory that attended his progress and recall.

Having but slightly touched on the circumstances attending the fall of this great man, I will repeat that after entirely approving the movement of the 4th Regiment in retiring their right wing, and feeling satisfied as to what would take place in the valley, Sir John Moore made straight for the village of Elvina, where the fight continued to be most bloody and most obstinately maintained. It had been repeatedly taken and retaken at the point of the bayonet. Just as the Commander of the forces arrived, the 50th Regiment, who were formed on the left of the village, commanded by Major Napier, and seconded by Major Stanhope, made a most desperate charge through the village ; but Napier's impetuosity carrying him forward through some stone walls beyond the village, he was desperately wounded, and fell into the hands of the enemy ; and Major Stanhope was killed. The general cheered the regiment during this charge, crying out, "Bravo, 50th, and my two brave majors !" Then perceiving the enemy coming forward to renew the struggle, he ordered up a battalion of the guards, directing at the same time that the two regiments already engaged should be supplied anew with ammunition. The 50th continued firm ; but the 42nd, mistaking this as an order to go to the rear for ammunition, began to retire. Seeing this, the general rode up to the regiment, exclaiming : "My brave 42nd, if you have gallantly fired away all your ammunition, you have still your bayonets—more efficient. Recollect Egypt ! Think on Scotland ! Come on, my gallant countrymen !" Thus directing the willing 42nd to meet the renewed attack on Elvina, he had the satisfaction to hear that the guards were coming up ; and, pleased with the progress of the 42nd, he proudly sat erect on his war-steed, calmly casting a satisfied glance at the raging war around. It was at this moment that he was struck to the ground by a cannon-ball, which laid open the breast of as upright and gallant a soldier as ever freely surrendered life in maintaining the honour and glory of his king and country. He soon arose to a sitting position, his eyes kindling with their usual brilliancy when informed that the enemy were victoriously repulsed at all points.

At this period the battle raged in its utmost fury ; and an active general movement was taking place from right to left of both lines, the enemy retiring, the British pressing forward ; and now Sir David Baird also was knocked down, receiving the wound for which he subsequently suffered the amputation of his arm.

On placing Sir John Moore in the blanket in which he was borne to the rear, the hilt of his sword got into the wound; and as they tried to take it away, he declined having it moved, saying, "It may as well remain where it is, for, like the Spartan with his shield, the Briton should be taken out of the field with his sword." The wound was of the most dreadful nature ; the shoulder was shattered, the arm scarcely attached to the body, the ribs over his heart smashed and laid bare.

Thus was Sir John Moore carried to the rear. As he proceeded, perceiving from the direction of the firing that our troops were advancing, he exclaimed, "I hope the people of England will be satisfied." On being taken to his house in Corunna, he again enquired about the battle, and being assured that the enemy were beaten at all points, exclaimed : "It is great satisfaction to me to know that the French are beaten. I hope my country will do me justice." Whether this well-founded hope was realised or not let the just and generous determine. He now enquired about the safety of several officers, those of his staff in particular ; and he recommended several for promotion whom he considered deserving. This exertion caused a failing in his strength ; but on regaining it in a slight degree, addressing his old friend Colonel Anderson, he asked if Paget was in the room. Upon being answered in the negative, he desired to be remembered to him, saying, "He is a fine fellow ; 'tis General Paget, I mean." This was a noble testimonial to that gallant officer's high character, rendered sacred by the peculiar circumstances in which it was called forth ; and it strongly marked the martial spirit and high mind of the dying hero, who, with his body writhing in torture, the veil of eternity fast clouding his vision and his lips quivering in the convulsive spasms of death, sighed forth his last words in admiration of the brave.

The battle of Corunna terminated at the same moment that the British commander expired. He was buried in the citadel. As the enemy's last guns were firing his remains were lowered into the grave by his staff, simply wrapped in his military cloak. No external mark of mourning was displayed ; the grief could not be withdrawn from the heart.

Thus, like a staunch general of the empire, Sir John Moore terminated his splendid career in maintaining its honour and crushing its foes. Yet his last act was peculiarly devoted to his own Scotland : it was cheering on the Royal Highlanders to a victorious charge. How Scotland has shown her recognition of the gallant and patriotic deed, or her admiration of the splendid career of the brightest ornament whom she ever sent forth on the glorious theatre of war, I have never been told.

CHAPTER XII.

ON January 18th, 1809, the British army sailed from
Corunna, and having encountered very boisterous
weather, the fleet were dispersed, and the regiments arrived
in England at different ports and at different periods during
the latter end of the month and the beginning of February.
One wing of the 28th Regiment landed at Portsmouth ;
the other, to which I belonged, disembarked at Plymouth.
Our appearance on landing was very ūnseemly, owing
principally to the hurry attending our embarkation at
Corunna, which took place in the dark and in the presence
of an enemy. Scarcely a regiment got on board the vessel
which contained their baggage ; and the consequence was,
that on quitting our ships we presented an appearance of
much dirt and misery. The men were ragged, displaying
torn garments of all colours ; and the people of England,
accustomed to witness the high order and unparalleled
cleanliness of their national troops, for which they are
renowned throughout Europe, and never having seen an
army after the termination of a hard campaign, were horror-
struck, and persuaded themselves that some dreadful
calamity must have occurred. Their consternation was
artfully wrought up to the highest pitch by the wily old
soldiers, who, fully aware of the advantage to be gained

by this state of general excitement and further to work
on the feelings, recited in pathetic strain the most frightful
accounts of their sufferings and hardships.   Interested
persons at home profited by this state of universal ferment.
One political party, eagerly catching at any circumstances
which could tend to incriminate the other, highly exagger-
ated even those already incredible accounts ; while the
other side, who felt that all the disasters attending the
campaign properly rested with themselves, joined in
the cry and with mean political subterfuge endeavoured
to throw the onus off their own shoulders on to the breast
of the silent, the unconscious dead.   A general outcry was
got up against Sir John Moore.   He was accused of being
stupid, of being irresolute, of running away, and of God
knows what.   His memory was assailed alike by those
politically opposed to his party and by those who once
were his supporters, and who, although aware of his
masculine genius, maintained their posts by basely
resorting to calumny and deceit.

During this campaign it was the opinion of many that
circumstances occurred which, under more favourable
auspices, would have induced some individuals to expect
promotion.   But the jarring and disturbed state of the
Cabinet, each individual endeavouring to counteract the
measures of his colleague, threw out a foggy gloom
damping all hopes ; and when the eminent services of
Sir John Moore and those of General Paget were passed
over unnoticed, it would have been a military heresy to
have accepted, much more to solicit promotion.

After remaining a few days at Plymouth, we proceeded
as far as Exeter, and there halted for the space of a week
to await further instructions from London.   During our
stay at this place we lived at the Old London Inn, and

here a curious scene took place. Two Spanish gentlemen stopped at the inn on their way to Falmouth ; and
when after dinner their bill was presented, a misunder-
standing took place. I should premise that at this, as at
many other inns in England, every edible article produced
on the table is charged separately. The Spaniards, after
carefully examining the bill, objected to pay it ; the waiter
reported to his master, who interfered, but since he was
as ignorant of Spanish as his guests were of the English
language, all was confusion. The arguments and assertions
of either party were totally incomprehensible to the other.
After fruitless clamour the landlord came into the room
where we, the officers of the regiment, dined, requesting
to know if any of us could assist him in his dilemma.
Although not very well acquainted with the Spanish
language at that time, I volunteered my services. The
Spaniards were very wrathful and boldly asserted that
the innkeeper attempted to extort payment for a dish
which was never brought to them ; this they were firm
in maintaining, having counted every article. One swore
that he never touched anything of the kind, and that,
if brought into the room, it must have been covered on
the sideboard ; the other accused the cook of having used
it himself in the kitchen, and of trying, that he might
conceal his gormandising, to make them pay, declaring
at the same time that the affair should be laid open
to the public for the benefit of future travellers who might
otherwise be taken in. By their accounts it was impossible
that I could fathom the affair ; and as soon as the
Spaniards allowed me to speak, I called the waiter to
bring his written bill, and on this one of the gentlemen
pointed out what he considered to be the cheat. I took
the paper from the waiter, when, lo ! upon examination

I discovered the viand in dispute to be the chambermaid, who was charged in the bill at two shillings. I could not restrain a loud fit of laughter, which roused the blood of the Castilians even more than the cheat; but when I explained the cause, they were as ready to enter into the joke as any others. Upon asking mine host how he could think of making a charge for the chambermaid in his bill, thus making a voluntary donation obligatory, he replied that, had he not done so, foreigners would never pay her; that his servants had no other wages than those which they got from customers. The Spaniards paid the bill most willingly, and joined our table, and the whole party laughed heartily during the remainder of the evening.

The order for continuing our route having at length arrived, we proceeded to occupy our old quarters (Colchester), where, after passing through Dorset, to avoid falling in with other troops on the move, we arrived after a march which including partial halts occupied one month and five days, giving an addendum to our campaign of from between three and four hundred miles without leaving a single straggler behind. This march bore heavily by lightening us of all our cash, and dipped us besides in the paymaster's books.

In less than three months after the regiment was united at Colchester, we again were ordered upon what we joyfully contemplated as active service. A magnificent expedition was sent out to carry off (if allowed) the Gallia Dutch fleet from the Schelde. The land forces, commanded by the Earl of Chatham, were composed of forty thousand men, the flower of the British Army. This force was accompanied by a not less imposing naval force: thirty-nine sail of the line, three dozen frigates and innumerable satellites, bombships, gunboats, brigs, etc., which, together with storeships, transports and other craft, amounted in the whole to upwards of six hundred sail.

To join this splendid armament the 28th Regiment marched from Colchester in the latter end of June, and reached Dover on July 4th. Thence we in a few days proceeded to Deal, where we embarked on board frigates— a squadron of that class of men-of-war under command of Sir Richard Keats being destined to carry the reserve of the army. This arrangement was adopted in consequence of the frigates drawing less water than ships of the line, thus enabling them to lie closer in shore and quicken the disembarkation of the reserve, who of course were the first troops to land. We remained upwards of a week anchored at Deal, awaiting final instructions and the junction of the whole. During this delay some thousand families, many of the highest lineage in the kingdom, visited Deal. All arrangements being finally terminated, this truly magnificent naval and military armament sailed on July 28th, 1809. Thousands of superbly dressed women crowded the beach ; splendid equipages were numerous ; all the musical bands in the fleet, as well military as naval, joined in one general concert, playing the National Anthem, which, with the loud and long-continued cheering on shore, enlivened the neighbourhood for miles around and caused the most enthusiastic excitement throughout the whole. Many beauteous fair, whose smiles were rendered yet more brilliant by the intrusive tear, waved their handkerchiefs in the breeze to the fond objects of their fixed regard, who responded with silent but steadfast gaze, burning with the two noblest passions which inspire the breast of man—love and glory. The show was august, the pageant splendid, the music enchanting.

Next morning we discovered the dykebound fens of
Holland, little anticipating that they were shortly to
become British graveyards. About noon we anchored;
and the remainder of the day was passed in preparing
the three days' cooked provisions always carried by British
soldiers on landing in an enemy's country.

The next day proved boisterous, and to our great mortification nothing general could be attempted. However
about noon the weather having somewhat abated, great
commotion was observed throughout the armament;
signals from ship to ship throughout the fleet portended
great events. Sir Richard Keats lowered his flag, followed
by Sir John Hope on board the *Salsette* frigate, which
carried the left wing of the 28th Regiment, with the
exception of the light company. The light company
embarked with the headquarters on board the *Lavinia*
frigate, commanded by Lord William Stuart.

After due consultation between the admiral and general,
a signal was made calling for all the carpenters of the
squadron with their tools. Some momentous affair was
evidently at hand. Four companies of the 28th Regiment
were lowered into boats, which, being joined by the light
company from on board the *Lavinia*, were placed under
the command of Major Browne of the regiment. We now
immediately pushed off, animated by the cheers of the
whole fleet. The shore was soon reached, the light company
leading the van, the first on hostile ground. Advancing
some way, we encountered a piquet, who, on our shooting
the fever (the ague only remained) out of a few trembling
Dutchmen, thought proper to retire. Upon this we proceeded to carry into execution the object of the expedition,
which, I forgot to mention before, was to destroy a signal-
post.

The carpenters now came in for a full share of the glory. Each axe that fell upon the staff was answered by cheers loud as salvos; but when the mast after repeated blows was seen to fall, so loud were the greetings that some ships passing at a distance on their way to England and reporting what they had heard, induced many there to think that Antwerp had fallen into our hands. After the fall and destruction of the telegraph, we returned triumphantly on board, carrying away all the machinery books and signals; and thus, and thus alone, the 28th Regiment signalised itself during this stupendous campaign!

Next morning (July 31st) a signal was made for all the troops to descend into the boats and prepare for landing. The rapidity of the current was such that the boats were carried away by the stream, and clung alongside of any vessel that came in their way. I recollect that Lieutenant-Colonel Woodford, with his light company of the Coldstream Guards, held on by the *Lavinia*, and was taken on board. The officers dined with Lord William Stuart, who, having been called away by Sir Richard Keats, requested me to do the honours of his table during his absence; and his guests, to relieve me from any embarrassment, freely and cheerfully partook of his lordship's fare. I more than once in later days met Colonel Woodford in London, and remember not only his polished address and courteous manner, but also his prompt recognition and ready kindness.

August 1st being fine, the reserve under Sir John Hope landed on the Island of South Beveland; while the other troops went ashore principally on the Island of Walcheren, and soon proceeded to besiege Flushing. On the 13th the bombardment of that fortress commenced. It was only on the morning of the 14th that, after many previous consultations, a squadron of frigates commanded by Lord William Stuart forced the passage of the Schelde ; and, notwithstanding the delay caused by considering the enterprise too dangerous to be attempted, only one vessel, the *Lavinia* which led, was struck by only one shot. On the morning of the 15th Flushing capitulated.

In the meantime the reserve in South Beveland stormed and took Fort Batz, a strong post occupied by the enemy. On the 11th an attempt was made by the enemy's gunboats to retake it ; but the guards, who originally took the fort, now successfully defended it.

Flushing having fallen, our frigates in the Schelde, and all the channels and passages round the islands scoured by our gunboats, the reserve expected hourly to be ordered to attack Antwerp and the enemy's fleet, who lay in our view and within our grasp, not far from Antwerp. However we were grievously disappointed. With the fall of Flushing fell all our warlike operations. After we had remained inactive a sufficient time to allow Fouché to collect and throw thirty thousand men into Antwerp and its defences, and to erect batteries along all the approaches which he armed with the guns taken from their now useless ships, the Commander of the forces, with the courtesy of manner which distinguished that nobleman, very politely requested the French to give up their fleet. But that surly son of a tubmaker, Bernadotte, sent a flat refusal ; and, finding too late that late Court hours and measured movements were ineffectual against rapid and early rising revolutionists, Lord Chatham with the greater part of the survivors of his fevered army returned to England on September 14th. A portion were left behind to favour the introduction of prohibited goods, but the fatality and expense attending the maintenance of this contraband establishment being found to more than counterbalance the advantages proposed, the project was abandoned, and those who escaped pestilence returned on December 23rd.

The splendid pageantry that attended, and the national joyous pride that greeted the departure of this superb armament, were wofully contrasted with its return. The unwieldy expedition, although it furnished cause of merriment all over the Continent, deluged the British empire with tears. There was scarcely a family in Great Britain which did not mourn the fate of a gallant soldier, without one cheering ray to brighten the gloom, one laurel leaf to be hallowed by their affectionate tears. The mortality among the troops was so great that bands of music were forbidden to attend the military funerals.

CHAPTER XIII.

WE RETURN TO THE PENINSULA.

AFTER having filled up some hundred vacancies caused by our Dutch expedition, we again received orders to prepare for foreign service ; and in January 1810 the 28th Regiment for the fourth time in four successive years marched from Colchester to go out and meet the foe in foreign lands. On this occasion we proceeded to Portsmouth, and with the 2nd Battalion of the 4th or King's Own Regiment embarked for Gibraltar, where we arrived towards the latter end of the ensuing month. In the April following, Major Browne of the regiment, with the light companies of the 9th, 30th, and 41st Regiments, a battalion company of the 28th which I accompanied, two guns and thirty gunners, the whole amounting to three hundred and sixty men and officers, marched to Tarifa, a small town at the entrance of the gut of Gibraltar, afterwards rendered celebrated by its noble defence under Colonel Skerrett against Marshal Victor.

Soon after our arrival I was sent by Major Browne with despatches to General Campbell, then Lieutenant-Governor of Gibraltar. Returning next day with the general's instructions, when I had got about half way, my attention was suddenly called by the peasantry, who pastured their flocks on the neighbouring hills, frequently crying out, " Beware of the French ! " Neither the dragoon

who accompanied me nor I myself could discover the
slightest appearance of an enemy, and I knew that the
French occupied no part within twenty miles of the place.
Under this conviction I proceeded forwards, yet cautiously,
for the shepherds, who seemed much excited, were running
in all directions collecting their flocks. On our advancing
a short way, we heard the shouts, " Beware of the French ! "
repeated with redoubled vehemence. I now stopped short,
when suddenly a French cavalry piquet, consisting of about
twenty men and an officer, darted from out the thickets,
which were so high and the patrol so well concealed
that, although within a hundred and fifty yards of us,
neither the dragoon nor I had discovered any appearance
of either man or horse. They were in their saddles in
an instant, and saluted us with their carbines and pistols
literally before we had time to turn our horses round.
My dragoon darted like lightning off the road towards the
coast, calling upon me to follow, and in an instant was
lost to sight. I felt much disinclination to trust my safety
to concealment in a country with one yard of which
off the road I was not acquainted. I therefore resolved
to rely on the abilities of my horse to make good my
retreat along the road ; I could depend upon him for
speed. The patrol gave me chase for upwards of four
miles. We always preserved nearly the same distance, from
a hundred to a hundred and fifty yards apart, losing sight
of each other only when a turn in the road or some high
brambles intervened. Our uniformly preserving nearly
the same distance did not depend on the equal speed
of our animals, but on the nature of the road which was
perhaps the worst mountain road in Europe ; and so deep
and so little apart were the ruts by which it was completely traversed that to push a spirited horse would

be to break his neck to a certainty and most probably
that of the rider also. On approaching the cork wood
not far from Algesiras, the ground being comparatively
level, I very soon left the dragoons far behind.

On my arrival at Algesiras, learning that two Spanish
regiments of cavalry had just arrived there, I immediately
waited on the senior officer, and informed him of what had
occurred, using every remonstrance which I could suggest
to induce him to march to the aid of Tarifa, which, even
before I entered the town, he knew from the peasantry
to be attacked. But all my prayers that he would aid
Tarifa, or at least cut off the retreat of the enemy, were
ineffectual, the Spanish commandant alleging that without
orders he could not move. Upon this I wrote to Lieutenant
Belcher, assistant military secretary to General Campbell,
stating all that had taken place, at the same time
remarking that from the fact, which I learned also from
the peasantry who from far and near drove their flocks
into Algesiras, that no sortie had been made by Major
Browne, I felt convinced that he was attacked by a force
much superior to his own. This letter I immediately sent
off by a boat to Gibraltar.

As soon as it became dusk I again mounted my horse,
if possible to get to Tarifa, attended by the same dragoon
who accompanied me in the morning. This man, who
was no coward, found his way into Algesiras about the
same time that I arrived there. He assured me that
he could conduct me by a coast road to within a hundred
yards of Tarifa without being discovered by any, as it was
a road or rather goat-track but little known. As a proof
of the confidence which he felt, he insisted on taking the
lead, for two horses could not move abreast, and like
a true Spaniard drew his sabre even before he left the

town. The only thing I obtained from the Spanish commandant was his gratuitous adieu, strongly recommending that I should not attempt to return to Tarifa until it should be thoroughly ascertained that the enemy had retired, to which advice, to avoid the enemy, I paid as much attention as he did to my recommendation to seek the enemy. I felt much anxiety to be at Tarifa, the more as I wished to tell Browne of what I had done, and that consequently he might expect a reinforcement.

We arrived before daybreak near the town, where meeting a friar we heard that we might advance with safety, for the French had retired. It appears that as soon as Marshal Victor, whose corps were lying before Cadiz, had learned that Tarifa was occupied by English troops, he sent out a strong patrol of infantry and cavalry to ascertain our strength. He felt very jealous of the post, as it threatened his foraging parties, who frequently came to the neighbouring fertile plains to procure nourishment for his army, and principally to collect forage for his cavalry. For this reason it was that he sent the party mentioned, who appeared before the walls of Tarifa on the morning of April 20th before daybreak, seven days after the place had been in our possession. The surmise stated in my letter to Lieutenant Belcher proved true. Major Browne, in consequence of the strong force brought against him, did not move out of the garrison until the evening, when the enemy drew off a part of their troops ; then, as they still occupied a large convent and some uninhabited houses close to the town, a sortie was made, headed by Captain Stovin, when they were soon dislodged and pursued for a considerable distance. This demonstration against Tarifa was attended with but few results or casualties, one man only, a gunner, being killed and a few more wounded.   Lieutenant Mitchell, a gallant officer, commanded the artillery.

On my arrival at Tarifa I acquainted Major Browne with all that had occurred to me during my absence, my useless endeavours to induce the Spanish regiments or any part of the garrison of Algesiras to intercept the enemy's return from Tarifa, and finally with my having written to Gibraltar. The major fully approved of all the steps I had taken; and, my letter being laid before General Campbell, he ordered four companies of the 47th Regiment, under the command of Captain O'Donoghue of that corps, instantly to embark for Tarifa, but the wind becoming contrary, they were obliged to disembark at Algesiras and proceed overland.   They arrived at Tarifa the night after my return there; and here they continued until the month of September.   Then the 28th Regiment, whose colonel, Belson, had gone to England in consequence of ill-health, were ordered to Tarifa; and Captain O'Donoghue's detachment, together with the light companies which originally had accompanied Major Browne, were then recalled to Gibraltar.

Shortly after this attack on Tarifa, an English merchant vessel was captured by a French privateer in the neighbourhood of Vejer, not far from Tarifa.   A midshipman, who commanded a gunboat detached from the guardship at Gibraltar, reported the circumstance to Major Browne, and applied to him for a detachment of soldiers to embark on board his boat, stating that so strengthened he might retake the vessel.   Browne, in whose estimation the honour of His Majesty's arms in whatever branch of the service was paramount to any other sentiment, hesitated not a moment, and ordered me, with as many men of the light company (28th) as the gunboat could stow, to embark immediately.

Leaving Tarifa in the evening and pulling all night, we found ourselves next morning at dawn in the celebrated bay of Trafalgar ; and as soon as light enabled us to see we discovered the vessel alluded to about two miles distant. We immediately swept towards her. Soon after a boat put off from the shore, now in possession of the French, with intention, as we afterwards discovered, to set the ship on fire. While some of the sailors and soldiers in turn used every exertion to row, or rather sweep, we kept up as quick a fire as possible with a long twelve-pounder and a twenty-four-pounder at the boat coming from shore. One shot having struck not far beyond her, whilst a shower of grape fell but little short, she thought proper to retire. Being thus freed from the enemy's boat, we made a wide offing to keep the vessel between us and shore, within musket-shot of which she was run aground. On boarding her, we placed bales of wool or cotton, which formed the principal part of her cargo, along her side next the shore to cover us from the fire of musketry ; for by this time a strong detachment of French infantry came down close to the water's edge, ranging themselves in loose order, so as not to offer any dense body to the fire of the gunboat, which, after putting the soldiers on board the merchantman, retired beyond musket range of the shore and kept up a fire of round shot and grape. The enemy on shore had a similar covering to our own, having the night before disembarked several bales of the cotton. Whenever any of these was struck by a round shot, its bounding from the beach presented a most fantastic appearance and caused shouts of laughter among the men, which tended to lighten their fatigue.

After working indefatigably for several hours, we at length succeeded in getting the vessel afloat. Our labour

was much heightened by our being obliged to work her
off by the windlass, since her capstan was unshipped and
carried away by the French, who had everything in preparation on board to set fire to her as soon as unloaded,
or if there were an attempt at rescue.

Having succeeded in carrying her off, we returned next
day to Tarifa, where we landed in triumph from our prize,
as she was termed. Next day she was sent to Gibraltar,
and condemned, I think, to salvage or some such term;
but never having on entering the army contemplated
becoming a prize-fighter, I may be mistaken as to terms.
On a distribution of this said salvage money being made,
I was put down to receive a portion such as is allotted
to a sailor, probably an able-bodied one. But on some
person in Gibraltar suggesting that probably it would not
be correct to class me, who was the only commissioned
officer present at the recapture or within sight of it, with
a common sailor, I was on reflection ranked with the
petty officers, cooks, etc., thereby gaining promotion from
the forecastle to the caboose, and obtaining the rank if not
the title of cook. I employed no agent, considering my
claim safe in the hands of the sister profession. Captain
Vivian, who commanded the guardship, the *San Juan*, at
Gibraltar, I was told, superintended the arrangement; and,
together with the whole of his officers and crew, shared
in the spoil, each officer having a much larger portion than
that dealt out to me, although neither he nor they aided
or assisted, or were or could be in sight, when the capture
took place. The midshipman who commanded the gunboat
was equally unfortunate as to the share to which he was
entitled as the only acting naval officer present at the
capture; but I heard at the time that to quiet him he
was otherwise rewarded. If true, I feel happy at it; and

we both should feel content, he at being promoted to
the rank of a commissioned officer, and I at receiving
a diploma as a master of gastronomic science, although to
this day I am ignorant how to compose even a basin of
peasoup.   Shortly afterwards I met Mr. William Sweet-
land, who was employed as agent on the occasion.   On
questioning him as to the extraordinary distribution, he
with professional coolness replied that he was employed
on the other side, that no person appeared on my behalf,
and that if anybody had, of course there could be no question
as to the sentence which must have been passed.   I was
strongly advised to appeal to the Admiralty, as I might
thereby gain a sum of money that would tend to my
advancement ; but I foolishly disregarded the counsel.
So I took my cook's wages, and therewith drank to the
health of my Sovereign, the honour and glory of my old
profession, and success for ever to the Royal Navy.   I
was afterwards informed that thanks were given to me
in public orders by Sir Richard Keats.   I never saw the
order, and therefore cannot answer for its existence; yet
the fact could easily be ascertained by any feeling interest
in the subject.   For my own part, I felt so dissatisfied
at the mercenary or jobbing part of the transaction that
I never took any step to ascertain whether the thanks
were or were not published.   Colonel Browne having
visited Gibraltar shortly after the transaction had taken
place, fully explained his and my sentiments to Captain
Vivian on the quarter-deck of the *San Juan*, among
other assertions upholding that he himself and the whole
garrison of Tarifa, from which Lieutenant Blakeney was
detached, had as strong a claim to participation in the
salvage as Captain Vivian and the crew of the guardship ;
and here he was perfectly right, for the garrison of Tarifa

was five-and-twenty miles nearer to the scene of action than the *San Juan* stationed at Gibraltar.

During our long stay at Tarifa few days passed on which I was not employed either in opposing the French foraging parties or in carrying despatches to and from Gibraltar. On one of these latter occasions, when returning to Tarifa after an absence of three days, detained by heavy rains, I was not a little surprised at finding a stream through the cork wood of Algesiras much changed in its aspect. But three days previously I crossed it when the horse's hoofs were scarcely wetted ; now it had become a roaring and rapid torrent. The passage of this torrent was very dangerous ; its bed, with which I was well acquainted having crossed it fifty times, was formed of large smooth flags much inclined, making it somewhat perilous at any time to ride over it. Within fifteen or twenty yards of this, the only part passable, the water-course suddenly wound round the base of an abrupt mountain, against which the torrent rushed with violence, and continuing its new direction soon disgorged itself into the ocean. To make a false step in crossing was certain destruction. The current passed rapidly downwards between the mountains, its foaming surf interrupted in its course by huge and prominent rocks, with which the mountain sides were studded down to the very bed of the torrent, which, now passing underneath, now boiling over the rugged and unseemly heads of those frightful masses of stone, gave them apparent animation ; like monstrous spirits of the flood, they seemed to threaten destruction to all who came within their reach. With such a picture before me and considering it a stupid way of losing one's life, I hesitated for some moments, when the Spanish dragoon, who always accompanied me on such excursions, boldly took the lead and entered the hissing foam. His horse made some few slips, and more than once I expected to see both dashed to pieces, which must have taken place had the animal made a really false step. Fortunately they got safe across ; but this did not induce me to follow. Few perils I would not have encountered rather than ride through that frightful torrent, knowing as I did the nature of its bed. Yet to return to Algesiras I considered degrading, especially when the dragoon had so boldly passed across. At length, and contrary to his advice, I determined to wade on foot, and flogged forward my horse into the water, which he unwillingly took, and like the other narrowly escaped. The last trial was my own. I recollected that, close above where the horses passed, a rock about two feet high stood in the centre of the stream, and to lean against that in case of necessity, I entered the water a little higher. Fortunately I thought of this precaution, for by the time I had with the greatest exertion got to where this rock was situated, I felt so spent and incapable of resisting the torrent that I could neither proceed nor retire. Placing both legs firmly against the rock, and feeling quite giddy from the glare and the rapidity with which the waters passed, I felt compelled to close my eyes for some moments.

My situation was now neither wholesome nor pleasant. Boughs and trunks of trees rapidly passed at intervals down the stream, any one of which coming upon me must have either smashed me on the spot or dashed me headlong against the rocks below. But luckily I was preserved by another rock, which stood in the centre of the channel not far above me, rearing its ample head over the water ; this dividing the torrent, sent the floating batteries on either side. The poor Spaniard appeared desperate, violently striking his head, but he did not attempt the water a second time, nor could I blame him. I wore a very long sash with its still longer cords, such as light infantry bucks then used. Untying it and holding one end, I flung the other towards the Spaniard, who anxiously prepared to catch it; but it proved too short. He now took off his sash, which was also long as all Spanish sashes are, and rolling up a stone within it flung it towards me with such precision that I caught it with both hands. I now tied the two sashes together, and fastened the stone within one end of the dragoon's sash, which I flung back to him. He caught it and gave a cheer. The only thing I now dreaded was that the Spaniard in his anxiety would give a sudden pull, which, with the heavy load of water I carried, might cause the silken bridge to snap or pull me off my legs, either of which things must be fatal. I therefore cautioned him to hold firm, but on no account to pull unless I should fall. He fully obeyed the directions, and I warped myself safely across. The faithful Spaniard hugged me to his breast, and having raped my cheeks of a kiss each, burst into a flood of tears, declaring that had anything happened to me he would instantly have deserted to the French; he said that, had I been drowned and of course carried into the ocean, no assertion of his could have prevented any one from considering him the cause, and that consequently he would have been torn to pieces by the English soldiers at Tarifa.

It was now about dusk, and the Spaniard having assisted me to mount, we started forward as fast as the badness of the road would permit, for we had several miles still to traverse. The expression of the inexpressible part of my dress at every stride of the horse resembled the sound made by steaks being fried in an adjoining room while the door is continually shutting and opening. This simile will now no doubt be considered excessively vulgar ; but at the period alluded to most officers were familiar with a frying-pan, and even a guardsman in those days could rough it on a beefsteak and a bottle of old port.

We arrived at Tarifa long after the officers had dined. Colonel Browne well recollects the circumstance, as it was on this occasion that I brought him a letter written by Lord Bathurst appointing him Lieutenant-Governor of Tarifa, with a pecuniary advantage attached which was not the least acceptable part of the communication.

In this expedition I lost the use of a gold repeater, which was so gorged by the mountain torrent that I never afterwards could keep it in order.

Soon after this I was again sent to Gibraltar with despatches, relative to which some notable occurrences took place. I should have previously mentioned that shortly after our occupation of Tarifa a corps or civic guard, composed of young men, inhabitants of the town, was formed. The command of this body, called the Tarifa Volunteers, amounting to from forty to fifty individuals, was confided to Captain Meacham, 28th Regiment, not only because he was a gallant and experienced officer, but also on account of his knowledge of the Spanish language, acquired at an earlier period when the regiment was stationed in Minorca. This corps in its infancy imperfectly drilled, without any established uniform and not very imposing in appearance owing to their diversity of dress, could not be relied on as an efficient force. For these reasons perhaps it was that they got the name of "Meacham's Blind Nuts," so baptised, if I mistake not, by Captain Allen of the 10th Regiment. However, to ascertain what might be expected from them in case of an emergency which was daily expected, Major Browne determined to put their alertness at least to trial, confiding his plan to the Spanish lieutenant-governor. After a jovial dinner-party he, about an hour before daybreak, ordered the drums and bugles to sound to arms and troops to line the walls immediately, stating that the French were rapidly advancing against the town. The first to be seen, sabre in hand, was the Spanish governor, previously warned ; then came forth the British garrison with firm and equal step ; and last and not too willingly appeared the rather tardy volunteers. They were to be seen in small groups scattered through the town, no kind of formation having taken place preparatory to their going to the walls ; and so they slowly moved along the streets. To hurry them up a gun was fired, when an extraordinary scene was presented. Suddenly all the doors in the town flew open, and out rushed a fiercer and more warlike body by far. The streets were instantly crowded with women, one seizing a husband, another a son, a third a brother ; some clinging to their dearly beloved, all endeavouring to snatch them by force from out their warlike ranks, loudly and bitterly exclaiming against the British, who, they cried or rather screamed, being fond of bloodshed themselves, would force others into fight whether willing or otherwise. At length, urged by some British officers and breaking away from their wives, mothers, sisters and lovers, in whose hands remained many cloaks, coats, hats and even torn locks of hair, the poor Nuts arrived half shelled upon the ramparts. Dawn soon after breaking, all the guns were fired off, but surpassed by the louder screaming inside the town. The rough music of the artillery was immediately succeeded by the more harmonious sounds of the band playing "God save the King." All was soon restored to tranquillity, save for a few contentious Blind Nuts, each claiming to be the first who mounted the walls and offered himself to be cracked in defence of his country.

Scarcely had this scene terminated when Colonel Browne received important intelligence of the enemy, and I was immediately sent with despatches to Gibraltar by water, the wind being rather favourable though strong, but the weather rainy. On my arrival at Gibraltar, to my utter astonishment I found the landing-place crowded with inhabitants, officers and soldiers, all greedy to know the nature of my despatches, especially as I had come away in such boisterous weather and in an open boat. All were in the greatest anxiety ; for an English man-of-war, happening to pass by Tarifa at the moment the guns were firing from the ramparts, reported the circumstance at Gibraltar, but as it was blowing hard at the time and there was no port, she had not been able to stop to ascertain the cause of the firing. This, since a second attack on Tarifa by a larger force was threatened by the enemy, caused the greatest excitement at Gibraltar.

The first person who addressed me on landing was Lieutenant Taylor, 9th Regiment (afterwards shot through the body at Barossa), demanding, without any prelude whatever, if Captain Godwin of his regiment was wounded. I dryly answered, " Yes." " Where ? " " In the shoulder." " Are they beaten off ? " " They are not there now." This was sufficient to extricate me from the surrounding crowd, which otherwise would have impeded my progress to the convent for at least an hour. As soon as Taylor got his information, he, followed by the crowd, whom I refused to answer, ran off to communicate his intelligence to his commanding officer, Colonel Mole, and Mole instantly galloped off with the news to General Bowes.

In the meantime I delivered my despatches to General Campbell at the convent. Proceeding thence to Captain Power, who temporarily commanded the 28th Regiment, I was there met by Captain Loftus, aide-de-camp to General Bowes, with a message from the general that I should immediately, and in writing, state my reasons for having propagated unfounded reports of an attack and battle fought at Tarifa. I instantly answered that I had propagated no reports ; that the words battle or Tarifa never escaped my lips ; that to get rid of an idle and troublesome multitude who surrounded me on landing, I muttered something in a low tone of voice to Lieutenant Taylor, telling him loud enough to be heard by many not to divulge anything until the contents of the despatches which I carried should be made known through the proper channel ; that Taylor promised secrecy ; and that my stratagem succeeded, for on his departure at a quick pace the crowd followed. I further added that, had I the slightest conception that anything thus communicated could be believed by a general officer, I should certainly have remained silent, however incommoded by the mob ; and that to free myself from them was my only object. This explanation seemed to have been sufficient. I had no further communication from the general ; but the circumstance having been privately communicated to General Campbell, he sent for Bowes and said, " So, general, I understand that you have had a flying despatch relative to a great battle being fought at Tarifa. I should think, general, that if such had been the case, this would have been the proper place for you to seek information, instead of sending in pursuit of the officer who carried despatches to me to know his reasons for any heedless conversation that might have taken place between him and any idlers by whom he was surrounded at the Mole. I understand also, general, that so pressing were you for his written explanation, that time was not allowed him to change his wet clothes, for which purpose it was I allowed him to go away, since he had been drenched with rain for several hours in an open boat." I met General Bowes the same day at the general's table. With a smile upon his countenance he very politely invited me to drink wine with him ; and the governor requested that, whenever I brought despatches, I should make the best of my way through the idlers, but should communicate with no one until I saw him. Thus the affair terminated as far as the generals were concerned.

But all my troubles were not as yet ended ; I had to encounter others on my return. During my absence Godwin had been told that I reported his having been wounded in the back of his shoulder ; but although he taxed me with the report in a laughing way, still he appeared not well pleased. His usual good-humour returned when I assured him that I never made use of such an expression ; and certainly Godwin was one of the last to whom I should attribute a wound in the back. The fact was that he had been hurt in the shoulder a short time previously by his horse running with him against a tree.

I frankly confess that while the affair was in agitation between the generals at Gibraltar I felt somewhat nervous, owing to a circumstance which took place five years previously. It may be recollected that in 1805 the regiment were encamped at the Curragh of Kildare. During the

early part of this encampment, when I was on duty on
the quarter-guard, it so happened that General Campbell
was general officer of the lines ; and unfortunately it
so fell out that the adjutant neglected to send me the
parole and countersign until a very late hour. In the
meantime came the grand rounds, who were rather hesitatingly challenged for the password, of which we ourselves
were in total ignorance. The general, noticing the not
very correct manner in which he was received and disre-
garding the challenge, rode up at once to the quarter-guard,
and, reprimanding me for the slovenly manner in which
the advanced files were sent forward, demanded the
countersign, adding that he believed I did not know it.
At the moment, as the general turned his head away,
the sergeant of the guard, having that instant received
the parole and countersign, stepped forward and whisper-
ing the words in my ear put the paper containing them
in my hand ; but the general perceiving some movement
rowed the sergeant for being unsteady under arms, and
called me forward rather briskly, repeating his belief that
I had not the countersign. I told him I had.

"And what is the countersign ?" quickly demanded
the general.

I now coolly replied, "I am placed here to receive, not
to give the countersign."

The general was evidently amazed at the reply, and
saying, "Very well, sir, we shall see about this in the
morning," turned his horse round to ride off.

This was the first quarter-guard I had ever mounted,
and from the novelty of the scene and my not having
the countersign when the grand rounds arrived, I felt
excessively nervous ; but although my knees at the first
onset beat the devil's tattoo against each other, yet, having

now gained full confidence, rather augmented by a titter amongst the general's staff one of whom was his son, afterwards Sir Guy Campbell, I told the general that my orders were to allow no person to pass without his first giving the countersign. Here the titter increased.

" What," said he—" not let me pass ? "

I made no reply ; but retiring the two paces which the general had called me forward, I remained on the right of my guard, looking most respectfully at the general. After a moment's thought he gave me the countersign, and having received the parole in ex-change rode away. I was in hopes that the unpleasant affair had ended here; but immediately after I was relieved from guard I was sent for by Colonel Johnson, who, although not my immediate commanding officer, commanded both battalions as senior lieutenant-colonel. To him therefore the general complained, and to him he seemed to attach most blame for allowing so young an officer, and so totally ignorant of his duty, to take charge of a quarter-guard. All the field officers of the two battalions were summoned on the occasion to Colonel Johnson's tent, and in their presence the general recounted the whole transaction. I remained perfectly silent. On his coming towards a conclusion, when he mentioned my having refused to let him pass, which he repeated with emphasis, I saw a suppressed smile on the faces of both Colonel Johnson and Colonel Belson. But Major Browne, impatient of restraint, broke into a laugh exclaiming, " Well, he is only one year in the Service ; I am many, yet I wish I knew my duty as well ; and," continued he with increased laughter, " it is the first time I ever heard of a boy ensign taking his own general prisoner." Browne was wrong as to my rank, for I had been five days a lieutenant.

However, the general did not seem to enjoy the joke as much as Browne did, and ordered Colonel Johnson to reprimand me. Johnson, who was brother-in-law to the general and one of the most gentlemanlike persons possible, bowed assent, but in some way gave the general to understand that he was at a loss to understand what particular part of my conduct it was for which I was to be censured. The general having retired, Johnson's rebuke to me was very slight indeed, particularly when I mentioned, as I refrained from doing while the general was there, that the countersign and parole, with which I should have been furnished before sunset, were not sent to me until midnight, just as the grand rounds advanced. But if the lieutenant-governor recollected this anecdote when at Gibraltar, it certainly caused no difference in his courtesy or hospitality towards me; for he insisted that whenever I visited Gibralter I should always make the convent my headquarters.

CHAPTER XIV.

A LITTLE CAMPAIGN FROM TARIFA.

TO relate the many and divers occurrences which took place during our stay at Tarifa, although all more or less interesting, would swell these pages to an imprudent size. I shall therefore pass over many and come down to the month of January 1811.

The Duke of Dalmatia, who directed the operations carried on against Cadiz and commanded the French force in Andalusia, was ordered by the Emperor to proceed into Estremadura, principally for the purpose of reducing the fortresses of Olivenza and Badajoz. Pursuant to these instructions he marched from Seville in the first days of the month with an army of sixteen thousand men, having withdrawn a part of the troops from before Cadiz. The British troops stationed in this fortress were commanded by General Graham. This active officer, indignant at seeing the gallant troops under his command ignobly and unnecessarily caged up in a fortress by an inferior force, (counting each Spaniard who wore military uniform a soldier), and anxious to shake off the dead weight of his sluggish ally, General La Peña, who impeded the Spaniards under his command both in working on the fortifications and fighting against the enemy, eagerly seized the opportunity offered by Soult's departure of bursting the trammels which fettered British valour and striking a decisive blow

against the enemy.   To carry into full effect his well-digested
plans, he proposed to the drowsy Spanish general, La Peña,
and to the active British admiral, Sir R. Keats, a sortie
from the Isla de Leon, purposing to attack the whole
French line, beat back the besiegers and bring the dis-
gracefully pent-up Spanish and British troops into open
air and active movement in the field.   This bold and
masterly project was eagerly embraced by Sir R. Keats,
and apparently so by La Peña.   It was therefore agreed
that whilst a bridge should be thrown across the River
Santi Petri, a general attack should take place by the
gunboats against the whole advanced French line from
Ronda to Santa Maria.   One obstacle however opposed :
the bank opposite the Isla, upon which the proposed bridge
was to rest, was with a strong force held by the enemy.
To obviate this it was determined that a diversion should
be made on the outposts in rear of the French lines,
to call off his attention, whilst the bridge was laid down.
In furtherance of this plan General Graham requested
General Campbell to allow Colonel Browne, who commanded at Tarifa, to move forward and attack Casa
Vieja.   Orders at the same time were sent by La Peña
to the Spanish general, Beguines, who commanded at
Alcala de los Gazules, to attack Medina Sidonia, distant
from his post about fifteen miles due west and directly
leading to Chiclana.

A despatch dated January 25th was late that night
received at Tarifa by Colonel Browne, containing orders
from General Campbell to move forward, with all the
troops he could take with him, to attack Casa Vieja,
and at the same time to favour as much as possible the
movement against Medina Sidonia by the Spanish troops.
Pursuant to his instructions, Browne, with four hundred

and seventy bayonets of the 28th Regiment and thirty artillerymen commanded by Lieutenant Mitchell, left Tarifa at three o'clock on the afternoon of the 26th and arrived at Fascinas—a distance of about twelve miles—at eight o'clock. Here we halted for a few hours ; and Captain Bowles of the regiment was detached with his company to watch the Vejer road and prevent our return to Tarifa being cut off by any troops coming from that direction, since Vejer was in possession of the French.

About twelve o'clock at night we again moved forward and at seven in the morning we came in sight of Casa Vieja, a large convent with some outhouses strongly fortified and garrisoned by French troops, amounting to upwards of a hundred men and having two twenty-four pounders on top of the building. This building is situated twenty-five miles from Tarifa, in the direction of Chiclana and Medina Sidonia, with which places it forms a triangle. We now moved forward, crossing the River Barbate immersed to our middle, when we were warmly saluted from the " Blessed old House," as the Spaniards called it, which at the same time sent out from twenty to thirty sharpshooters. The regiment circled round to get in rear of the convent, while the light company driving in the sharpshooters took a more direct line and soon gained the crown of the hill immediately over the building. We now lay down, after descending to within pistol-shot of the place, and opened so hot a fire that even a sparrow could not live on the walls. A parley was now sounded and the garrison summoned to surrender, which the commandant without any hesitation resolutely refused to do. Colonel Browne thought of attacking the convent by storm, although he had no scaling ladders and the walls were very high ; but reflected that even though we should succeed (which must be attended with severe loss from the great strength of the works lately constructed), its possession to us would be useless. He judged correctly that his instructions would be more effectually carried out by allowing the post to remain in the hands of the enemy, and by continuing to threaten it so as to induce the French at Medina to detach a force to its aid. Since it was no part of our object to come upon the place by stealth, the commandant there had time in the morning, previous to the investment, to apprise the garrison at Medina of our approach and of his own danger ; and consequently both infantry and cavalry were immediately sent to his succour.

Leaving the light company to look down on the convent and prevent all communication, Colonel Browne, with the rest of the regiment, marched towards Medina to favour any attack on that place. As he advanced he encountered the detachment sent from Medina, whom he attacked and put to the rout. He then halted giving his harassed men, who were soaked through with mud and rain and with wading rivers, an opportunity of refreshing and hoping also to induce the enemy at Medina to come forward. In both he fully succeeded. We had already with us some mounted guerillas, who were of more or less use ; and during Colonel Browne's halt he was fortunately joined by from thirty to forty Spanish cavalry commanded by an officer, who gallantly did their duty as long as they remained with us ; and it was a well-authenticated fact in those days that a small body of Spaniards attached to or acting with a British force, when there were no Spanish generals with false pride to interfere, would proudly imitate the heroic conduct of their allies.

The French force who now advanced from Medina were

at least equal in infantry and far superior in cavalry to that commanded by Browne, who, his men now refreshed by their halt, retired steadily on Casa Vieja, followed by the enemy, whose numbers increased every moment, particularly in cavalry. The light company were now imperceptibly withdrawn from the high ground, which prevented those within the convent from seeing either our troops or those who were advancing to their aid. A few of the company, in very extended order and partly covered by the brushwood, were left, and these fired at any showing themselves on the walls, so that those in the fort were in total ignorance of what was passing so near them; and thus we dreaded no attack from our rear. The light company having joined the regiment and the Spanish dragoons closed in, Colonel Browne formed line, placing some cavalry on either flank. The main body of cavalry, together with the few baggage horses and those which carried our provisions, were judiciously posted on a gently rising ground immediately in rear of our centre, which gave an imposing appearance. On coming closer the enemy halted, no doubt awaiting still stronger reinforcements, or probably imagining that we did not show our entire force.

As the dusk of evening advanced, Colonel Browne, covering his whole front with the Spanish cavalry who commenced skirmishing with that of the enemy, and considering that he had a French garrison in his rear, a superior force in his front, and the ground favourable for cavalry in which the enemy exceeded him by far, silently retired in the dark, recrossed the Barbate, and entered the gorge of the mountain pass, which being thickly planted with wood secured us against an attack of horsemen. On this night the Spaniards were to attack Medina; but reports coming in frequently during the night and down to a late hour on the morning of the 28th, showed us that the enemy's troops, whom we had drawn on at such risk, had not retired, and therefore that Medina had not been attacked.

Among the many messengers we sent out to collect information as to the movements of the Spaniards, one returned that forenoon, bringing a letter from the Spanish general stating that his troops were still in Alcalá, but that he intended moving forward immediately. Thus all our hardships and risk counted for nothing. We felt much mortified, and would willingly have returned to Tarifa from a scene where in appearance at least deceit had been used. But Browne, faithful to his instructions, moved out of his stronghold as soon as he learned that the enemy, whom we had drawn forward, had commenced a retrograde movement. Succeeding again in drawing them back, he again retired. The opposing cavalry were by this time much increased. On this day we were joined by forty men of the Tarifa Volunteers. Our situation was comfortless, neither houses, tents nor huts to shelter us, and the rain falling heavily. It was the first time that Meacham's corps were ever washed clean, and the Blind Nuts began to see what was the varied life of a soldier. However we kept up a blazing fire. Frequent reports during the night stated that the enemy were collecting in considerable numbers in our front with intent to attack us ; but, confiding in the vigilance of the Spanish cavalry, we felt no alarm.

Between three and four o'clock on the morning of the 29th our attention was suddenly called by the trampling of horses quickly approaching. Springing up from our seats round the fire (lying down was out of the question from the heavy rain), we were instantly under arms, when an officer, two orderly dragoons, and a couple of armed guides rode up, whom we immediately recognised as Spaniards.

The officer was aide-de-camp to General Beguines, by whom he was sent to Colonel Browne to inform him that untoward circumstances prevented an earlier attack on Medina Sidonia, but that it was his decided intention to storm it next morning, and he requested the colonel to make every exertion in his power to aid the assault. From what had already passed we felt very dubious as to Beguines' intentions. But there was something so noble and ingenuous in the deportment of the aide-de-camp, who solemnly pledged himself for the attack taking place, that for the first time we strongly suspected a Spanish general of sincerity ; in this instance we were not deceived. Colonel Browne told him that his support might be relied on, and instantly gave orders to prepare for march. The aide-de-camp having sparingly partaken of our greatest luxuries— salt pork and rum—mounted his steed with all that grace so peculiar to a Spaniard (and he was as fine-looking and handsome a man as I ever met), and bidding us a cordial farewell commended us with religious fervency to God and Saint Anthony and so rode off over bad roads and through French vedettes to inform his general that the English troops were already under way.

Groping our way in the dark, we advanced, and, having crossed the Barbate, were informed that the enemy were again retiring. Hurrying on to the convent, where we arrived at daybreak, we instantly opened a roaring fire of musketry against the building, more to make a noise than with the expectation of producing any other effect. Leaving the Tarifa Volunteers with a few red soldiers interspersed, Colonel Browne with the regiment moved towards Medina. We had not proceeded far before we encountered a party of about sixty men, infantry and cavalry, who, upon hearing our fire at the convent, had turned

round. They were instantly put to flight. Pressing
forward towards a mill about a league and a half from
Medina, our cavalry and guerillas, now exceeding sixty in
number, were detached to the mill, as we knew it to be a
post occupied by the enemy. On their approach the enemy
fled, when the mill, together with strong fieldworks and
extensive stabling recently finished, was set fire to, thus
informing the enemy at Medina of our advance. Upon
this, a formidable detachment were sent against us.
Coming close, they halted for a short time, but soon
displayed their boldness by a menacing advance, while we
showed our judgment by steadily retiring, covered by our
cavalry and the light company. As we fell back on
Casa Vieja, firing was heard in the direction of Medina
Sidonia. The enemy halted ; we conformed. On both
sides the cavalry skirmished by long shots. This petty
warfare continued nearly two hours, when we retired
gradually to our position over the convent. Here Colonel
Browne received a despatch from General Beguines informing him that he had taken Medina, but that the enemy
were in strong force before him, and that he anxiously
awaited the result of the sortie from the Isla de Leon.

Soon after this despatch had been received, the garrison
in the convent were made acquainted with all that had
happened in a very extraordinary manner. A large body
of the enemy's cavalry bore directly for our position. So
menacing was their aspect that our attention was entirely
directed towards them, and Colonel Browne prepared to
form square. In the meantime a French officer, winding
unperceived round the base of the high ground which
overlooked the convent, had the boldness to approach it
so near as to be enabled verbally to communicate with
the garrison. The verge of the hill, as I have already

stated, was lined by the Tarifa Volunteers, who, not being accustomed to active warfare and being drenched by incessant rain, did not use that vigilance which such hostile close neighbours required ; and it was the loud voice of the French officer which first called their attention. Many of them now fired, and some of the light company running up followed the example ; but, the mischief being done, we all rejoiced to see that the gallant officer escaped unhurt. It was subsequently ascertained that the communication thus heroically conveyed directed the commandant on no account to surrender, for although Medina had fallen that morning, it would be attacked during the night and the commandant strongly reinforced next morning. However we conjectured at the moment from the fact of the enemy having lost Medina, that the communication directed the commandant to seek an opportunity of escape with his garrison. The light company therefore resumed their old position over the convent, and the few guerillas now with us were ordered to be excessively alert. The regular Spanish cavalry, with the greater part of the guerillas, were skirmishing with the enemy in our front.

From the time we left Tarifa, about three o'clock on the 26th, up to the same hour on the 29th, the weather was so rainy and boisterous as to frustrate all the plans of the British general commanding at Cadiz. In consequence of this, double despatches were sent to Colonel Browne, one from Sir R. Keats (I could never learn why), the other from General Graham, stating that from the boisterous state of the weather the intended movements and the sortie from the Isla were postponed, and therefore directing his return to Tarifa as soon as possible. The gunboat which carried these despatches arrived at Tarifa only on the morning of the 29th. The naval officer in

charge was strictly enjoined to give his despatches into
no other hands than those of Colonel Browne, or in his
absence to a commissioned officer, who should be held
responsible personally for their delivery to the colonel.
There was no officer left in Tarifa except Lieutenant Light
of the Grenadiers (shortly afterwards shot through the
body at Barossa), and he but just recovering from a severe
fit of illness. He, though willing to undertake the duty,
was incapable from weakness ; and as the naval officer
insisted on the absolute necessity of delivering the despatches immediately, Assistant-Surgeon Johnson, who had
charge of the sick, volunteered to be the bearer and
unhesitatingly set forth. Having arrived at a small
hamlet about two miles short of Casa Vieja and rather
out of his direct road (he had no guide and was never
there before), he enquired where the British troops were,
when he was answered, " At Casa Vieja " ; and they
pointed to the convent. He rode directly to the gate, and
was instantly fired at from within. This took place at
the very moment when, as I have mentioned, the light
company were replaced immediately over the convent
and the guerillas ordered to maintain a vigilant look-out.
As soon as the doctor was fired at by the French from
within, he, as was natural, wheeled round and galloped
away at full speed, but not knowing what direction to
take, he unfortunately took the road to Vejer, of which
place in our present situation we felt particularly jealous.
As the convent intervened, the doctor's approach from
the hamlet had not been seen by us ; but when we saw
him gallop away from it at full speed, the light company
would certainly have fired at him had he not been instantly
covered by the mountain round which he rode. To protect
himself from the inclemency of the weather, which continued

wet and stormy, he wore a blue greatcoat buttoned up to the chin, over which he carried a loose camlet cloak. His cocked hat was covered with oilskin, strapped also under his chin ; and in all he showed no appearance of a British officer. In his flight he was unfortunately discovered by some of the guerillas, who like us mistaking him for a French officer endeavouring to escape, rode at him with their lances. On such occasions the lower end of the lance, which is formed of an iron slide or wedge, is driven into a box of the same metal fitted to receive it, and is always attached to the saddle. The horse, when an attack is made, is put to his full speed thus adding his velocity to his strength ; and with this full force Johnson was struck by a lance under the elbow, breaking one of the bones of the forearm, and striking him to an incredible distance from his horse. So far the act admitted of some shade of justification ; but while the doctor lay on the ground he received many wounds before it was found that he was a British officer ; and before any of the regiment came up the guerillas had actually commenced sharing his garments ; one took his hat, another his cloak, and so on. Johnson declared that on the advance of the guerillas, whom he knew to be such, he pulled open his outer vestments to show his British uniform, while his assailants asserted that they themselves opened his surtout to take it away, and only then discovered the red coat by which his life was saved. However that might be, the act was cowardly, as they were told at the time, for eight or nine of these butchers attacked him at once with full intent to kill him. Their duty as soldiers was to take the doctor prisoner, supposing him to be a French officer which I firmly believe they did at the onset, and to ascertain what information he possessed ; but they then would have lost the spoil, being well aware that in our presence they would not have been permitted to rob a prisoner naked.

On perusing the despatches carried by the ill-fated doctor (who received all the attention and assistance possible and was immediately forwarded to Tarifa), Colonel Browne immediately saw the perilous situation in which we were placed. He was open to attack in front by an overwhelming force from Chiclana, where the failure of the sortie from Cadiz must have been known long before the information could have reached us, and the object of our advanced movement consequently discovered. His return to Tarifa was liable to be anticipated by pushing a force through Vejer, which, by moving along the coast road would have a much shorter distance to get to Tarifa than we had ; and that town, being left without any troops for its defence, except a few sick in hospital, must immediately surrender. Or again, should the enemy force Captain Bowles' company, detached to watch the Vejer road, they could come immediately in our rear and cut off our retreat over the mountain road which alone was left to us. Any one of these measures could easily have been carried into effect had the enemy been a little more lively. They had the intelligence of the failure of the sortie from Cadiz long before we had ; and when General Graham's despatch was received we were then upwards of eight miles from Bowles, and therefore could give him no support were he attacked. Under these circumstances Browne hesitated not a moment how to act, and instantly marched from the convent, exposed to its fire, the Spanish cavalry still remaining behind as a check on the garrison. During our march Browne wrote to General Beguines, informing him of his communication from Cadiz and demanding to know whether, notwithstanding the failure of the sortie, he could maintain Medina Sidonia, at the same time candidly stating that he felt compelled to retire to prevent being cut off from Tarifa but that, although the risk was great, yet he would at all hazard await the general's answer on the skirts of the wood.

We remained during the night in the comfortless and slobbery gorge. The despatch to Beguines was never answered ; but next morning the colonel received a report from the cavalry officer left behind to awe the convent, that the French had again entered Medina the previous night at twelve o'clock, that Beguines was retiring to Alcalá, and that he himself with the whole of his detachment had been recalled to cover the retrograde movement. This report was dated three o'clock on the morning of the 30th, but reached us only at ten o'clock. An hour's time would have been sufficient to bring it from where it was dated. Whether this delay of six hours was made designedly to keep us from retiring, which would prevent the troops in the convent from coming out, we could not say ; however, it looked suspicious, and to us, critically situated as we then were, might have proved fatal. Orders were immediately sent to Captain Bowles to retire along the mountains and meet us at Fascinas, while we retired direct to that place.

Soon after Bowles joined, which was some time after our arrival at Fascinas, we all pushed forward for Tarifa and about dark arrived at Torre la Peña. Here we came on to the plain of Tarifa, which in consequence of the late continued rains now presented a sheet of water extending to the town, a distance of from three to four miles. Our way seemed a continuation of the ocean close on our right, the waters frequently intermixing ; however, wade it we must.

This operation to strangers would be attended with much danger from the numerous pits and deep ruts throughout ; but as scarcely a day had passed during nine months upon which some of us had not ridden or walked from the town to the tower, we trusted to our recollection and pushed forward to Tarifa, where we safely arrived late at night without any serious accident. While we were wading through the waters a lieutenant of the regiment was soused over head and ears, and when drawn out ejaculated, 'twixt joke and earnest, " Ah, if my poor mother saw me now ! " This pathetic speech caused a general laugh, and whenever any similar accident befell, some mother sister or lover was called upon, which kept up the merriment until we arrived. A laughable or humorous expression coming from a fellow sufferer has more effect in rousing the energies and diverting the men from bending under fatigue than the most studied and eloquent harangue delivered by any who do not actually participate in their hardships. Were I to undertake a long and fatiguing march with a body of soldiers, I should prefer being accompanied by a man in the ranks who could and would occasionally sing a humorous or exhilarating song than by a Demosthenes or a Cicero travelling at his ease. Those who have accompanied soldiers in long and forced marches must have remarked how quickly and cheerfully the men fall into their proper places, timing their step to the cadence of the song, and with what renovated vigour they press forward.

In this expedition, as in all others which we made from Tarifa (too numerous to be mentioned), we were accompanied by Lieutenant Mitchell, Royal Artillery. In Tarifa he was an artilleryman, pointing the guns from the bastion most exposed ; in the field he was a light bob, foremost in prick-

ing for the foe ; and on the occasion just mentioned he
acted in a third capacity, for he reconnoitred the fort of
Casa Vieja, guessed its capabilities from outward demonstration, ascertained the strength of its defences by personal
observation and formally reported thereon with all the
inherent pomp and acquired gravity of a Royal Engineer.

Although our little campaign lasted no more than five
days, yet it was very severe from our having suffered much
hardship and privation. We were sparingly fed ; during
the whole time drenched through by continual exposure to
rain, without any sort of shelter whatever. Six times we
crossed the Barbate River up to our middle ; we approached
no habitation save the " Blessed old House," its fire not
wholesome ; we had enough of marching over infamous
roads ; and we finally terminated our expedition on the
evening of the fifth day by wading for the last three miles
through a lake. Yet as soon as we changed our dress and
sat down to a smoking mess dinner, all our hardships were
forgotten, and long before we retired to repose our thoughts
and conversation were occupied alone in speculations on
our next enterprise. So lives a soldier ! Our men were
again ready for the field on the next day but one. Poor
Meacham was sadly annoyed at being recommended to
expose his Nuts to the sun for at least a fortnight to save
them from perishing by mildew.

CHAPTER XV.

ON the day following that upon which we returned to
Tarifa I was sent to Gibraltar with despatches giving
an account of our late movements to the lieutenant-governor,
who was much pleased with the conduct of the regiment
in general, but particularly with that of Colonel Browne
for the determined and judicious manner in which he
conducted the whole of the operations, as was fully testified
by General Beguines in a despatch written to General
Campbell on the subject.

Rather excited than depressed by the failure of the
intended sortie from Cadiz, General Graham, the resources
of whose mind multiplied in proportion as difficulties
appeared, still insisted not only on the local advantages
to be gained by a sortie before Soult should return with
reinforcements, but also that to boldly march out from the
strongest hold in Spain and undauntedly maintain the war
in the open field would inspire the nation with confidence
and stimulate the whole population to the deeds of national
glory which Spaniards were wont to perform. He con-
tended that with such sentiments properly directed the
Spaniards alone were an overmatch for any invading nation,
and would shortly succeed in freeing their country and
driving every Frenchman in Spain down the northern side
of the Pyrenees. These arguments could not be opposed

even by General La Peña, who opposed everything except the enemy. It was therefore arranged that seven thousand Spaniards and three thousand British troops should embark at Cadiz and sailing to Tarifa there descend, since that was the nearest place which the allies possessed in rear of the enemy's lines. To facilitate this enterprise General Graham made a sacrifice not easily paralleled. He ceded the chief command to his ally, thus patriotically giving up the certainty of personal fame as a leader for the honour of his country's arms and the prosperity of the general cause ; and such was the confidence he felt in the valour of the British troops under his command and in the happy results, if La Peña would only do his duty towards his country, or do anything except what was glaringly wrong, that he condescended to serve under the Spanish general, and that too against the opinion of Lord Wellington, who recommended him never to move out of Cadiz to execute any movement except in chief command. The duke well knew by dearly bought experience of what leaven Spanish generals were moulded. He knew that it required the utmost exertions of a British general to persuade those of Spain to save their own corps, without calculating on more. Of this Cuesta gave convincing proof by his movements before the battle of Talavera, by his inertness and incapacity while the battle raged and above all by his disgraceful conduct after the battle was fought, on account of which his lordship felt compelled for the safety of his own troops to separate from the Spanish army, bidding them farewell with feelings of respect for the gallant soldiers, of contempt for the vanity and ignorance of their commanders, and of distrust of the government who would have devoted their allies and compromised the honour and independence of their country for personal ambition and mean self-interested

motives. Spanish character in the different branches was
discovered rather too late for his advantage by Sir John
Moore, who portrayed it in its true colours for the information of His Majesty's counsellors and the guidance of his
successors in Spain.

It was now agreed that Generals La Peña and Graham
should march immediately after disembarkation against
the rear of the enemy's lines, force a passage to the con
tinental bank of the Santi Petri River, and by dislodging
the French from the posts which they there occupied cover
the construction of the bridge and the sortie from the Isla
de Leon. The Spanish general, Zayas, who was appointed
to the command at Cadiz during La Peña's absence, was
directed to second the project if the opportune moment
should arrive.

All being now ready, General Graham with the British
troops sailed from Cadiz on February 21st for Tarifa.
This place presenting only a roadstead and the wind
blowing fresh on the 22nd, when the general came before
it, a descent was found impracticable, and he therefore
proceeded to Algesiras, where he landed, and marching
over an excessively bad road arrived on the evening of the
23rd at Tarifa. The weather continuing boisterous, the
troops halted to await the Spaniards ; and Major Duncan's
brigade of guns, which had been disembarked at Algesiras,
had to be put on board again and brought by water to
Tarifa on account of the state of the road, over which a
wheelbarrow could not be rolled without disaster.

At Tarifa the 28th Regiment were garrisoned under the
command of Colonel Belson, who had rejoined a few days
previously from England. General Graham being well
acquainted with the old corps, particularly during the
campaign of Sir John Moore, requested General Campbell's

leave to lead it during the expedition, which was granted ; but the lieutenant-governor, not forgetting Colonel Browne's eminent services during his long command at Tarifa under many critical circumstances, sent the flank companies of the 9th and 82nd Regiments from Gibraltar, which, together with those of the 28th Regiment, were to be placed under the command of Colonel Browne, thus giving him an independent flank battalion, subject to no orders but those coming direct from General Graham.

During the few days which the British troops spent at Tarifa our time was passed in that jovial conviviality always to be observed among British soldiers on the opening of a campaign. This formed a remarkable era in the history of the 28th Regiment, never equalled in any other corps. They formed the proper garrison of Tarifa, and having been quartered there for some time were the only regiment which had an established mess. The town furnished but one posada, or inn if it may be so called ; and this afforded but little accommodation to so large a concourse as that now assembled. Upwards of a hundred and fifty officers dined at our mess daily ; those of the regiment, together with those of the flank companies sent from Gibraltar, who were of course honorary members, amounted to nearly fifty, for the officers of the 28th Regiment, never being much addicted to depôt duty, always mustered strong at headquarters.

Our mess-room was very spacious, and at either end was a room which entered into it ; not only these three, but in fact every room in the house, had tables put down ; and many there were who felt glad to procure a dinner even in the kitchen. The draught on our cellar was deep, and profiting by the experience of the first day of the jubilee, on the second day, the 24th, we passed a restriction act limiting each officer to a pint of port and half a bottle of claret ;

but notwithstanding this precaution, we ran a pipe of port dry in less than four days. Porter and brandy, being easily procured, were not subject to restriction ; a great part of these was disposed of in the kitchen and the small rooms by the mess-man as his private speculation. It was calculated that, including port claret brandy and porter, two thousand bottles were emptied in our mess-house within the week. Our wine accounts, as must be evident under such circumstances, were much confused and difficult to keep, since it was no easy matter to ascertain with whom each visitor had dined. The mess waiter was sent round daily to ascertain this fact, so necessary for the guidance of the wine committee. Discrepancies not unfrequently occurred between the highly favoured host and the too obliging guest. I recollect the mess waiter telling Colonel Belson one day that Lieutenant-Colonel A——n said he dined with him, upon which Belson remarked to the guest, loud enough to be heard by many, " A——n, you do not dine with me." The other very humorously replied, " Oh, I beg pardon—1 made a mistake ; now I recollect, it was for to-morrow I was engaged to you." " There you are mistaken again," said Belson ; " it was for yesterday, when you did not forget." These circumstances I recollect well, as I happened to be president of the mess for that week. Colonel Belson would not allow me to cede the chair, and always sat on my left hand. Our mess-man, a sergeant of the regiment named Farrel, although he piqued himself on an acquaintance with algebra, yet with all the aid of the assumed numbers, A B C, could never discover the unknown quantities consumed. He went into the field at Barossa, but was never heard of afterwards. Among the slain he was not ; and, enquiries being made at the French headquarters, he was not one of the few prisoners taken with a part of our baggage which fell into the hands of the enemy previous to the commencement of the action, "when the Spaniards in their way lived to fight another day." It is more than probable that in the annals of warfare no regiment has ever had an opportunity of enjoying themselves to such an extent as the 28th Regiment while General Graham's army remained at Tarifa. We were happy to see our friends, who, to do them justice, waiving all ceremony showed us extraordinary attention.

Even the sergeants contrived to procure a room, where they enjoyed themselves as much as the officers in the mess-room ; and their jokes, if not equally refined, were not the less entertaining. Being a member of the mess committee, my avocations obliged me to keep a vigilant look-out through all parts of the house, which gave me an opportunity of hearing unobserved many of the jests and repartees which took place in the sergeants' room, or debating society, as it was termed. But although these were at times rather sharp, still perfect good-humour prevailed throughout. The principal spokesmen, if my memory fail not, were a Sergeant Turnbull of the Guards, and a Sergeant O'Brien, of the 87th Regiment. They were most determined opponents, and each had a bigoted attachment to his own country, in support of which he poured forth witty and pungent repartees to the great entertainment of the auditors.

On one occasion, while I was on my way to our cellar, which was fast falling into consumption, my steps were arrested by loud bursts of laughter issuing from the debating-room. The first words which I distinctly heard were, " O, O, O ! You are all ' O's ' in Ireland !"

This remark evidently came from the Guardsman, when O'Brien drily replied, " ' O ' means ' from,' or ' the descendant of ' ; therefore I am not surprised at its being ridiculed by persons of your country, where long line of descent is so difficult to be traced."

" And pray, Mr. O, from whom are you descended ? "

" From Bryan Boro, the Great Boro."

" And surely ' Boro ' must be a corruption of the Spanish word ' Burro,' which signifies ' an ass' ? "

Then Pat grew eloquent on the deeds of his great ancestor, who at the age of eighty gained a most glorious victory over the invading Danes on the celebrated plains of Clontarf. Equally eloquent was he also on the demerits of the Englishmen of that ancient time, until cried out the British sergeant with a fine scorn :

" I like to hear a fellow of your kind, with your beggarly Irish pride, talking of records and historical facts ! Look to the history of your own country to learn its disgrace. What have you ever done or achieved except through murders, robbery, cruelty, bloodshed and treachery ? Have you not always been fighting amongst yourselves, or against your masters, since we did you the honour of conquering you ? "

" If we compare notes about murder and treachery, you need not fear being left in the background," retorted the Irishman ; " and as to the honour of being conquered, faith ! I cannot cope with you in your dignities there, for I cannot deny that you have been honoured in that way by Romans, and by Danes, and by Saxons, and by Picts, and by Scots."

" Your arguments," at last said the Englishman, after some further exchange of historical fragments, " might pass without contempt had they not been delivered with such a disgusting brogue. I should recommend you to go back again to some charity school—I mean, in England."

"If I intended to go to a charity school, it should certainly be in England. In my country it is only the destitute who go ; but in yours it is the rich men who send their sons on to the 'foundations' of the public schools which were originally intended for the education of poor clergymen's sons. With respect to my brogue, which you civilly term disgusting, it is our national accent and not disgusting to native ears, although to us the language is foreign. But I should like to know with what accent your countrymen spoke bastard French when it was crammed down their throats with a rod of iron for upwards of three hundred years ? "

"A language does not go down the throat," said the Englishman ; " it comes up, at least in every other country except Ireland. I make you a present of the bull, although there is no necessity for the donation, for all bulls are Irish."

"How are all bulls Irish ? "

"Because England, your mother-country, has ceded all bulls to you as being legitimately Irish."

"I don't understand how you make out England to be our mother-country. Step-mother is the proper term to give her ; and, faith ! a true step-mother she has proved herself to be."

Thus raged the fight amid the laughter and encouragement of the hearers, until, being president of the mess, I was reluctantly obliged to return to the mess-room.

During the stay of the British army at Tarifa strong working parties were constantly employed in levelling the roads, which the French engineers had frequently reported impassable for artillery ; however, profiting by our exertions in the present instance, they subsequently brought guns against Tarifa.

The stormy weather having somewhat abated, the second division of the fleet, laden with La Peña and seven thousand Spaniards, arrived off Tarifa on the morning of the 27th. It still blew fresh ; but owing to the indefatigable exertions of the navy the astonished Spaniards found themselves all disembarked before the evening. Again they were startled at the activity of the British general, who would have marched that night. The forward state in which the British were induced the Spaniards to proclaim their army also in movable condition. La Peña and his troops thus prepared and the roads made passable for artillery, the march was announced for the morrow.

The night of the 27th being the last jovial one the army were to pass at Tarifa, one hundred and ninety-one officers dined at the mess. The exhilarating juice of the grape was freely quaffed from out the crystal cup, and the inspiring songs of love and war went joyfully round, and the conclusion of each animating strophe was loudly hailed with choral cheers ; for such is the composition of a soldier that the object of his love and his country's foe alike call forth the strongest and most indomitable effusions of his heart, so closely allied is love to battle. Hilarity and mirth reigned throughout. Lively sallies of wit cheerfully received as guilelessly shot forth added brilliancy to the festive board. Officers having entered their profession young, mutual attachment was firmly cemented, genuine and disinterested. Each man felt sure that he sat between two friends ; worldly considerations, beyond legitimate pleasures and professional ambition, were banished from our thoughts. The field of glory was present to our view and equally open to all ; none meanly envied the proud distinctions which chance of war fortunately threw in the way of others. Oh, what an odious change I have lived to witness! But the days of our youth are the days of our friendship, our love and our glory. A fig for the friendship commenced after the age of sixteen or seventeen, when the cool, calculating and sordid speculations of man suffocate the fervid and generous feelings of youth!

CHAPTER XVI.

FROM TARIFA TO BAROSSA.

OUR revels continued until the morning; and in the morning, while many a Spanish fair with waving hands and glistening eyes was seen in the balcony, we marched out of Tarifa with aching heads but glowing hearts.

Towards evening we halted, and the army was modelled. The leading divison was placed under the command of General Lardizabal, an officer in every way qualified for the post. The Prince of Anglona was appointed to the centre or principal body of the Spaniards; but with this body La Peña remained. Two regiments of Spanish guards, the Walloons and that of the Royal City, were attached to the British troops, commanded by General Graham; this corps were termed the reserve. The artillery were attached fortunately to the troops of their respective nations; but by some courteous mismanagement two squadrons of German hussars were united to the Spanish cavalry under the command of Colonel Whittingham, and thus attached to the Spanish army. This officer held higher rank in the Spanish army, and, if I recollect right, commanded a corps of Spanish cavalry, clad and paid by England; but their movements were peculiarly Spanish.

On March 1st La Peña moved towards Casa Vieja, and marched the whole army in column of companies

nearly within gunshot of that post; and while moving
along the plain close to the " Blessed old House," the
column was reduced to subdivisions, giving the enemy full
opportunity of counting every man in the army. Whether
this extraordinary mode of procedure arose from treachery
or ignorance cannot be asserted, for at that time it was
difficult to distinguish one from the other in the movements
of Spanish generals. However that may be, the circumstance was loudly censured by all. As soon as the army
halted, General Graham mentioned this oversight to La
Peña ; yet it was not until next morning and after the
whole allied army had passed the post mentioned on its
route to Medina Sidonia, that the British general obtained
permission to dislodge the enemy from the convent. The
light company of the 28th Regiment, having made close
acquaintance with the post not long previously, were sent
on this duty. On our approach the enemy evacuated the
convent. As we were not able to come up with them, a
party of the German hussars were sent in pursuit, by whom
they were soon overtaken. But although thus threatened
by cavalry, they considered it unadvisable to form square
as the light company were fast approaching ; they therefore turned round and formed line. Here some untoward
work took place on both sides. The French, seeing no
possibility of escape, remained steady until the Germans
were close upon them, when they deliberately fired a volley
at them and then threw down their arms ; two of the
cavalry were killed and others wounded. The Germans,
enraged at their loss and justly considering it an act of
wanton and useless bloodshed, charged the unfortunate
defenceless wretches, sparing not a man ; all were cut
down. I never in my life witnessed in so small an affair
such mutilation of human beings. When they were carried

into the convent yard the doctor of the 82nd Regiment, attached to the flank battalion, declined to dress their wounds, as it was totally impossible that any one of them could survive. The light company were left on piquet or rearguard in the convent during the day, with orders to join the army after dusk at Medina Sidonia. Not long after this we were all astonished at seeing the whole army retiring, but could descry no enemy to account for the movement ; however, it appeared that as La Peña moved on Medina he was informed by some roving Spanish soldiers whom he met that Medina had lately been reinforced. Upon this information alone he made the retrograde movement, which cost the Spaniards many lives and might have been fatal to the Spanish cause ; but of this in its place· Thenceforth La Peña was distrusted by every British soldier, and the constancy of General Graham in accompanying him farther is to be much admired. At nightfall the piquet joined its own battalion, not at Medina, but on the very ground whence the army moved that morning.

On the morning of the 3rd, taking nearly an opposite direction to that of Medina, the army moved towards Vejer. This day's march was excessively harassing. A causeway, along which we must pass, was constructed over the edge of a lake ; and the heavy rains had so swollen the waters that not a vestige of the causeway was perceptible. Our guides were guerillas, but imperfectly acquainted with the place ; and thus many of our men in attempting the passage fell into the deep. Even along the causeway, when discovered, we were up to our middle in water ; the track was marked by placing men on the submerged road. The British general with his staff stood in the water to guide and animate the soldiers during their aquatic movement. Having passed this obstacle, which occupied much time, we pushed on to Vejer, from which we dislodged the enemy there posted. The town is built on a high conical hill looking down on the celebrated Bay of Trafalgar, where every breast was filled with thoughts of the immortal Nelson. From this eminence the enemy had a full view of the surrounding country, and not only could discover all our movements as we approached, but, as on the preceding day when we were passing the convent, were enabled to ascertain our exact strength.

On the afternoon of the 4th, about three o'clock, the army again moved forward, before the men's clothing and appointments were dry. General Graham, previous to leaving Tarifa, requested La Peña to make short marches, and thus bring the troops fresh into action. But the Spanish general, as is common with the weak, imagining that genius was marked by diversity of opinion and mistaking mulish obstinacy for unshaken determination, disregarded this sound advice. He acted on the principle of differing from the British general in everything ; and accordingly he marched the army for sixteen hours, the greater part of the time during a cold night, making frequent momentary halts, which always tend to harass rather than refresh troops.

On the dawn of the 5th our advanced guard of cavalry (Spanish) were encountered and worsted by a few French dragoons ; the affair was trifling, yet its moral influence was sensibly felt throughout the day. Cold, wearied, dejected but not disheartened, we still moved forward, until the sun, rising with unusual splendour and genial warmth, dissipated the drowsiness, which but a moment previously bowed down every head, and roused us to wonted animation. On opening our eyes to broad daylight, we found ourselves on the south-west skirts of Chiclana plain.

On the evening of February 27th La Peña had written from Tarifa to General Zayas communicating his intention to move forward next day, and stating that Medina Sidonia would be in his possession on the 2nd of the ensuing month, and that he would be close to the Isla de Leon on the evening of the 3rd. Zayas, acting on mail-coach time, regardless of unforseen contingencies, badness of roads or any other obstacles which might retard La Peña's advance, and without ascertaining whether that general was close at hand or not, trusting only to his watch for regulating his measures, laid down the bridge on the night of the 3*rd*. The following day passed without any appearance of La Peña or the British troops. The enemy, taking advantage of this delay, attacked the bridge on the night of the 4th with their piquets and small detachments, killed and wounded many Spaniards, took three hundred prisoners and broke two links of the bridge. It was through mere good fortune that the Isla did not fall into their hands. At the critical moment Captain A. Hunt, R.A., with the ten-inch howitzers, arrived and supported a charge made by a Spanish regiment over the bridge of boats, and so the enemy were repulsed. But if Marshal Victor had been more active, and had marched down six or eight thousand men during the 4th and screened them behind Bermeja Castle until night, and then made his attack with such a force, instead of with some six or seven hundred, there is not the slightest doubt but that he would have taken the Isla, and then either defended or destroyed the bridge. Under such circumstances the allied army would have been compelled to retire to Gibraltar to avoid Sebastiani, who, upon learning that Victor was in possession of the Isla, would of course have come forward with an overwhelming force.

It was in consequence of the losses sustained at the bridge on the night of the 4th and morning of the 5th, together with the imminent danger in which the Isla de Leon was of being taken, that I ventured to say that La Peña's dastardly retreat from Medina Sidonia cost the Spaniards many lives, and might have been fatal to the Spanish cause. La Peña's proceedings on our arrival at the plain of Chiclana were equally absurd and dangerous. Early on that morning (the 5th) he ordered General Lardizabal down to the Santi Petri point without giving or receiving any information whatever. Not even a gun was fired to give notice to those in the Isla of our arrival, nor was it ascertained whether the bridge was strongly defended or in whose possession it actually was. The proceedings of Zayas and La Peña offer a correct specimen of the manner in which combined movements were executed by Spanish generals ; all acted independently and generally in direct opposition to each other. On this occasion Lardizabal acted gallantly. Having beaten away a strong force of the enemy from the Santi Petri point, he established communication with Zayas, thus enabling him with three thousand Spanish troops and an immense park of artillery to pass from the Isla over the bridge.

The army, as already mentioned, entered the plain of Chiclana early on the morning of the 5th, close to a low mountain ridge called Cerro de Puerco, or " the boar's neck," from its curving shape bristling with pine trees, and from the number of those animals always to be found there. This ridge, distant from the point of Santi Petri about four miles, gradually descends for nearly a mile and a half to the Chiclana plain. On its north side the plain is broken by ravines, pits and rugged ground ; a large pine forest hems it on all sides at unequal distances.

Situated midway between the hill and Santi Petri point, close to the western point of Cerro de Puerco, stands La Torre, or the Tower of Barossa. The eastern point of this ridge looks upon the space between Chiclana and the Santi Petri; whilst its western boundary looks down upon the boat road leading from Vejer to Bermeja and the Isla de Leon, passing within less than half a mile of the tower above mentioned.

In preparing for the battle General Graham, like an experienced soldier, pointed out to La Peña all the advantages which the ground offered, insisting on the absolute necessity of occupying the ridge of Barossa with their strongest force, it being the key of the whole ground. But the Spanish general, indignant at having his proper line pointed out by a *foreigner*, spurned his advice and being borne out by his Adjutant-General Lacy, ordered the British general to proceed to Bermeja to maintain the communication between the allied troops in the field and those in the Isla. General Graham, although naturally courteous and through policy yielding, yet on this occasion absolutely refused obedience until the Spaniard pledged himself to post on the heights of Barossa a Spanish force at least equal to that commanded by the British general. Long before his movement down to Bermeja, he detached Colonel Browne with his battalion to occupy the western point of Barossa. There we were shortly afterwards joined by the Walloon and the Ciudad Real regiments of guards. To this body were subsequently added three other Spanish battalions, four guns, and all the allied cavalry, commanded, as I have already said, by Colonel Whittingham. The whole were under the orders of General Cruz-Murgeon, accompanied by Brigadier-General Beguines, and all, as we thought, determined to do their duty.

Soon after General Graham with the British division
had moved from the plain through the pine grove
towards Bermeja, Marshal Victor, who anxiously watched
the movements of the allies, seeing their troops at three
different points, Barossa, Santi Petri and Bermeja, moved
forward from Chiclana towards the road which leads from
Vejer. This movement was not immediately perceived by
us, the Spaniards being placed between our battalion and
the point mentioned ; but a confused and hasty movement
on their part induced the colonel to send me to ascertain
the cause. I was told by General Cruz-Murgeon that they
merely wished to take ground to our left ; but seeing
the hurry of the Spaniards increase, I instantly galloped
beyond their extreme flank, and now discovered the French
cavalry moving towards the coast road and rather inclining
towards our position. Retiring quickly, I reported the
circumstance to Colonel Browne.

By this time the greater part of the Spanish troops
had passed between us and the coast road and were soon
in rapid march towards the beach leading to Bermeja.
Colonel Browne strongly and rather indignantly remonstrated against their conduct. At this period Colonel
Whittingham rode up, and addressing Colonel Browne said,
" Colonel Browne, what do you intend to do ? " The reply
was, " What do I intend to do, sir ? I intend to fight the
French." Whittingham then remarked, " You may do
as you please, Colonel Browne, but we are decided on a
retreat." " Very well, sir," replied Browne ; " I shall stop
where I am, for it shall never be said that John Frederick
Browne ran away from the post which his general ordered
him to defend." Generals Murgeon and Beguines were
present during the conversation, and as they expressed a
wish to know its exact import, I informed them word for

word in plain Spanish, which I pledge myself was a correct
and full interpretation, and could not be misunderstood.
Colonel Whittingham again addressed Colonel Browne,
saying, " If you will not come with us but wish to retire
on General Graham's division, I shall give you a squadron
of cavalry to cover your retreat." Browne wheeled round,
making no answer ; and thus a formidable corps, compoucd
of two regiments of Royal Spanish Guards, three regiments
of the line, a park of artillery and a strong force of cavalry,
all well armed clad and appointed, undaunted by the
scowling frowns of their allies and the reproachful taunts
of their own countrymen, were not afraid to run away.
They retrograded with firm tread ; nor faltering step nor
slow was seen, and not one longing lingering look was
cast behind.   They left four hundred and seventy British
bayonets bristling on the neck of the boar.

The Spaniards being now out of the way and soon out
of sight, Colonel Browne directed Lieutenant Sparks, 30th
Regiment, who acted as engineer, to loophole a chapel
which stood on the summit of the hill. Some men were
loosely thrown in, and the remainder of our little battalion
formed three sides of an oblong square, the low tower
or chapel supplying the fourth face.

By this time the French cavalry had gained the coast
road, probably either to cut off the retreat of the allies
by that route or to prevent any troops coming by way
of Vejer. Be that as it may, they now turned directly
towards us. On approaching nearly within musket range,
they opened right and left, apparently to gain both
our flanks ; and now for the first time their artillery
were discovered not far behind, and at the same moment
their infantry were seen moving forward, darkening
the distant part of the plain which skirts the town of

Chiclana. Hesitation would now be madness. Our men were instantly withdrawn from the chapel, and forming column of quarter distance we proceeded quickly down the hill towards the pine forest which shut out Bermeja from our view. The enemy's horsemen were soon on every side of our little column and kept gradually closing in; but dreading that, before we could get away to a sufficient distance from the hill, the artillery, which we had seen whipping over the plain, would open their fire upon us, we durst not halt to form square ; our situation was rather perplexing, but we were determined. In this order we moved rapidly down the hill, which being uneven and woody favoured our retreat ; but on crossing a ravine we became more exposed, having entered on comparatively level ground, scarce of wood. Colonel Browne now threw out a few loose files, but not far from each angle of the column, to warn the cavalry off, some few of whom were hurt by their fire. To say the truth, the cavalry showed rather a wavering inclination than a firm determination to charge us. Having passed over the level ground, we touched the skirts of the forest, and on our forming line the cavalry drew off.

During these operations General Graham, entangled in the pine forest, was pressing forward towards Bermeja, when two peasants rode breathless up to him, stating that the whole French army, headed by Marshal Victor, were rapidly crossing the plain of Chiclana and coming down on his rear. Upon this he immediately turned round and soon perceived the Spaniards, who had fled from the hill, posting along towards the coast ; and since these were mistaken for French, the English troops were on the point of firing into them. At this moment Captain Calvert, having discovered something red through the thick foliage

of the wood, cried out, "That must be Colonel Browne's
flank battalion," and darting forward soon discovered his
surmise to be fact.   General Graham came forth instantly
to meet us, saying, "Browne, did I not give you orders
to defend Barossa Hill ? "   " Yes, sir," said Browne ; " but
you would not have me fight the whole French army with
four hundred and seventy men ? "   " Had you not," replied
the general, " five Spanish battalions, together with artillery
and cavalry ? "   " Oh ! " said Browne ; " they all ran away
long before the enemy came within cannon-shot."   The
general coolly replied, " It is a bad business, Browne ; you
must instantly turn round and attack."   " Very well," said
the colonel ; " am I to attack in extended order as flankers,
or as a close battalion ? "   " In open order," was the reply,
and the general returned to the troops in the wood.

All this time we never saw our English comrades, though
they were close before us, so dense was the wood.   The flank
battalion were instantly extended into skirmishing order,
which had scarcely been done when the general again rode
back to Colonel Browne, saying, " I must show something
more serious than skirmishing ; close the men into compact
battalion."   " That I will, with pleasure," cried the colonel ;
" for it is more in my way than light bobbing."   The order
to close on the centre was instantly bugled out, during
which movement the colonel sent to know from the general,
who had again retired, if he was to advance as soon as
formed, and whether he was to attack immediately in his
front or more towards his right.   The answer was, " Attack
in your front, and immediately."

All being now ready, Colonel Browne rode to the front
of the battalion and taking off his hat said in a voice to be
heard by all, " Gentlemen, I am happy to be the bearer
of good news : General Graham has done you the honour of

being the first to attack those fellows. Now follow me,
you rascals!" He pointed to the enemy, and giving the
order to advance broke into his favourite air :

> "Now, cheer up, my brave lads! To glory we steer,
> To add something new to this wonderful year."

Thus we moved forward with four hundred and sixty-eight
men and twenty-one officers to attack the position, upon
which but three-quarters of an hour previously we had
stood in proud defiance of the advancing foe, but which was
now defended by two thousand five hundred infantry and
eight pieces of artillery, together with some cavalry. To
this force were added two battalions of chosen grenadiers,
commanded by General Rousseau, the whole under the
orders of the General of Division, Rufin.

CHAPTER XVII.

THE result of the conflict between such a force and our
lone little battalion, whose strength I have already
mentioned, must be anticipated. The enemy, seeing so
small a force, detached from any apparent support, advancing against them, allowed us to approach close; and the
orders given by Colonel Browne were that not a shot
should be fired, but to proceed to work as soon as possible
with the bayonet. As soon as we crossed the ravine close
to the base of the hill and formed on the opposite side, a
most tremendous roar of cannon and musketry was all at
once opened, Rufin's whole division pointing at us with
muskets, and eight pieces of ordnance sending forth their
grape, firing as one salvo. Nearly two hundred of our men
and more than half the officers went down by this first
volley, thus opening the battle propitiously for them. We
now literally stood in extended order; the battalion was
checked. In closing on the centre and endeavouring to
form a second efficient line, upwards of fifty more men and
some officers were levelled with the earth; and all the
exertions of Colonel Browne could not form a third line.
We had by this time lost upwards of two hundred and
fifty men and fourteen officers, between killed and wounded;
the remainder of the battalion now scattered. The men

commenced firing from behind trees, mounds or any cover
which presented, and could not be got together.

When I say that out of twenty-one officers—the whole
number who originally went into action—fourteen were
put *hors de combat*, this latter number might be given as
nineteen ; for two officers only of the battalion were now
to be seen standing on the field, Colonel Browne and the
humble author of these Memoirs (wounded). The colonel
now addressed me, saying, " I shall go and join the Guards ;
will you come ? " I declined the proposition, remarking
that not being just then firm on my legs, it would take
me some time to arrive at where the Guards were ; that
he was unhurt and mounted and could confidently go.
His character for bravery had been established throughout
the army for many years ; but as for me, although I
had seen a good deal of service, particularly during the
campaign of Sir John Moore, still I was a very young
man, and I therefore told him that so long as three men
of the battalion stood together and I was able to stand with
them, I should not separate from them.

The colonel galloped off and joined the Guards, who
were at that moment passing at some distance in rear of
where our right flank originally stood, now marked only
by our dead. The Guards moved forwards with astonishing
celerity and steadiness, although not formed and exposed
at the time to a tremendous fire of grape and musketry.
To this new scene of slaughter it was that Colonel Browne
directed his course.

When the flank battalion were first ordered to advance,
we were not in sight of the other British troops ; but as
we approached the ravine, casting a glance behind we
discovered the Guards emerging from the forest. They
presented neither line nor column, a confused mass showing

no order whatever, one order alone excepted, and that they gallantly maintained throughout the day : it was the order to advance against the foe.   Every roundshot which struck their mass passed over our heads, we then being close under the hill upon which the enemy were posted.

The first advance of General Dikes' brigade was directly in our rear. This direction was continued until the wood, which stretched forward immediately on his right flank, was cleared. His brigade then brought up their left shoulders until our right flank was passed. Dikes now brought forward his right, and extending his line gallantly pressed on to attack the left of Rufin's division, made heavy by General Rousseau's grenadiers.

Soon after Colonel Browne's departure, Captain (long since lieutenant-colonel) Calvert, General Graham's aide-de-camp, rode up to where I was carrying on a kind of fight with a very few men about me. Perceiving the destruction around, and seeing some soldiers straggling and firing some way in the rear, he requested me to go back and bring them up. This I positively refused, stating that I was wounded in the thigh, and were I to proceed to the rear I could never regain my place with an army advancing ; I added that as he was mounted he would be safe in making the attempt. Calvert smiled and rode off, but not to the rear. Again I was left comparatively alone.

By this time the near approach of the Guards claimed a large portion of the enemy's fire, which previously had been directed to the place where the remains of the flank battalion still continued to fire from behind defences. I now contrived to get eight or ten of the men together, principally 9th Grenadiers and 28th Light Infantry ; to this little force I proposed charging a howitzer, which was pouring forth destruction immediately in our front. The proposition being well received, I seized a firelock (there were many spare ones), and on this a drummer named Adams, of the 28th Grenadiers' Company, said that were he not afraid of being obliged to pay for his drum, he also would take a musket. Upon my telling the boy that I would pay for his drum, he flung it away and armed. I have always thought Adams the bravest man, or rather boy, whom I ever met—not for seizing a musket and gallantly charging, for in excitement that was natural enough ; but that he should stand calmly calculating the price of a drum when hundreds of balls were passing close to his body is scarcely credible ; but so it was.

We now darted forward and were so fortunate as to capture the gun at the very moment when it was being reloaded. Two artillerymen were bayoneted ; the others rode off on their mules. This was not a gun fallen into our hands—it was taken at the point of the bayonet ; and however I may be criticised for saying it, I was the first person who placed a hand on the howitzer ; and afterwards with some chalky earth I marked it "28th Regiment."

Scarcely had the gun been taken when we were joined, as if through magic effect, by upwards of a hundred men of the flank battalion—a proof that they were not far distant. They darted forth from behind trees, briars, brakes and out of hollows ; I could imagine myself standing on "Benledi's Side." We now confidently advanced up the hill, and unlike most advances against a heavy fire, our numbers increased as we proceeded, soldiers of the flank battalion joining at every step. On capturing the gun, I threw down the firelock and bayonet which I carried; but Adams retained his and putting on a pouch did good service during the remainder of the day.

Soon after the movement of General Dikes in rear of the flank battalion, Lieutenant-Colonel Barnard, also commanding a flank battalion, and Lieutenant-Colonel Bath, leading the two flank companies of the 20th Portuguese Regiment, pushed forward to the left, and were immediately in fight with the enemy's tirailleurs. Colonel Wheatley, who commanded those troops together with the 28th, 67th and 87th Regiments, disentangling himself from the pine forest and at the same time prolonging his left flank, soon found himself opposed to the division of General Laval, who, debouching from the Chiclana wood, advanced so far as to form an obtuse angle with Rufin's division, already in line and engaged on the hill. Laval bore heavily forward in dense column, sending forth a continued peal of musketry, reckless of the destructive fire of our artillery, which took him in front and flank. Previous to these movements of Dikes and of Wheatley, Major Duncan was sent forward with his brigade of artillery consisting of ten guns. He came up rather close in rear of Browne's flank battalion soon after we were engaged, and next to our own battalion the artillery were the first British troops in action. The guns were soon embattled in rear of our left flank; their murderous fire was quick, and heavily pitched into Laval's advancing columns. Yet Laval still pressed forward, until Wheatley's brigade advancing, firing and deploying, came in contact with them; then the 87th Regiment, commanded by Major Gough, making a desperate charge, completely overthrew the 8th French Regiment, capturing their Eagle. In the meantime Laval, moving forward his right wing,

13

whom he strengthened with a battalion of grenadiers, attempted to turn Wheatley's left flank; but Colonel Belson, with the 28th Regiment, who formed the left of Wheatley's brigade, coming up, forming and firing by companies, kept back his left wing in a diagonal direction, and by making a vigorous charge of the whole regiment served Laval in the manner in which the French general would have served him; he completely turned his flank.

At this period the strife was fierce, but, the British cheer passing through the entire brigade, the whole line now pushed forward. A general charge took place, and Laval's division were upset. Wheatley's brigade, now bringing forward their left, and whilst in full pursuit, fell in with the enemy's corps of reserve, who were instantly put to flight at the point of the bayonet. In the meantime the Guards, led on by General Dikes, pushed gallantly forward with lengthened step and lofty bearing ; and I make bold to say that never did the household troops witness a day more honourable to their corps, nor one upon which they more brilliantly maintained the glory of their prince. Surmounting all difficulties presented by the roughness and inequalities of the ground, heedless of the enemy's menacing attitude, reckless of the murderous fire which swept their still unformed ranks, they bore steadily onward and having crossed a deep broad and rugged ravine, wherein many a gallant soldier fell to rise no more, they climbed the opposite bank. Here they were encountered by Rufin's left wing and Rousseau's grenadiers, which latter gallantly descended from their position to give that reception which to such a warlike visit in martial country was due. But the Guards having gained firm footing on the base of the hill, and no obstacle opposed save men in arms, British blood and British prowess soon prevailed. The chosen

grenadiers recoiled from the shock. Rufin, or rather Victor
who was present, tried to retrieve the disaster by bringing
forward his right ; but these were furiously attacked
and driven backwards by the remnant of Browne's flank
battalion, now amounting to nearly two hundred men and
one wounded officer. Both the enemy's flanks were thus
turned round in rear of his centre.

And now the battle for a moment hovered in the zenith
of its glory ; the contending foes were not above ten yards
asunder, and scarcely were the enemy seen to move.
Tenaciously maintaining their hold of the hill, they fought
with desperation, defending every inch of ground; for the
precipice was near. Their hardiest veterans stood firm ;
their bravest officers came forth displaying the banners of
their nation ; the heroic example of Marshal Victor was
imitated by all. Conspicuous in the front the marshal
was recognised by both armies waving his plume in
circling motion high above his head, to fasten his troops
to the hill ; but his gallant deeds and surprising valour
were vain against his more than equal foe. General
Graham at this critical moment darted to the front, and
by one short word, loud and inspiring, made nought of
all the marshal's bravery and combinations. The word
was, "Charge!" Like electric fluid it shot from the
centre of the British line to the extremities of its flanks,
instantaneously followed by the well-known thundering
British cheer, sure precursor of the rush of British
bayonets. The Guards and flankers now rushed forward,
when with loud and murmuring sounds Rufin's whole
division, together with Rousseau's chosen grenadiers, were
instantly in whirling motion rolled down into the valley
below, leaving their two brave generals mortally wounded
on the hill, which was now in possession of their blood-

stained conquerors. The battle was won ; and the gallant Graham triumphantly stood on the bristling crest of Barossa's blood-drenched hill.

Now, since both flanks of the enemy had been turned, they came back to back on the plain ; and this steadied them, so that they continued to fire. I therefore requested Colonel McDonald, our Adjutant-General, to allow me, with the survivors of the 28th Regiment's flank companies, to go out and skirmish with the enemy, whilst our line should be got ready to advance. To this, with the concurrence of Colonel Browne who had just rejoined the battalion, he consented. We then moved forward. I saw no other troops go out. Colonel Browne was now the only officer with the remaining part of the flank battalion. After skirmishing for a short time, we were recalled. On our return, Colonel McDonald remarked that Major Northcote, having come up with the Rifles, would cover the line ; that he therefore recalled us, especially as Colonel Browne wished to have me with the battalion, at the same time saying in the most flattering manner that he should never forget my services throughout the day, and would always be ready to testify to them when called upon.

The enemy's divisions, now united, were soon formed, and seemed determined to seize the boar by the tusks ; but the boar was now metamorphosed into a lion. On Major Duncan arriving with his guns and sending some beautifully directed shots with mathematical precision to dress their line, Marshal Victor retired his troops beyond the noxious range. The hill being gained, and the enemy inclined, although ashamed, to retreat, General Graham sent his aide-de-camp Captain Hope to General Beguines, requesting him to bring up the two Spanish regiments originally attached to the British division; even this turned out unpropitious. When Duncan's fire prevailed on the enemy's column to retire, Colonel Ponsonby, of the Quarter-Master-General's Department, by permission of General Graham sought out the allied cavalry and brought away the German hussars. Having wound round the western point of the disputed hill, they were seen sweeping along the plain in beauty of battle; and it is my firm belief that had they not appeared at that moment we should have been immediately in motion to the front. We gave the Germans a cheer as they passed in front of our line, now formed. The enemy's cavalry turned round and faced them stoutly, their commander placing himself some distance in their front. As the Germans closed on the enemy our cheers were enthusiastic. The brave French leader was instantly cut down; our cavalry charged right through their opponents, then wheeling round charged them from rear to front, one red coat always conspicuous, Colonel Ponsonby. The French dragoons thus broken, Rousseau's grenadiers came to their support, and forming square covered the horsemen in their retreat. Again the British troops were on the point of advancing, when a staff officer came galloping up to say that a fresh column of the enemy were coming on the right flank of the Guards. This information alarmed us. Looking through my glass and observing them for an instant, I assured Colonel McDonald that they were Spaniards and that I knew the regiments. However some hesitation followed; thus the Spaniards who betrayed us in the morning deceived us in the afternoon. It was General Beguines who, glad to get away from La Peña, was hastily advancing with the two regiments before mentioned.

A second column were seen advancing from the opposite direction—Chiclana. This was supposed to be Villatte's division, who had not been engaged during the action, having remained near the Almanza creek, in front of General Zayas. But they turned out to be the sick, marched out from the hospitals of Chiclana, who thus succeeded as a ruse in covering the retreat of the vanquished Victor.

Although at this critical juncture every British soldier felt confident that a strong body of six hundred Spanish cavalry, fired by the example of the gallant Germans, would ride forward against the reeling columns of the retiring enemy, yet they never appeared. Abandoning their calling as soldiers they remained behind, mouthing the pebbles of the beach and thus preparing with oratorical effect to extol as their own those heroic deeds in which they bore no part and from which they studiously kept aloof.

Notwithstanding the arrival of Beguines, General Graham evidently saw the difficulty and danger of making an advanced movement. The enemy, though beaten and having suffered severe loss, still retired with a stronger force in the field than the British numbered before the battle commenced. Villatte's division were fresh, and could easily have joined Victor. Our army was crippled, half its numbers being put *hors de combat*; and the survivors had been for twenty-four hours under arms, sixteen of which had been passed in marching, and chiefly during the previous night. After having gained so brilliant a victory, and defeated the enemy at all points, the British general fully expected that La Peña, awaking from his torpor, would take advantage of Victor's overthrow and lay the drowsy Spaniards on the track of his discomfited and retiring columns ; but he was mistaken—such was never La Peña's intention. At the

time when Colonel Browne took up his position on the
hill, the principal part of the Spanish artillery were moved
along the beach road and halted about midway between
the two points whence the enemy could move on to attack,
the one by the western point of Barossa, the other by the
eastern side of Bermeja. On this position they halted,
but with their drivers mounted, ready to start at a moment's
notice for that point, whence the enemy advanced *not*.
Thus, when Victor was perceived advancing against Colonel
Browne, the great guns flew along the beach road, nor
stopped until Bermeja was left far in their rear. Later,
when the British troops were exposed to the hottest fire,
perilously situated, their rear left open to attack by the
early flight of the Spaniards from the hill, yet La Peña
gave no aid, although, had he moved forward by the eastern
side of Bermeja and come on the plain in that direction
towards Chiclana, he would have got in rear of Marshal
Victor, when the whole French army must have been
destroyed or taken. But neither the roaring of cannon,
his duty towards his allies, the pride of his profession, nor
the independence of his country was sufficient stimulant
to rouse him forward into action : La Peña was determined
not to move. Yet when subsequently cashiered for his
disgraceful conduct, he had the unparalleled impudence
to declare that it was a great hardship to be dismissed the
Service after *he* had gained so brilliant a victory with
the allied army. And soon after the battle General Cruz-
Murgeon unblushingly asserted in the public prints at
Cadiz that he took both prisoners and guns during the
action. Colonel Ponsonby, who undertook to refute this
unfounded statement, asked me (all the other guns captured
being accounted for) whether any Spaniards even seemingly
assisted or were in sight when the gun, which he said he

saw me in the act of charging, was captured. I replied
that there was not a Spaniard in the field at the time, and
that with the exception of himself and Colonel McDonald,
the Adjutant-General, who rode past at the time, no
individual of any corps was in sight of the flank battalion
when the gun was taken, not even the Guards, who, though
immediately on our right, were shut out by the intervening
inequalities of the ground. But with respect to his taking
four guns, General Cruz-Murgeon was partly right, the
term "taking" only being erroneous. After the action
was over, the Spanish general found his own guns on the
same spot where he had abandoned them in the morning,
silent and cold, though they should have been loudly
pouring forth their hottest fire against Rousseau's division
when they were advancing against Colonel Browne's position.
This I said that I was ready to prove, having seen the guns
after the Spaniards had fled. This statement being made
public, the controversy ceased, and Cruz-Murgeon shrank
from the paper warfare as disreputably as he had fled from
the field.

Until late in the evening the British general maintained
his position on the hill, when, seeing no prospect of a
forward movement on the part of the Spaniards, he, as
soon as it was dark, to prevent his movement being
discovered by the enemy, retired down to Santi Petri
point, and passed over the bridge of boats into the Isla
de Leon.

CHAPTER XVIII.

WE RETURN TO TARIFA AND THENCE TO LISBON.

THUS terminated the celebrated battle of Barossa, by Spaniards termed the bloody fight of the wild boar, fought under extraordinary difficulties against a gallant foe more than double in number, by harassed British troops, whose gallantry called forth the admiration of all Europe and the malignant jealousy of their allies— a battle which immortalised the genius and valour of the commanding general, who coolly directed our movements until all was prepared for the bayonet, when, laying aside the personal prudence of the experienced old commander, he displayed the vigour and impetuosity of the young soldier, leading us on to the final glorious charge. It was during this charge, and when the Guards and flank battalion united on the top of the hill, that Colonel Browne and I again met, he on the left of the household troops and I on the right of the flank battalion, with whom, from the departure of the colonel until his return, I was the only officer and consequently in command. The time of my command, as well as I can recollect, was about an hour, and that during the hottest part of the action. After mutual congratulations, my gallant colonel shook me cordially by the hand, declaring that he never could forget my services on that day, and adding that, should we both survive the action, he would in person present me to General Graham and bear full testimony to my

conduct throughout the whole day. The colonel was
fully aware that, had the author of these Memoirs lagged
behind in consequence of a wound received early in the
action, he, on his arrival on the hill, instead of finding
nearly two hundred bayonets of the flank battalion well
into the charge which reeled the enemy off the hill, would
not have had a single man of that battalion present to
command, and must consequently have been still a
volunteer with the Guards. I reported to him my having
charged and taken the howitzer. Here I feel called upon
to state that when Colonel Browne parted to join the
Guards there were not ten men of the flank battalion to
be seen and not above four or five standing near us ; there
was nothing for him to command, and I feel thoroughly
satisfied that it was by sheer bravery he was moved.
Although the battalion when they originally moved forward
had not the slightest prospect of success, still it was
absolutely necessary for the safety of the British army
and the Spanish cause to push us forward ; and had
we not undauntedly pressed on to attack Rufin in his
position, that general would have come down in perfect
order on the British troops, then in a confused mass and
so entangled in the pine forest as to render any attempt
at formation totally impracticable. To await an attack
under such circumstances must have been attended with
the most fatal results.

The extremely critical situation in which the British
troops were placed cannot be more forcibly expressed than
by General Graham's own words in his orders of the
following day :

"ISLA DE LEON, *March 6th*, 1811.

"The enemy's numbers and position were no longer
objects of calculation, *for there was no retreat left.*"

Under these circumstances to hesitate in pushing forward the flank battalion, not only as select troops, but also as the only British troops regularly formed, since they had not yet been entangled in the pine forest, would have shown culpable weakness and want of resolution, although the movement was consigning us as a body to certain destruction. At the commencement of the action our battalion formed a little more than a tenth of the army; yet at the close of the action our casualties both in officers and men amounted to nearly a fourth of the entire loss sustained, although every regiment was well into the fight.

The officers killed and wounded in the flank companies of the 9th and 28th Regiments alone exceeded a fifth of the total loss of officers; they were sixty-two, and of the flank companies there were thirteen, six of the 9th and seven of the 28th. But the carnage which the flank battalion suffered was never brought before the public. The casualties which took place in the different flank companies were in the official despatches put under the heads of their different regiments; thus the officers killed and wounded of the 9th Regiment flankers were returned as a loss sustained by the 9th Regiment, although at the time the 9th Regiment were doing garrison duty in Gibraltar; and the 28th Regiment, who formed the extreme left of the line, returned eight officers killed or wounded, whereas seven of those were of its flank companies with Colonel Browne's battalion, who were led into action on the extreme right, though the Guards having moved by our rear and subsequently forming on our right, we at the close of the battle stood between the two brigades.

The battle, although it lasted little more than two hours, was extremely fierce and bloody, and its results marked the gallantry of the two nations by whom it was fought.

Two thousand French, with three general officers, were either killed or wounded; and they lost six guns and an Eagle. The loss on our side consisted of five lieutenant-colonels, one major, sixteen captains, twenty-six lieutenants, thirteen ensigns, one staff, fifty-one sergeants, eleven hundred and eighty rank and file, making a total of twelve hundred and ninety-three put *hors de combat*. But of all the army the severest loss sustained was by the grenadiers and light bobs of the 28th Regiment ; and it may truly be said that the young soldiers who filled ·up the vacancies left in those companies by the veterans who fell in the mountains of Galicia or at Corunna or who sunk through the swamps in Walcheren, were this day introduced to a glorious scene of action. Two-thirds of the men and all the officers lay on the battlefield : one alone of the latter was enabled to resume his legs, for he had no bone broken ; he continued through the fight,—'twas the system of the old Slashers.

The flank officers of the 28th Regiment who fell in the battle were Captain Mullins, Lieutenant Wilkinson and Lieutenant Light (Grenadiers) ; and Captain Bradley and Lieutenants Bennet, Blakeney and Moore. Poor Bennet was shot through the head whilst gallantly cheering on the men through an incessant shower of grape and musketry. On seeing him fall I darted to the spot and too plainly discovered the cause. It grieved me that I could not stop for an instant with my dearest friend and first companion of my youth ; but friendship, however fervid, must yield to imperative duty. The men were fast falling and it required the utmost exertion to keep the survivors together, exposed, as they then were, to a murderous fire of round-shot, grape and musketry. My exertions at the moment were rather limping, as I had just been struck by a grape-shot under the hip, which for a moment laid me prostrate. I could only cast a mournful look at Bennet, poor fellow. It may be that our firm friendship conduced to his fate. A vacancy occurred in the light company a few days before the action, and I saw that Bennet would willingly fill it up ; but it was an established rule, at least in the regiment, that a senior lieutenant could never be put over the head of a junior already serving in the light company. Perceiving that his delicacy prevented his asking, I prevailed upon Colonel Belson to appoint him, although my senior. With the battalion two officers only were wounded, Captain Cadell and Lieutenant Anderson. In the flank companies no officer escaped, and poor Bennet fell, to rise no more. But after all man must have a final place of rest, and the appropriate bed of a soldier is the battlefield ; and it will be some consolation to his friends to know that never did a soldier fall more gallantly or on a day more glorious, and never was an officer more highly esteemed when living, nor, when he fell, more sincerely regretted by the whole of his brother officers. He was wounded about noon on the 5th ; the brain continually oozed through the wound ; yet strange to say he continued breathing until the morning of the 7th, when he calmly expired with a gentle sigh. A marble slab was subsequently erected in the chapel of the Government House at Gibraltar, to the memory of Bennet and of Lieutenant Light of the Grenadiers, by their affectionate brother officers who unfeignedly regretted the early fall of the two gallant youths.

A few days after the battle the 28th Regiment returned to Gibraltar and the flank battalion to Tarifa, where we joyfully reoccupied our old quarters in the houses of the truly hospitable inhabitants. I was billeted in the house of an old priest, Don Favian Durque. His sister, an old maiden lady, lived with him, and it is impossible to express the kindness and attention which I received from both. When the old lady heard that the grape-shot which struck me had first passed through an orange, a ration loaf and a roast fowl, with tears in her eyes she knelt down and with religious fervency devoutly offered up her thanks to the Blessed Virgin, who, she said, must have fed the fowl which so miraculously saved my life.

A week had not elapsed after our return to Tarifa when Colonel Browne received a letter from General Graham requesting that he would recommend any officer of the flank battalion who had distinguished himself in the late action. This was in consequence of some circumstances having come to the general's knowledge, principally through his Adjutant-General, Colonel McDonald, and his Quartermaster-General, Colonel Ponsonby, as well as through his aide-de-camp, Captain Calvert. Colonel Browne then recommended me to the general.

Having had occasion to go to Cadiz on private affairs, I carried the colonel's letter, upon presenting which the general delayed not a moment in sending a report on the subject to the commander-in-chief, with a strong recommendation ; and during my stay in the Isla I had the honour of dining every day at the general's table. In Colonel Browne's letter, which he read to me, the capture of the howitzer is stated, but is not mentioned in General Graham's report. In fact he could not well have mentioned it, having already reported the capture of all the guns in his official despatch. I cannot help thinking that had Colonel Browne not forgotten his promise to me, solemnly and spontaneously pledged on our meeting on Barossa Hill, and had he mentioned my name to General

Graham before that gallant officer sent off his despatches,
my promotion to a company would not have been the
result of a subsequent action.

We remained at Tarifa a few months longer, continually
fighting for our bread (the crops), when many a lively
and serious skirmish took place. It is a pleasant little
town, and famous as the point where the Moors made their
first descent into Spain, invited by Count Julian to avenge
the insult offered to his daughter, the beautiful Florinda,
by Roderick the last of the Visigoth monarchs.   When
the Moors had been expelled from Spain, a watch-tower
was erected here, in which towards evening a bell rings
every hour until dark ; it then sounds every half hour
until midnight,—from that hour until three o'clock in the
morning it rings every quarter, and after that every five
minutes until daybreak. This custom continued down to
the period when we were quartered there and probably
does so to the present time ; and this bell to our great
annoyance hung close to the officers' guardroom.

Nothing offends a Spaniard, particularly in Andalusia,
more than to insinuate even that he is in any way connected
with the Moors.   Should you through doubt ask a Spaniard
to what country he belongs, he answers that he is a pure
and legitimate Castilian, not intending to say that he is a
native of either of the Castiles or that he was born in
wedlock, but giving you to understand that his veins are
not contaminated with any mixture of Moorish blood.
Yet in Tarifa, where they are most particular on this
point, they still continue a Moorish custom peculiar to that
town and not practised, I believe, in any other part of
Spain. The ladies wear a narrow shawl or strip of silk,
called a mantilla, generally black ; the centre of this
strip is placed on the crown of the head, the ends

hanging down in front of the shoulders, the deep fringe, with which they are trimmed, reaching close to the ankle. So far this dress is common throughout Spain ; but in Tarifa the ladies cross the mantilla in front of their faces, by which the whole countenance is concealed, with the exception of one eye ; this is done by dexterously lapping the mantilla across at the waist, and so gracefully that the movement is scarcely perceptible. I have seen many English and even Spanish ladies of the other provinces endeavour to imitate this sudden and graceful movement, but never without awkwardness ; whereas every female in Tarifa accomplishes it in a moment. This temporary disguise is resorted to when the ladies go out to walk ; and so perfect is the concealment and the dress of the ladies so much alike, that the most intimate acquaintances pass each other unknown. Thus accidents may happen and husbands fail to know their own wives.

Spanish ladies in general are very fine figures, for which reason, as I have been told, their under garments, far from flowing, are very narrow, and tied down the front with many knots of fine silk ribbon.

The order for the flank companies to join headquarters having arrived, after a long and happy sojourn we bade a final adieu to this pleasant and hospitable little town, and proceeded to Gibraltar.

After remaining a few days in Gibraltar to exchange our tattered Barossa clothing for a new outfit, which the flank companies had no opportunity of doing previously, the regiment sailed for Lisbon on July 10th, on board two men-of-war ; but a calm setting in, we were carried by the current to Ceuta on the African coast. Dropping anchor, the officers landed to dine with our old friends, the 2nd Battalion 4th or King's Own, who were quartered there ;

but the weather promising fair, Blue Peter and a gun
summoned us on board before the cloth was removed.

Next morning we found ourselves off Tarifa. The whole
population were on the beach kissing hands and waving
kerchiefs in the breeze ; we recognised them all ; and a
recollection of the many happy days we passed there, where
so oft we played and sang and danced the gay fandango,
called forth from all a tear or sigh. The Tarifa ladies were
famed throughout Spain for their beauty. But the charmed
city soon receded from our view ; and on we plodded
listlessly, until we came abreast of Barossa Hill, when we
all hurried on deck and drank a flowing bumper with three
times three cheers to the health of the gallant Graham.
Continuing our course towards the land, where dwell the
brown maids with the lamp-black eyes, we arrived at
Lisbon on the 20th and next day disembarked.

Our field equipments were immediately put in preparation ; our baggage animals were procured as soon as the
market supplied, and as cheap as the Portuguese sharpers
would sell, who next to Yorkshiremen are the greatest
rogues known in regard to horses. Our wooden canteens
were well soaked, securely to keep in what the commissaries
cautiously served out. A portable larder or haversack was
given to each to carry his provisions in, and a clasp knife
which was both fork and spoon. Our little stock of tea,
sugar and brandy was carefully hoarded in a small canteen,
wherein dwelt a little tin kettle, which also acted the part
of teapot; *two* cups and saucers (in case of company), two
spoons, two forks, two plates of the same metal, a small
soup-tureen, which on fortunate occasions acted as punch-
bowl but never for soup. This was termed a rough-and-
ready canteen for officers of the line only. Hussars,
lancers and other cavalry captains would doubtless sooner

14

starve than contaminate their aristocratic stomachs with
viands, however exquisite, served on such plebeian utensils ;
however a frying-pan was common to all ranks.

Our equipment being completed, the march was announced
for August 1st. Many conflicting sentiments jarred in our
breasts the night before. Thoughts of the bloody battles
we had gained and the prospect of a glorious campaign
before us were gloomed by the recollection that not long
before we had taken the same route with Sir John Moore
at our head ; that since that period the ranks of the
regiment had been thinned or swept away at Corunna,
Oporto, Talavera, Albuera, Barossa. Many a gallant soldier
and sincere friend had been laid low since last we met at
Lisbon. With these recollections we sat down to table, and
eating seemed but a work of necessity, which passed in
mute action. The cloth being removed, a bumper was
proposed to the memory of the immortal Moore. It was
drunk in perfect silence and, as it were, with religious
solemnity. The martial figure and noble mien of the
calumniated hero stood erect in the imagination, and was
perfect in the memory of all ; but a painful recollection of
the mournful state in which we last beheld him saddened
every countenance. We seemed to see him borne in a
blanket by the rear of the regiment, the moon acting as
one big torch to light the awful procession as it moved
slowly along, our men falling around him as if anxious,
even in death, to follow their gallant leader, and the enemy's
guns firing salvos as if to cheer the warrior's last moments.
He knew that they were beaten. Thus Sir John Moore
bade his final adieu to the regiment, all shattered save his
martial spirit and lofty mind,—these were unbroken and
remained inflexible. He yielded his last breath with a sigh
of love for his country and of yearning for his profession.

After this toast was drunk the band with muffled drums played, " Peace to the Fallen Brave "; but either the instruments were out of tune or our souls not tuned to harmony. The music sounded mournful and low ; a dark gloom like a Pyrenean cloud hung cold, damp and clammy around ; we tried to shake it off but in vain.

Our next bumper was to the memory of our late gallant comrades, who gloriously fell since our last march from Lisbon, gallantly maintaining the honour of their country and corps. This toast was also drunk in solemn silence, while many an eye swam at the recollection of scenes and friends gone for ever. I thought of my poor friend, Bennet. This toast led to the mention of several anecdotes, wherein the deceased bore the principal part. The gallant feats of our departed friends insensibly revived sentiments of a less mournful nature ; the foggy vapour somewhat cleared away.

Our third and last bumper was " To our next happy meeting ; and whosoever's lot it be to fall may the regiment soon and often be placed in a situation to maintain the glory of their country, and may they never forget the bravery and discipline which won the ' back-plates.' " This sentiment was received with wild enthusiasm, and so loudly cheered by all that gloom and melancholy were frightened out of the room. The festive board gradually resumed its wonted cheerful tone ; the merry song went round drowning the doleful funeral dirge ; past misfortunes and useless regrets were forgotten. We sat late and drank deep, and thoughts of the fair and of future glory alone occupied our minds. Heedless of the obstacles opposed to reward of personal merit by an all-grasping aristocratical interference, our heated imaginations presented nothing but blood, wounds and scars, ribbons and stars to our dancing vision now becoming double and doubtful ; and at last we retired—but to prepare for advance. Such was the custom of gallant gay soldiers the night previous to opening a campaign ; in their breasts the reign of *ennui* is but short, and they spurn presentiments and foreboding, harboured only by the feeble nerve, the disordered brain, the shattered constitution, or by those whose vices conjure up frightful phantoms to their troubled conscience.

CHAPTER XIX.

NEXT morning at dawn we commenced our second campaign in Portugal. Crossing the Tagus, we continued our route through the Alemtejo, and arrived at Villaviciosa on the 10th. Here we joined our 2nd Battalion, commanded by Lieutenant-Colonel Abercrombie. It was the first meeting of the battalions since our separation at the Curragh of Kildare in 1805, and was very interesting. The old veterans of the 1st Battalion with measured phrase recounted their feats in Denmark, Sweden, Holland, Portugal and Spain, cunningly leaving many a space to be filled up by the warm imagination of their excited young auditors. On the other hand the gallant striplings of the 2nd Battalion, with that fervent and frank ingenuousness so inseparable from youth and so rare in advanced manhood, came at once to the bloody fight. They long and often dwelt upon the glorious battle of Albuera ; they told of the Spaniards coming late ; that Blake would neither lead nor follow ; of brigades being cut up through the over-anxiety of their commanders ; of colours being taken ; in fine, of the battle being all but lost, until their brigade, commanded by their gallant Colonel Abercrombie, in conjunction with the brave Fusiliers, came up and by a combined and overwhelming charge bore down all opposition and tore away the palm of victory already twining round the enemy's standard.

The two battalions had been so severely cut up, particularly at Barossa and Albuera, that one battalion alone remained efficient for service. All the men of the 2nd were transferred to the 1st. Their officers and sergeants returned to England ; but since Colonel Belson was obliged to go home for the benefit of his health, Colonel Abercrombie was retained. And now, and contrary to my wishes, the colonel appointed me to the command of a battalion company ; but he pledged himself that whenever the regiment should be about to come in contact with the enemy, I should have it at my option to join the light company.

We shortly afterwards removed to Portalegre, General Hill's headquarters. Here we remained some time enjoying all the luxury of campaigning, inviting even to the most refined cockney, keenest sportsman, or most insatiable gourmand. Races were established, partridge-shooting was good, and General Hill kept a pack of foxhounds, and entertained liberally. He felt equally at home before a smoking round of beef or a red-hot marshal of France, and was as keen at unkennelling a Spanish fox as at starting a French general out of his sleep, and in either amusement was the foremost to cry, " Tally ho ! " or, " There they go ! "   As his aide-de-camp, Captain Curry, was married, the amiable Mrs. Curry always dined at the general's table, so that we neither forgot the deference due to beauty nor the polished manners of the drawing-room.

But a union of so many sources of happiness is transient in the life of a soldier. Towards the middle of October a division of the French 5th Corps, commanded by General Gerard, moved through Estremadura to collect forage and provisions for the army at Portugal, crossing the Guadiana

at Merida, and approaching the Portuguese frontier near
Caceres and Aliseda.   In consequence the British troops
marched out of Portalegre on the 22nd, and the head of
our column reached Albuquerque in Spain on the evening
of the 23rd.   General Hill was here informed that the
enemy had retired from Aliseda to Arroyo de Puerco, and
that Aliseda was again in possession of the Spaniards.
However, to secure that country, Aliseda was entered
on the night of the 24th by a British brigade, some
Portuguese artillery, and a portion of cavalry ; whilst at
Casa de Santillana, about four miles distant, a similar
force was stationed.   The enemy's advanced guard were
driven out of Arroyo de Puerco on the morning of the 25th
by the Spanish cavalry, commanded by Count Penne
Villamur ; the fugitives moved upon Malpartida, their
main body being still at Caceres.   The British and
Portuguese troops following the route of Villamur's
cavalry, after a forced march which continued throughout
the night of the 25th, arrived on the morning of the 26th
at Malpartida ; and here we learned that the enemy had
during the night moved upon Caceres.   During this
morning General Hill was informed that Gerard, with
the main body of his troops, had moved from Caceres,
but in what direction none could tell.   In this uncertainty,
together with the inclemency of the weather and the
fatigue caused by our previous night's forced march,
the general judged it expedient to halt for the day.
The Spaniards however moved on to Caceres.   Towards
night the general having received positive information
that the French had directed their course upon Torremocha,
we were put in motion at three o'clock on the morning of
the 27th ; but during our march we were informed that
the foe had evacuated Torremocha that very morning,

with the avowed intention of occupying the town of Arroyo
Molinos for that night. All our information seemed to
be at variance; yet all was perfectly correct. General
Hill now bent his line of movement, and by a forced march
arrived late that evening at Alcuescar, unperceived by the
enemy. Both armies marched nearly in parallel lines
during the greater part of the day, and not very far
asunder; but intervening mountains and a thickly wooded
country prevented each from seeing the other.

We now felt certain that the enemy, whom we had so
ardently and arduously sought, were at length within our
reach. Our advanced post was not above two miles from
Arroyo Molinos, where Gerard rested in fancied security,
flattering himself that he had deceived us by his movements, and that we were then at Caceres, toward which
we had bent our course in the morning.

On arriving at Alcuescar we were all excessively fatigued
from our forced marches; but while we were pitching
our tents and anticipating some repose, I received an
order to proceed to San Antonio, between six and seven
miles distant, to carry despatches to General Hamilton,
who commanded a Portuguese brigade halted at that
place. I strongly remonstrated, pointing out that during
a halt of some hours by which the whole army gained some
repose, I had been sent far into the country to collect information from the peasantry; that carrying this despatch
did not fall to me as a regular tour of duty; and above
all, that I felt excessively unwilling to proceed to the
rear at that late hour, knowing that the army were to
move during the night and would more than probably be
engaged before the dawn. However all my remonstrances
were vain. Lieutenant Bailey, then on the quarter-master-
general's staff (now commandant in the Island of Gozzo),

told me that I was particularly selected by General Hill
to carry the despatch ; that his orders were peremptory ;
and that not a moment should be lost in communicating its
important contents to General Hamilton. Bailey then read
the despatch, which imported that, from the position which
the British army occupied, the enemy could not possibly
escape except through San Antonio. General Hamilton
was therefore directed to place every car and cart in his
possession, and everything which he could collect in the
place, as an obstacle across the road, and in every way to
impede the enemy's progress, should they attempt to pass
him during the night, and thus to give time to the British
troops to come up on the first alarm. The despatch was
read to me with the view that, should I be pursued by
any French cavalry patrols, I should tear it, and if I
fortunately escaped, deliver its contents verbally, or if
I were driven out of my road, communicate its import in
Spanish to any peasant I might meet, who could perhaps
creep his way to San Antonio, although I should not be
able to get there. I had an order from General Hill to
the Spanish General, Giron, to furnish me with a party of
dragoons. The Spanish general offered me three men
when like Phocion I remarked that for the purpose of war
they were too few and for any other purpose too many.
I therefore took only one man, strongly recommended as
a guide, and set off in very threatening weather for San
Antonio.

Arriving there without any adventure and safely delivering my despatches, I immediately wheeled round to regain
the camp, when, in addition to the lateness of the hour
and the difficulty of finding my way through a dense
forest, the darkened clouds suddenly burst and torrents of
rain poured down, accompanied by a tempest of wind so

furious as nearly to blow me off my horse. All traces
of our route having disappeared, I called to the dragoon
to go in front and point out the way, upon which he
very coolly but respectfully replied that it was for the first
time in his life he was there. My rage and consternation at this astounding declaration was such that I could
have shot the fellow. I asked him how he could think of
coming as a guide through a thick forest, and over ground
with not one foot of which he was acquainted, beset too
by the enemy's patrols ; and expressing my conviction that
he must be a countryman of mine, I asked him if he were
born in Ireland. The man replied that he was not selected
as a guide ; that he and the other dragoons, whom I had
declined taking, were simply warned as an escort, but the
word guide was never mentioned. As to his place of
birth, he, after appropriate adjustment in his saddle and
assuming true quixotic mien, announced himself a
"Castillano puro"; but judge my mortification at his
asking me, with simplicity apparently genuine, if Ireland
was in Portugal ! I indignantly darted my spurs into the
flanks of my unoffending high-spirited Andalusian steed,
which, although never attached to the commissariat, I had
selected from the breed of Bucephalus or bullock-headed,
still common in Andalusia, and remarkable for the bones
which protrude above the eyes and resemble stumps
of horns.

We still moved forward and after wandering some time
in the dark perceived a fire. This was cautiously approached. The dragoon, being in front, was challenged by
a sentry, whom he declared to be French ; and instantly
turning we both galloped off. We were wandering to and
fro, scarce knowing where we were; but the Sierra
Montanchez, rearing its head high above the trees and

appearing black amidst the dark clouds, prevented us at least from turning our backs to the place we sought, and warned us not to approach too near lest we should come upon the French army. Again we discovered a fire, which we conjectured to be that of a piquet. It rained torrents ; the wind blew furiously tearing the trees from the roots. Troops of howling wolves stalked around ; and although they sometimes passed nearly between our horses' legs, we durst not fire even in our own defence, lest in so doing we should awaken the attention of a more formidable foe.

Soaked through with rain, not knowing where I was, I struck my repeater, which I never failed to carry, and found that the army would be in motion in little more than an hour and a half. I became desperate; I resolved at all hazard to ascertain our true position. With this determination I alighted, leaving my cloak on the saddle, since it was too heavy to support from the quantity of rain it had imbibed ; my pistols I carried in my breast, to keep the locks dry. The Spaniard I prevailed upon to remain behind, between thirty and forty paces distant from the fire which burned in our front, with orders not to move unless he should hear a shot fired, when he should take it for certain that I was attacked ; then he was to ride forward at full speed, taking care not to leave my horse behind. All thus arranged, with doubtful step I approached the fire. My preceding the dragoon arose neither from personal bravado nor from want of full confidence in the Spaniard, who, I felt convinced, would do his duty gallantly : in fact, I had some difficulty in prevailing upon him to remain behind ; and he anxiously pleaded to accompany me, although he still felt offended at being taken for a Portuguese-Irishman. My taking the lead was in consequence of the haughty Castilian having been too proud to learn any language but his own; and I happened to have had a tolerably good acquaintance with the languages of the four nations whose troops were in the field, English, French, Spanish and Portuguese. Silently and cautiously I moved forward, until I arrived within a few yards of the fire ; then lying down flat on the ground, and forming a kind of funnel with both hands close to the ground and laying my ear thereto, I now plainly heard words which I joyfully discovered to be Portuguese. Getting on my legs I approached the fire with confidence. A Portuguese sentry, lowering his bayonet, demanded who I was ; this being soon explained, I holloaed out to Don Diego, the Spanish dragoon, who instantly galloped forward with his sabre drawn, but not forgetting my horse. Upon asking the Portuguese corporal, who commanded the piquet, where the English were encamped, I was much astonished at his replying, " Here." I could discover no sign of an army or a camp, until moving forward about forty yards in the direction which the corporal indicated, I came upon the very spot upon which my own tent had been pitched. Here I found Lieutenant Huddleston, of the company, lying under the folds of the tent, which had been blown down. I asked the cause of the darkness which reigned around and which was the chief cause of my wandering for some hours close to the army without being able to discover it. He told me that immediately after my departure a general order was issued that not a light should be lit, except one in the commissariat tent, and that only while they served out an additional allowance of rum, granted in consequence of our long march and the dreadful state of the weather ; and that the furious tempest, which I must have encountered in the forest, blew down almost every tent, which added to the obscurity.

I had still upwards of two miles to ride through incessant wind and rain to reach the village of Alcuescar, where the generals took up their quarters with the light companies of the division and some Spanish cavalry. Immediately on arriving there I reported to General Hill my having executed the duty with which I was entrusted. This report I made through Captain Clement Hill, the general's brother and aide-de-camp. He told me that the general felt excessively well pleased at my having succeeded, wondered at my having returned so soon, or at all, in such dreadful weather, and directed that I should not depart until I had dined (rather a fashionable hour, past one in the morning), adding with his usual urbanity that he regretted not being able to see me, as he was engaged with two Spaniards, who were making communications of a very important nature.

Having swallowed some cold roast beef and a tumbler of port, I retired to the next house, where fortunately the light company of the 28th Regiment were stationed. Here I procured food for my wearied horse ; but, although steeped with rain, I could make no change in my dress, my baggage being upwards of two miles in the rear, where the regiment were encamped. Change of stockings I could procure, but my boots teeming with water I durst not take off, knowing that I should not be able to draw them on again.

Shortly afterwards the army from the camp came up and joined us. Company states being collected, the adjutant told me that the colonel remarked that No. 1—the company to which I had been attached—was not signed by me. I had previously fallen in with the light company. I immediately signed the state and fell in with the battalion company. I perceived that the colonel rather avoided me.

All being prepared, the light companies of the brigade

were ordered to advance. I could restrain my feelings no longer, and went to the colonel, reminding him of the promise which he made when I was unwillingly appointed to the command of a battalion company in Portugal ; and repeated what I then said, that since October 14th, 1808 (the day we marched from Lisbon under Sir John Moore), to the present time the light company, although they had been innumerable times in fight, had never fired a shot nor seen a shot fired when I was not present, and I trusted that I should not now be left behind. " Oh ! there it is, Mr. Blakeney—every one wishes to leave me. You are more respectable commanding a company with the regiment than 2nd in a company detached." Being rather hurt at the (for the first time) cool manner in which he addressed me, I merely bowed and said that with whatever company I was ordered to serve I hoped to be able to do my duty. The colonel rode away, but immediately returned and said : " Blakeney, I very well recollect my promise, but thought you would never mention it. I wished to have you near myself. However I now speak to you as your friend : do as you please ; either join the light company or remain, but do not hereafter say that I marred your prospects, which on the contrary I pledge you my honour I would most willingly advance." Encouraged by the colonel's friendly and sincere manner, as well as by the kind regards which he always showed towards me, I felt emboldened to express my sentiments freely ; and although I held Colonel Abercrombie in the highest estimation, as indeed did every officer in the regiment, I told him candidly that I wished to join the light company. Shaking me cordially by the hand, " God bless you, my honest fellow ! " said he, " and may every success attend you." Another officer was appointed to command the battalion company and mounting my horse I soon overtook the light bobs, who greeted me with a cheer, saying that they knew Mr. Blakeney would not remain behind. This anecdote, in itself of no consequence, I introduce, as it gives me an opportunity of doing justice to the noble feelings of the gallant generous Colonel Abercrombie, of whose disinterested friendship I soon had a still stronger proof.

CHAPTER XX.

ABOUT dawn, weather still dreadful and favoured by a dense fog, the troops were formed under rising ground within half a mile of the enemy, who, strange to be said, did not present even a single vedette. They occupied Arroyo Molinos, a small town situated under the northern extremity of Sierra Montanchez, a broad chain of mountains which receded from Arroyo in a semicircular form, its extreme points being upwards of two miles asunder. It is everywhere impassable, even by goats, except within about a quarter of a mile of its eastern point, where persons desperately situated might by climbing, scramble across. The road leading from Arroyo Molinos to Merida lies at right angles to that from Alcuescar, while the road to Medellin intersects the one leading from Merida to Trujillo. To prevent the escape of the enemy by any of these roads was the anxious care of the general. The rising ground, under which our troops united, prevented our near approach being discovered by the enemy and favoured the distribution of the army for the attack.

Major-General Howard's brigade, composed of the 1st Battalions 50th, 71st and 92nd Regiments, one company 60th Rifles, and three six-pounders, supported by Morillo's Spanish infantry, formed the left column, and, commanded by Lieutenant-Colonel Stewart, were pushed forward direct

upon the town ; the 50th and the guns remained a short
distance in reserve. Colonel Wilson's brigade, consisting
of the 1st Battalion 28th, 2nd Battalions 34th and 39th
Regiments, one company 60th Rifles, the 6th Portuguese
regiment of the line, commanded by Lieutenant-Colonel
Ashurst, with two six-pounders and a howitzer, formed
the right column. The cavalry, commanded by Sir William
Erskine, formed a third column ; these were placed in the
centre, ready for any emergency. All being prepared, all
suddenly moved forward, favoured by the elements, which,
but a few moments ago furiously raging, now as if by
command became perfectly calm ; and the dense fog
clearing away, our left column were absolutely entering
the town before the enemy were aware of our vicinity.
Although one of their brigades had marched an hour
previously for Merida, their main body were only now
getting under arms to follow. The 71st and 92nd
Regiments cheered and charged through the town,
making a few prisoners, but had some men cut down
by the opposing cavalry. The enemy, driven out of the
place, formed in two columns on the plain outside, under
the base of Montanchez, protected by their cavalry.
Casting a glance to the north, they perceived the 50th
Regiment with the guns advancing. The fire from the
71st Light Infantry, issuing from the gardens, disturbed
their close formation ; and in the meantime the 92nd
Regiment filed through the streets and formed line
on the enemy's flank, who, upon this double assault,
commenced a rapid retreat, as they thought, reducing
the front of their columns, who were headed by their
cavalry. This, advance or retreat, was performed with
such celerity that they were soon lost sight of by our left
column.

At this juncture the Spanish cavalry commanded by
that active officer, Count Penne Villamur, rode into the
plain and separated the enemy's horsemen from their
infantry. The count steadily, though not furiously,
maintained his part until the British cavalry came up, who,
in consequence of the rude darkness of the night and
roughness of the roads and ground, had been delayed in
their advance. There was also an equestrian Spanish band,
clothed like harlequins and commanded by a person once
rational, but now bent on charging with his motley crew
the hardy and steadily disciplined cavalry of France ; and
yet, however personally brave their commander, Mr.
Commissary Downy, little could be expected from this
fantastic and unruly squadron, who displayed neither order
nor discipline. Intractable as swine, obstinate as mules
and unmanageable as bullocks, they were cut up like
rations or dispersed in all directions like a flock of scared
sheep.

The British cavalry having at length come up, accompanied by the German hussars, the affair became more
serious. A brisk charge by two squadrons of the 2nd
Germans and one squadron of the 9th English Dragoons
led by Captain Gore, the whole commanded by Major
Busshe of the Germans, put the French cavalry to flight.
Their infantry still pushed forward with uncommon
rapidity, yet in perfect order, fancying without doubt that
all their danger was left behind. But as they approached
the eastern horn of the crescent range of the Sierra
Montanchez, by passing round which they expected to gain
the Trujillo road, they were met directly in front by our
right column, headed by the light companies of the 28th,
34th and 39th Regiments. Here a rather unfortunate
circumstance took place. About ten minutes before we

saw the head of the enemy's approaching column, four of
their guns whipping at speed crossed in front of the
light companies who formed the advance guard of our
column. We were immediately ordered to follow and try
to overtake them; and we consequently brought forward
our left shoulders and attempted a double quick movement
through ploughed ground, soaked by several days' previous
rain, every step bringing the men nearly up to the knee
in clammy mud. When we had made a mock run for
eight or ten minutes, General Hill, who saw the movement,
ordered us to desist, as the cavalry would take the guns ;
they were soon afterwards captured by the 13th Light
Dragoons.

We now brought up our right shoulders and faced the
enemy's column, the head of which was by this time close
at hand. A low ridge or rising ground was between us,
and, the 28th Light Company leading, I galloped up the
ascent, urged by the ambition natural to youth to be the
first to meet the foe. In this however I was disappointed ;
for on gaining the summit I discovered immediately on
my left General Hill with his aide-de-camp, the late
Colonel Curry, attended by one sole dragoon. The light
company came quickly up and commenced firing (the
enemy not above a hundred yards distant), upon which the
general showed his disapprobation in as marked a manner
as a person could do who never, under any excitement
whatsoever, forgot that he was a gentleman; at
this moment he felt highly excited. The enemy perceived it impossible to pass by us, and as our left column
were moving up in their rear every eye was casting
a woeful look up the side of the dark and stubborn
Montanchez, which forbade access ; they saw no mode
of escape. Becoming desperate, and arriving at where

the mountain began to dip, they made a rush at the broad and high stone wall which ran along its base, and tearing open a breach, the head of their column, led by General Gerard, entered the opening at the very moment that the light company topped the rising ground and saw them. Thus did Gerard make his escape, which he could not have effected had we not been sent trotting after the guns, by which we lost upwards of twenty minutes' time.

But there was still a remedy left, had it been taken advantage of, as will afterwards be shown. I observed the displeasure which our men's firing gave the general, who at the moment used the remarkable words, "Soldiers, I have done my duty in showing you the enemy ; do you yours by closing on them." Upon this truly eloquent and inspiring appeal, which must have fired the breast of the most phlegmatic, I instantly placed my cap on the point of my sword, and waving it over my head I rode between the contending troops to prevent the light company from firing, exhorting them to come on with the bayonet, a weapon which they well knew from experience the enemy could never resist. The men whom I addressed, 28th Light Company, had fought at Barossa and Albuera, and some still there were of the hardy old veterans of Galicia. I mention the 28th Light Company, since they were the company who led and whom I commanded ; they instantly obeyed the call, and I need scarcely say that the other light companies of the brigade were not less prompt. All knew the efficiency of the weapon mentioned, and knowing it came forward undauntedly, although at the moment the odds against them were fearful. The three companies could not muster two hundred bayonets ; the column to be charged amounted to nearly fifteen hundred.

As the captain of the company, not knowing the enemy to be so near, had remained behind to behold a charge made by the harlequin equestrians, I had an opportunity of leading the 28th Light Company into the body of General Gerard's column, the head having unfortunately previously escaped through the breach in the wall.

Having brought the company in collision with the enemy, and being a pretty fair fox-hunter and well mounted, I jumped the wall, my horse carrying me stoutly over, although, with the exception of few and short intervals, I had been on his back for six and thirty hours. The wall being crossed, absurd as it may appear, alone I met the then head of the enemy's column. A scuffle ensued ; I lost my horse and cap, but not my sword.

My address to the light company, as well as what followed, was in the presence of General Hill, who as I write commands the army in chief ; and I trust to escape a suspicion of exaggeration in my recital of what took place, for however inclined I might feel to extol my own services on the occasion, anything I could allege would fall short of Lord Hill's testimony, stated in his letter to Lord Fitzroy Somerset, Military Secretary, dated Portalegre November 24th, 1811.

Soon after I crossed the wall, Lieutenants Potter, 28th, and Sullivan, 34th Regiments, at the head of some men of their respective light companies, charged through the breach, now almost choked with French, when all who had not previously escaped were made prisoners ; and Lord Hill may recollect that, whilst as yet only the light companies of Colonel Wilson's brigade were come up and engaged, his lordship made upwards of a thousand prisoners, who threw down their arms, all or most of whom would have escaped had not those companies undauntedly and quickly rushed forward. Had we been so fortunate as to come up twenty minutes sooner, General Gerard and every man in his army must inevitably have been taken. No military enterprise throughout the Peninsular War was more judiciously planned or more promptly executed.

The light companies now pushed forward in pursuit of Gerard and the fugitives ; every yard we advancèd prisoners were made. Having continued the chase to beyond the crest of the hill, I was amazingly surprised at seeing Gerard descending down the road leading to Merida, about two hundred yards beneath us ; he was accompanied by very few men, for the ground was broken and rocky and very difficult to pass over. Some French officers, who rushed through the wall on horseback, had been immediately obliged to dismount, and, formation of any kind being impossible, groups of the enemy continually descended in small numbers, who, on reaching the road, ran forward to join those who had already arrived. But my astonishment was caused at seeing a squadron of British cavalry drawn up on the road who moved not at all, although within a hundred yards of where Gerard and the enemy descended in these small bodies from the mountain. Some time afterwards I asked the officer who commanded the squadron how it was he did not charge the fugitives, remarking that he lost an opportunity which most probably would never again present itself, that of taking prisoner the enemy's commanding general. He replied with perfect seriousness that his orders were to halt on that road, and that therefore the escape of the enemy was no affair of his ; that had he been ordered to charge, he would have done so willingly. This I firmly believe ; and he was not very long afterwards killed while gallantly charging with his regiment. What increased my astonishment was that the enemy descended on to the road exactly in his front, and moved away from him ; for the squadron were drawn up to face the direction which the French took, being the only one by which they could escape.

The British loss in the action was trifling : seven rank and file killed ; seven officers and between fifty and sixty rank and file wounded. On the part of the enemy, General Gerard's corps were almost totally destroyed or dispersed. General Le Brun, Colonel the Prince D'Arenberg, both of the cavalry, Colonel Andrée, Adjutant-General, Lieu-tenant-Colonel Voirol, and another lieutenant-colonel whose name I forget, Gerard's aide-de-camp, one commissary, thirty captains and subalterns, and upwards of fifteen hundred rank and file were made prisoners. The whole of their guns, waggons, baggage and magazines were captured. Their loss in killed and wounded could not be ascertained from the nature of the ground, but it must have been considerable. The light companies were firing during four hours, while they chased the fugitives up the hill of Montanchez and down the other side until we nearly reached the road. When General Morillo returned next morning, having continued the pursuit all night, he reported that, exclusive of those who fell on the plain, upwards of six hundred dead or dying were found in the woods and among the mountains.

In consequence of the severe fatigue which the army had suffered immediately before the action, as well as the necessity of bringing the prisoners together, the light companies were called in. On arriving on the plain I was not a little surprised at the general greeting I met from the whole regiment, who with the 34th had been some time in the plain. When the regiment had approached the breach in the wall, my horse was found in possession

of a French soldier and my cap at the foot of the hill
where it had rolled down. I was consequently put down
as either among the slain or made prisoner ; and upon
this Colonel Abercrombie had said that he was excessively
sorry for the circumstance, but that it was all my own
seeking, because I declined remaining with him.

CHAPTER XXI.

I AM MADE BEAR-LEADER.

THE troops now entered the town of Arroyo Molinos, and I proceeded directly to the Prince D'Arenberg's quarters, to which I was called by General Hill, who requested that I would accompany the prince to Lisbon, and this too at the prince's request. Upon my expressing an unwillingness thus to go to the rear, the general paid me a very flattering compliment, saying that had he not deemed it necessary to retire in a day or two at the farthest, he would not request, nor even consent to my leaving the army even for a day ; but that Soult's corps were advancing, which rendered it necessary for him to retire. Colonel Rook, the adjutant-general, being present, asked me with what escort I would undertake the charge, and if I thought twenty men sufficient. I offered to be responsible for the prince's safe conveyance with four men and two dragoons. Rook replied that he would double the number of infantry which he proposed, but could not grant a single dragoon. I then consented to go with a corporal and six men of my own regiment. He agreed to the number but not to the regiment ; the bulk of the prisoners were to be escorted by a suitable detachment of the 34th, and he could not break up a second regiment. And so with Corporal Hughes and six men of the 34th I commenced my march for Lisbon.

I very soon repented of having taken so small an escort, not on account of the prince, but of the French commissary, whom, at the particular request of the prince, I allowed, though unwillingly, to accompany him; had I foreseen the annoyance and danger which his presence caused I certainly should have refused the request. In proceeding through the Spanish frontier we passed through the same towns which Gerard occupied during his foraging, or rather marauding excursion immediately before; and it required all my exertions to protect the commissary from being torn to pieces. The peasantry collected round the houses where we halted for the night, loudly demanding the commissary; and although I harangued them and pointed out the national disgrace that would attend any outrage committed on the prisoners, and the insult it would be to England whose prisoners they were and consequently under her protection, still I felt it always prudent to make the guard load in their presence, and to place double sentries over the house, with orders, loudly delivered, to shoot any who should attempt a forcible entrance.

Although the escort consisted but of ten persons, the corporal and his party of six, my servant, bâtman, and self, and the prisoners amounted to the same number—viz., the prince, a captain of his regiment, his secretary, two cooks, his Swiss coachman, three other servants and the commissary—still I allowed them all to carry arms. I felt no dread of their escaping, being fully convinced that they were much more inclined to remain my prisoners than think of escape, for they were fully aware that they would be torn to atoms by the enraged peasantry; moreover the prince, in whose honour I confided, held himself responsible for all. I remarked to the prince with a smile in the presence of the whole party, that I felt certain his pledge was not endangered, stating the reasons above mentioned ; yet I told him plainly that if his authority were not sufficient to oblige the commissary (who was present) to keep more retired, and not with imprudent gasconade to present himself at the doors and windows and thus irritate an enraged population, I should reluctantly be compelled to make him a close prisoner and place a sentry over him, not so much for his safety as for that of others, whom I held in higher consideration. But although I gained my point, yet until I got across the Spanish frontier I was in continual alarm, all owing to our graminivorous companion. Albeit though this commissary certainly was as impertinent and forward a fellow as I ever met with, still he could not in justice be held personally responsible for the outrages which drew upon him this general odium ; for when he robbed the peasantry of all their grain, cattle and provisions of every kind, and as much specie as he could grasp, he acted under superior command ; he was therefore but a simple machine. But the lower orders, solely interested in present good or evil, rarely investigate the remote cause which produces the present effect.

The last Spanish town through which we passed was Valencia de Alcantara ; and here I had the honour of reporting our arrival to the captain-general of the province, General Castanos, a fine fat jolly-looking fellow. Being about to quit the Spanish territory next day, the prince and I entered into a conversation about the general character of the inhabitants.

In allusion to the late action and the movements which led to that event, I warmly expatiated on the praiseworthy fidelity of the Spaniards, particularly those of Arroyo Molinos and Alcuescar, in never having communicated our near approach to the French army. The prince replied

that they did not use such fidelity as I imagined, for the
night previous to the action two Spaniards came to his
quarters in Arroyo Molinos and informed him that we
were much nearer than the French general seemed to be
aware of; that upon this he immediately imparted the
information to Gerard, who replied : " Prince, you are a
good and active soldier, but you always see the English in
your front, rear and flank. I tell you they are eight leagues
distant, for I know to a certainty that they were seen in
the morning marching hastily towards Caceres, thinking
to find us there ; and so confident do I feel as to the
certainty of what I tell you that I shall delay the march
to-morrow an hour later to give the men more time for
repose." Much hurt at the general's remark, which had
the appearance of insinuating that he entertained a dread
of encountering the English, the prince returned to his
quarters. About an hour before dawn next morning the
general sent for him, according to custom, to take a glass of
old rum ; this he declined, the conversation of the previous
evening being still painfully in his recollection. In less
than an hour afterwards he heard a loud and confused cry in
the streets, when instantly his adjutant darted breathless
into the room holloaing out, " Mon prince ! mon prince !
nous sommes attrapés ! " The English were driving
through the town. At the heels of the adjutant in rushed
Gerard, aghast and foaming at the mouth, and exhorted
the prince to use every exertion to get the cavalry out of
the town. " Ha ! " said the prince, " do I always see the
English where they are not ? " " For the love of God,"
replied Gerard, " do not add to my distraction. This is not
a time for badinage or reproof; exert yourself to the
utmost or we are undone. The English are forcing
their way through the town. Get the cavalry out and

form on the plain as quickly as possible." The rest I
knew.

Next morning we left Valencia before dawn and were
soon in the Portuguese territory. The prisoners now
breathed freely, not having felt very secure during our
route through Spain. The mountains we had now to cross
were very steep and excessively difficult of ascent,
especially with a wheeled vehicle. The prince travelled
very comfortably in a handsome carriage taken at Arroyo
Molinos, in which fortunately he was always accompanied by his graminivorous friend, whom the prince
and I used facetiously to call Bucephalus. Four large
Spanish mules which drew the carriage being insufficient
to haul it up those hills, I directed that a couple of bullocks
which were ploughing alongside the road should be added
to the team. The harnessing was attempted in a violent
manner by the Swiss coachman, an immensely stout and
large person ; but one of the animals becoming very restive,
severely wounded him with one of his horns. The wound
was excessively severe and dangerous, but being ignorant
of technical terms I must decline attempting a description.
The coachman, becoming furious from pain, drew his sabre,
and cutting and slashing right and left so wounded the
bullock that I ordered the guard to disarm him, and never
after allowed him to carry any other weapon than his
whip, although he frequently entreated the prince to inter-
cede for the recovery of his sabre. The owners having
interposed, the animals were quietly harnessed, and after
a long pull we at last reached the summit. Owing to
its great height and the season being rather advanced
(the middle of November), the atmosphere was excessively
cold. We halted on this our first Portuguese mountain
for some hours, and I cannot forget our delicious repast

upon roasted chestnuts and goats' milk, plentifully supplied
by the Portuguese shepherds. Thunderstruck on hearing
that one of their guests was no less a personage than a
prince, they crowded round the blazing fire before which we
were feasting to have the illustrious stranger pointed out,
no doubt expecting to see in a person of such exalted rank
something superhuman.

Continuing our route tranquilly and without any adventure, we arrived at Portalegre, which again became General
Hill's headquarters. Here we halted for a few days, during
which we were visited by Prince Pierre d'Arenberg, who had
procured General Hill's permission to come and see his
brother, in whose regiment he was a cornet. Prince
Prosper felt some delicacy in conversing with him except
in my presence; but as I received no decisive instructions
on the subject, I declined intruding on their conversation ;
and feeling in no way anxious to pry into their family
concerns, I remarked to Prince Prosper that he had nothing
of military consequence to communicate, and as to the
treatment which he met with from the British it was but just
that he should have an opportunity of declaring it to his
brother, free of all restraint which my presence might
impose. The princes expressed their thanks in the
warmest manner; and Prince Prosper remarked that it was
well that he should have a private opportunity of telling
his brother of the kind and generous manner in which he
had been treated, which was of such a nature that, recounted in the presence of an Englishman, it must have
the appearance of exaggeration and flattery, and more
particularly if told in my presence, who stood first in
courtesy and generous conduct. I imbibed the potion and
retired to the next room.

Before we continued our route towards Lisbon, Colonel

Abercrombie sent me a message from Albuquerque to say
that, not being present at what took place with the light
company in the late action, it being detached from the
battalion, he could not *directly* recommend me for my
conduct on the occasion ; but he requested me to forward a
memorial of my general services through him, thus giving
him an opportunity of giving his testimony to my services
throughout.   This generous communication I of course
acted upon immediately ; and I wrote to Lord Lynedoch
on the subject, from whom I shortly after received the
following letter :—

"LEGIORA, November 19th, 1811.

"MY DEAR BLAKENEY,—I did you all justice, I assure you,
before at the Horse Guards, and have just written again to
Colonel Torrens to remind him of all I said after Barossa, and
to request that he will state my testimony to the Duke of York
in aid of your memorial.   Excuse this hasty scrawl, And believe
me truly yours

"THOMAS GRAHAM.

"LIEUTENANT BLAKENEY, 28<i>th Foot.</i>"

However flattering such a letter was to me, or must be to
any officer however high his rank, when coming from such
a person as Lord Lynedoch, yet it is not from motives of
vanity that I give it publicity, but rather to reflect its true
merit back to the pure fount whence it sprung.   Any
attempt at eulogy from so humble an individual as myself
could add but little to the brilliancy which his splendid
achievements throw around Lord Lynedoch.   I shall therefore confine myself to saying, in the unsophisticated phrase
of an old campaigner, that the zealous officer who willingly
and conscientiously discharges his duty, though naked of
other patronage or support, will always find in his lordship
his most willing supporter and unswerving friend.   Here

will be seen an officer, high in rank and still higher in reputation, commanding a corps of the most uniformly victorious army which ever graced the military annals of any nation whatever, writing in familiar language to a subaltern officer, showing anxiety for his interests and using every exertion to forward his promotion from no other motive than the belief that he had fully discharged his duties to his king and country to the utmost of his abilities. I had no introduction from influential friends to his lordship, nor had I the honour of his acquaintance previous to the expedition from Tarifa and the occurrences which took place in the battle of Barossa. No doubt generals in high or chief command willingly forward the claims of officers whom they consider deserving while they continue to serve under them; but I am ignorant of any other instance where claims on patronage have been invited and called for, such as in the letter written by Lord Lynedoch to Colonel Browne at Tarifa, requesting the name of any officer of the flank battalion under his command who had distinguished himself at the battle of Barossa. How much more in unison with the genius of Britain and with the spirit of her free and liberal institutions, and how much more nobly is the general employed who, like Lord Lynedoch, diligently and openly seeks through his ranks for objects worthy his protection, than he who indefatigably searches for pretexts for a clandestine representation, generally a misrepresentation! And it is not a little to be wondered at that England, which ever was and ever will be inimical to the introduction of the inquisition in any country, should harbour that wicked and degrading institution throughout every branch of her Service which is smoothly termed "*confidential* reports," thus turning the Army in particular, whose constitution is based on the most scrupulous adherence to the highest and nicest principles of honour, into a graduated corps of spies from the ensign up to the general. Great Britain does not reflect that by encouraging these confidential or clandestine reports she is inflicting an insulting and severe censure on the laws and morals of the nation, as not being sufficient to govern by open and legitimate means.

To remove an officer from the Service upon a confidential report is both unjust and impolitic, and answers no good end. It is but natural to suppose that when a senior officer accuses a junior by means of clandestine reports, with the hope of having him removed from the Service without trial, that this dark mode of procedure arises from inadequacy of matter to bear him out, or for reasons still darker than the foul means adopted. But supposing even that it should be made evident to His Majesty that the officer so reported is unworthy of continuing in the Service, is it politic to remove him from it without assigning a cause or making his delinquency public? When a robber or even murderer is executed, it is not from a vindictive motive, it takes place as a dreadful warning to deter others from committing a similar crime; therefore due punishment cannot be made too public, or its imperative necessity too strongly impressed on the minds of the people. The injustice of these secret proceedings was clearly shown at Malta in 1821, at which time I was quartered there. A commanding officer in the garrison so blackened the characters of a large portion of his officers through confidential reports that it was determined to have the greater number of them removed from the Service. This was discovered by means of a lady of the regiment, who carelessly said to another that she would soon see the junior captain become the senior; this being

16

repeated soon became known throughout the corps, when
the officers fortunately arrived at the true cause of the
threatened removal.   Consequently, and very naturally,
they spoke openly.   To avert the evil they asserted that
tyranny, oppression and falsehood had been used towards
them.   This coming to the knowledge of the commanding
general, Sir Thomas Maitland, he ordered a court of
inquiry.   He clearly stated that from the reports which he
had received from the commanding officer he had intended
to recommend that many officers of the regiment should
be removed from the Service ; but in consequence of its
coming to his knowledge that the commanding officer
was far from immaculate, and that oppression or unfounded
reports might have been resorted to, he thus gave the
officers an opportunity not only to exonerate themselves
from the charges alleged against them, but also to declare
their grievances.   What was the consequence ?   One
subaltern was brought to court-martial by the commanding
officer and was acquitted ; but the commanding officer
was brought to trial upon two-and-twenty grave charges,
on one-and-twenty of which he was found guilty, and as
a matter of course publicly dismissed the Service.

So much for *confidential* reports.   Who can count the
number of high-spirited noble and gallant youths who
have fallen victims, or whose prospects have been blasted
through this dastardly mode of proceeding ?   It is the
noble-minded and high-spirited alone who call for protection against such an iniquitous system ; the fawning
and servile are sure to escape, and not unfrequently with
rewards.   The duties of a commanding officer are manifold ;
and he who does not execute them with temperance, justice
and impartiality is not for that responsible post.

I had the good fortune of being intimately acquainted

with that gallant and sterling soldier, General Ross, who should be held up as a model for commanding officers of regiments. He at once was the father and brother of every officer in his corps, and was on the most familiar and intimate terms with every officer down to the junior ensign; yet none ever dared or attempted to take the slightest liberty which could be considered, even by the severest martinet, as derogatory in the slightest degree to the respect due to the commanding officer or injurious to the maintenance of the strictest discipline. The respect entertained by all for Colonel Ross was entirely matter of sentiment and good feeling. The lively, though sometimes imprudent sallies of a glowing mind were by him rather laughed away than harshly or even seriously chided; the feelings of a gentleman were never wounded in cooling the fervid ebullitions of youth. He felt fully sensible that the military laws, as sanctioned by his country, were sufficient for the ends desired, and therefore never resorted to the cowardly subterfuge of stabbing in the dark by means of clandestine reports, which are never resorted to except by those who from meanness of capacity or want of resolution shudder at a fearless and open discharge of their duty, or whose vicious and vindictive natures induce them to strike the deadly blow unseen. Such a liberal and just commanding officer did exist, I know, in the person of the late General Ross when commanding the 20th Regiment; and such a commanding officer does exist, I have been told, in the person of Sir Edward Blakeney, commanding the Royal Fusiliers.

CHAPTER XXII.

I CONTINUE TO PLAY THE GAOLER.

AFTER a short halt at Portalegre Prince Pierre returned to his regiment, and we continued our route to Lisbon. On arriving at Abrantes Prince Prosper was splendidly entertained by Colonel Buchan, who commanded there. The roads being here impassable for a carriage, that in which the prince travelled was left behind; and we proceeded in a comfortable boat down the Tagus to Lisbon, where we safely arrived.

The orders which I received immediately on my arrival were that the prince should never leave the Duke de Cadoval's palace, in which we were lodged, except in my company; and I was never to go out with him in other than my scarlet uniform. These orders came direct from the Duke of Wellington. The strictness with which I was directed to attend so particularly upon the prince did not arise from any want of confidence in his parole; it was the better to protect him, for such was the state of public ferment at the time in Lisbon that nothing but British protection could save him from public and most probably serious insult and outrage. This state of general excitement was caused by reports in the Spanish papers, as also by the assertions of many Spaniards then in Lisbon, that when Ballesteros was defeated by the French at

Ayamonte, the prince, who served there with his regiment of cavalry, cut many hundred Spaniards to pieces who were unarmed and who never carried arms in their lives. At his own particular request I showed him the Spanish gazettes in which his alleged cruelty was most severely reprobated. On perusing the papers he remarked with a laugh, "How stupid these Spaniards in thinking that by thus abusing me they do me injury! The fools are not aware that the more they accuse me of cruelty the stronger will be the conviction in the breast of the emperor that I did my duty zealously." I merely asked if the emperor *required* such mode of performing duty. A momentary reserve ensued ; it was but of short duration. In truth, from the commencement of our acquaintance to our parting we lived on the most friendly and intimate terms, and seemed more like two intimate young gentlemen of equal rank than simple Mr. and a Serene Highness.

The prince was entertained by all the British authorities in Lisbon. On one occasion he was invited to dine with Major-General Sir James Leith, but I was not included in the invitation. The prince would rather have declined, but I persuaded him to go, and accompanied him to Sir James's house. Asking for an aide-de-camp, I gave the prince to his care, telling him that I expected that he would not return except accompanied by an officer ; I then immediately retired. I was very happy at having this opportunity of going out to see some old friends ; I had many, having been twice previously in Lisbon. On my return, which was rather late, I found the aide-de-camp asleep on the sofa, and the prince sitting by his side laughing. On awakening he told me that he received Sir James Leith's positive injunctions not to quit the prince until my return home ; and he gave me a very polite

message from the general, stating his regret that he was
unacquainted with the mutual obligation that existed
between the prince and me or he would certainly have
invited me to dine. Sir James called next day, and
repeated what the aide-de-camp had previously said. A
nearly similar occurrence took place the second time we
dined with Marshal Beresford.

These invitations were highly honourable to me ; but
it was complete servitude, and made me as much a prisoner
as the prince, with the additional weight of responsibility.
The strict obligation of always accompanying the prince
in my uniform interfered with many amusements. In
going to the theatres he was instantly recognised and
rudely stared at ; and even had we risked going in plain
clothes, contrary to our instructions, there still remained
an obstacle. The prince wore mustachios, by which he
would be immediately known, and with these he was very
unwilling to part. I told him that if he shaved them
off, I should run all hazard and accompany him in plain
clothes in some of our nocturnal rambles. After urgent
expostulations on my part and profound sighs on his, he
consented to have them removed. He sat down before a
mirror, determined, despite of cavalry pride, to cut down
the long, long cherished bristly curls of war. His hand
trembled. He shrank from the first touch of the razor,
yet he bore the amputation of the right wing with tolerable
fortitude ; then, turning to me with a deep sigh, he held
up the amputated member clotted with lethal soap. He
looked mournful and pale ; but however I may have com-
miserated his grief, for the life of me I could not refrain
from laughing aloud at the appearance of his face with
one mustachio only, which, deprived of its old companion,
appeared double its former length. I requested him to

give the hanger-on no quarter, but instantly to cut him
down; the operation soon followed. The mustachios were
washed, cleaned and dried, then carefully wrapped up in
silver paper and forwarded with a pathetic letter to the
duchess, his wife. The prince declared that he never again
would act the soldier either for Napoleon or any other.
This determination arose entirely from his being tired of
the army, not from cutting off the mustachios, which act
bore no analogy to the story of Delilah; and although I
was instrumental in cutting off the hairs of war if not of
strength, he never found in me a Philistine. A tailor was
now sent for to make him a brown-coated gentleman.

We now felt no obstacle to our enjoyment of many
amusements from which we previously were debarred.
For such was the metamorphosis from the splendid cavalry
uniform, highly decorated breast, blackened and curled
whiskers and mustachios and the fierce *tout-ensemble* to
the simple brown coat and the plain civic face, that had
I not been present at the barbarous deed, I scarcely could
have believed him to be the same person; and such was
my reliance on his word that I felt no hesitation about his
going out, even alone.

The prince entertained very liberally whilst in Lisbon;
when he was not dining out, there were twelve covers at his
table for the officers, his fellow prisoners, who were invited
in rotation. One officer alone, a lieutenant of artillery, was
never invited. It was alleged that when we attacked on
the morning of the action, this unfortunate young man,
who commanded the artillery, had no matches lit, and that
had he been prepared we must have lost more men in
killed and wounded while filing through the town; in
consequence, he was cut by every French officer in Lisbon.
I felt much for him, and mentioned to the prince that

where they were all alike unfortunate, it appeared invidious to single out one for neglect ; for whatever his fault might have been, it could not have had the slightest effect in changing the result of the action. The prince, although a stern soldier, somewhat relented ; but there was such a person as Napoleon to be taken into consideration. However, he mentioned the circumstance to General Le Brun, expressing an inclination to become reconciled to the artillery officer. Le Brun would not listen to it, alleging that it would be setting a dangerous example to look over or in any way countenance gross neglect of duty, at the same time casting a scowling look at me, knowing that it was I who spoke to the prince on the subject. Annoyed at his obduracy and a little nettled by his indignant look, I asked him if he did not think that, had there been mounted patrols on the look-out to give alarm in proper time, the artillery officer, thus warned, would have had his guns in battle array ; instead of which, we came absolutely into the town without encountering a single French dragoon. The general treated my observation with haughty silence ; but the French adjutant-general, also a prisoner, being present, darted a fiery glance at Le Brun, and would no doubt have applied his censure of the artillery officer to himself, had he not been restrained out of consideration for the prince, who was second in command of the cavalry. Le Brun was disliked by all from his haughty and overbearing manner. When after the action the officers made prisoners were required to sign their parole, Le Brun refused, saying that the word of a general of the French was sufficient. Our quartermaster-general, Colonel Offley, a gallant and determined soldier, a German by birth, soon settled the affair in a summary way by giving orders that if the general refused to sign his parole, he was to be marched with the bulk of the prisoners. This order cooled the general's hauteur : he subscribed.

On one occasion, when a large party of French officers dined with us, the prince asked me to what town in England I thought it likely he would be sent as prisoner of war. This I could not possibly answer. He then asked which I considered the second town in England. I said that from a commercial point of view we generally ranked Liverpool next to London ; but as places of fashionable resort Brighton, Bath and Cheltenham ranked much alike. I inadvertently asked him which he considered the second town in France. " Rome," said he, " ranks the second and Amsterdam the third." I remarked that then we had no longer an Italy or a Holland. " Yes," replied the prince, " we have both ; but by a late edict of the Emperor those two towns are annexed to France, but it is not the policy of England to recognise it." I made a low bow. In compliment to me, I suppose, the prince changed the topic immediately, saying that he dreaded a ship so much that he would sooner fight the battles of Talavera and Albuera over again than undertake so long a voyage as that to England. I told him to quiet himself on that head, for he might get to England in two hours. The whole company stared, but particularly Le Brun, who was always a standing dish at the prince's table. Speculation ran high. A balloon was generally suggested, but the velocity even of this was doubted. I denied the agency of a balloon, and maintained that it was to be accomplished by wind and water solely. As I still withheld an explanation, the prince got off his chair, and flinging away his little foraging cap said, " If you do not tell us I shall give you a kiss, and I know that you would sooner get a slap on the face than be

kissed by a man." On his advancing towards me, I requested
that he would sit down and I would give him an explanation
which I felt persuaded would convince all present that
my assertion was perfectly correct. At this a general laugh
followed. The prince being re-seated, I addressed him
thus : " In less than two hours after you leave the
quay, you will have got rid of all the boats which impede
your passage down the Tagus, and immediately after you
will steer clear of Fort St. Julian at the influx of the
river. You are then at sea and arrived ; for by an *old*
edict, recognised by every sovereign in Europe, ' All the
seas are England.' " The whole company endeavoured,
although awkwardly, to force a laugh, except Le Brun,
whose scowling frown indicated his chagrin, and I fancied
that I distinguished the word *bêtise* muttered between
his teeth. I longed for an opportunity of paying him off ;
it soon occurred.

Le Brun called next morning, as usual big with nothing.
Perceiving that he wished to be alone with the prince,
I retired to the next room. Soon after the prince requested
me to come back. He was much excited, and flinging
his cap on the floor, " Only think," said he, " what the
general has been telling me as an undoubted fact. Some
rascally Portuguese has persuaded him to believe that
above a hundred sail of French line of battleships have
appeared before Cadiz ; that the British squadron, stationed
there, were compelled to fly ; that the fortress must
immediately surrender, and consequently all Spain must
soon be in our possession. In the first place," added the
prince, " all the navy of France do not amount to the
number which the general says are before Cadiz, without
taking into consideration the utter impossibility of their
being enabled to form such a junction unmolested in the

face of the British navy. If a corporal of my regiment
told me such a story, believing it, I should turn him into
the ranks." At this remark the general became highly
indignant, and the prince's excitement much increased.
To restore tranquillity I asked the general about the
appearance of the person who gave him the important
information ; and nodding assent to his description, I
exclaimed, " The very man who spoke to me this morning."
" There," said the general, happy to have anything like
corroboration ; " and what did he tell you ? " I looked
round with much apparent precaution, and after anxious
pressing on his part and affected hesitation on mine, I
got quite close to the prince and the general, who took
a chair. I then in a low tone of voice, our three heads
nearly touching, said : " When I came to Lisbon this same
Portuguese was pointed out to me as a person who always
possessed much information, but sold it dearly." All this
time the prince was staring at me, knowing that I bore
no great affection for the general. " But," said the general,
" what information did he give you ? " " He told me that
he knew to a certainty, from a source which could not
be doubted—I think you said one hundred ? " " Yes," replied Le Brun, " one hundred sail of the line." " He told
me," I resumed, " that there were two hundred thousand
British troops absolutely on the boulevards of Paris, but
not a single soul could tell whence they came. I gave my
informant six gros sous : how much did you give, mon
général ? " At this the prince absolutely became convulsed
with laughter. The general darted from his chair, snatched
up his hat, and turning his head half round gave us the
most ungracious *bonjour* that I ever heard escape the
lips of a Frenchman, and then strode out of the room.
Scarcely had he left when the prince ran forward and

absolutely embraced me, saying that I had done him the
greatest favour which I could possibly confer, as he felt
sure the general would torment him no more. He was
right ; Le Brun never again called.

About this time a very laughable scene took place in
Lisbon. An announcement was published in the papers
that an English officer would walk across the Tagus with
cork boots. At the hour specified the concourse was
immense ; twenty thousand persons at least were collected
at Belem, the place indicated. Every boat on the Tagus
and every vehicle in the town, of whatever description,
was hired for several days previously. A Portuguese guard
were posted to keep the cork-boot platform clear, and a
military band attended ; it was in fact a magnificent
pageant. At length the hour of execution arrived, but no
cork boots ; hour after hour passed, but still the principal
actor was wanting. The spectators, wearied by fruitless
expectation, began to retire ; and here the ingenuity of
the hoax was displayed—for when some thousands had
moved off, a sudden rush was made towards the platform.
Those who retired instantly returned, but only to be disappointed. This ruse, strange to be said, repeatedly succeeded ; back came the crowd, but the great Earl of Cork
never came forth. At length and after dark all retired
in the worst possible temper ; many did not reach their
homes until after midnight, although Belem was not more
than five miles from Lisbon, such was the throng both on
the Tagus and along the roads. Next day all Lisbon was
in uproar at being thus insulted by the English, who denied
all knowledge of the affair ; and in reply to a remonstrance
made by the Portuguese Government on the subject to the
English authorities, it was asked rather acrimoniously how
such an absurd article had been permitted to appear in the

public prints when the censorship of the press was entirely
in the hands of the Portuguese Government. This was
rather a poser, and the affair died away in languid laughter.

The time having arrived for the prince's departure for
England, Captain Percy, in whose ship he was to proceed,
mentioned to me that he had some hope of procuring an
exchange between the prince and his father, Lord Beverley,
who was detained in France ; requesting also that I would
ascertain from the prince what he wished put on board for
his little comforts. The prince in reply commissioned me
to tell Captain Percy that as to the exchange he felt fully
persuaded that Napoleon, although the uncle of his wife
the duchess, would never consent to the exchange ; that
as to his comforts on board he felt extremely obliged to
Captain Percy for his polite and kind attention, and the
only thing he requested was a little old rum. I delivered
his message, but told him that it was scarcely necessary,
for there was always sufficient rum on board a man-of-war.
On parting, he told me that whenever I should come to
Brussels I should have no formal invitation to his father's
palace ; I should live there and invite whom I pleased,
for I must consider myself as a master in the house. How
I treated him while we lived together as prisoner and
guard may be seen in a letter which I had the honour
of receiving some years afterwards from his late Royal
Highness the Duke of Kent.

It was at my option to accompany the prince to England ;
I was strongly recommended to do so, and the prince warmly
urged me to the same effect. The bait was tempting ;
but although better success would undoubtedly have attended
a campaign in the luxurious Green Park, surrounded by
magnificent mansions, traversed by splendid equipages,
studded with groups of noble courtiers and glittering

flatterers, yet I preferred the uncompromising discharge
of my duty and the wild scenery and extensive plains
of Spain, in company with my gallant companions of the
war, whose hearts were open as the boundless tracts they
traversed, their friendship fervid as the genial sun which
glowed over their heads, and their sincerity pure and
unsullied as the mountain breezes they inhaled. All this
was good enough for me.

CHAPTER XXIII.

ON the departure of the prince I immediately joined my regiment at Albuquerque. On my arrival I had the honour of dining with General Hill. He congratulated me on my good fortune in carrying the prince safely to Lisbon, remarking that had I not been able to harangue the peasantry in their native language, sixty soldiers instead of six would scarcely have been a sufficient guard. The general had heard from several Spanish officers of the difficulty and danger which I had encountered. He then congratulated me on the certainty of my immediate promotion ; was pleased to say that I should soon reap the reward which I so well merited, and then handed me the following letter, which he requested me to keep by me : —

"GALLEGOS: *January 16th,* 1812.

"SIR,—I am directed to transmit to you the annexed extract of a letter from Lieutenant-Colonel Torrens, in reply to your recommendation in favour of Lieutenant Blakeney.

"The Commander-in-Chief will take an early opportunity of recommending Lieutenant Blakeney for promotion.

"I have the honour to be, etc.,

"FITZROY SOMERSET,
"*Military Secretary.*

"LIEUTENANT-GENERAL HILL."

Towards the latter end of February my name appeared in the *Gazette,* promoted to a company in the 36th Regiment, dated January 16th, 1812. After endeavouring in vain to accomplish an exchange back into my old corps, I forwarded a memorial to the Duke of Wellington applying for permission to join the 1st Battalion 36th Regiment, then in the Peninsula. His Grace answered that he could not interfere with the appointment of an officer from one battalion to another ; that being promoted I must join the 2nd battalion, to which I properly belonged ; and that I must therefore proceed to England and report my arrival to the adjutant-general. A copy of this answer was forwarded from headquarters to the officer commanding the 1st Battalion 36th Regiment, then at Almendralejo. It was matter of surprise to many that whilst hundreds of officers were vainly applying for leave to go to England, I could not procure leave to keep from it; but such, no doubt, were the arrangements between the Horse Guards and the army in the Peninsula.

In the beginning of March General Hill moved upon Merida, endeavouring to surprise a detachment of the enemy there stationed. He approached within a short distance without being discovered ; but an advanced guard being at length perceived, the enemy hastily evacuated the town. As we neared the place we saw their rearguard of cavalry crossing the bridge. Our cavalry and light artillery had previously forded the Guadiana, and it was confidently expected would soon come up with the retiring foe. No longer doing duty with the 28th Regiment, I rode over the bridge as the German dragoons were closely pressing on the enemy's rear, passing by their flank. I soon came in view of their main body. They proceeded hesitatingly, having no doubt been informed by their patrols that our cavalry had already forded the Guadiana. They halted on a conical hill, or rather rising mound, which they occupied

from its base to its summit, apparently expecting to be
charged. I immediately wheeled round and returning at
full speed informed General Hill of what I had seen. The
general, whose coolness was never more apparent than
when the full energy of the mind was called into action,
replied in his usual placid manner : " Very well ; we shall
soon be with them. Gallop over the bridge again and tell
General Long to keep closer to the wood." Instantly
setting off I soon recrossed the bridge, at the far end of
which I met Lord Charles Fitzroy returning after having
delivered a similar message. The cavalry general's reply
was that he wished to keep clear of the skirts of the wood,
when one of us remarked that the wood must have skirts
more extensive than a dragoon's cloak to keep them at
such a distance. The enemy, perceiving how far they
kept away, descended from the mound on which they had
expected to be charged, and rapidly pushed forward without
any molestation ; for as our dragoons moved they still more
deviated from the enemy's line of march, and seemed to be
en route for Badajoz. Had our cavalry closed upon the
wood and even menaced a charge, the progress of the enemy
would have been impeded ; but had our cavalry and light
guns, by which they were accompanied, pushed forward
rapidly, which they could have done since the plain was flat
and level, and headed the enemy, they would have kept them
until our infantry came up. But nothing of the kind was
attempted, and so every French soldier escaped, though
every one ought to have been made prisoner, and this
affair of Merida would have been more complete than even
that of Arroyo Molinos ; for when I reported the position
of the enemy to General Hill, they were not more than two
miles distant from our advanced guard. This affair caused
an era in the life of General Hill ; for I heard many of his

17

oldest acquaintances remark that before the evening of this day they never saw a cloud upon his brow.

All hopes of being permitted to remain in the Peninsula having vanished, I resolved to return to England. With heavy heart I parted from the regiment in which I first drew my sword, in which my earliest friendships were formed and my mind modelled as a soldier. In Colonel Abercrombie's quarters at Merida many of the officers were assembled. Sorrowful, I bade adieu to my gallant old comrades, and quaffed a goblet to their future success whilst I clasped the colours to my breast—those colours which alone throughout the British army proudly display the names of the two bloodiest fought battles in the Peninsula, Barossa and Albuera; and in each of these battles the regiment claimed a double share of the glory. At Barossa, while Colonel Belson at the head of the 1st Battalion charged and turned the chosen grenadiers forming the right of the enemy's line, Colonel Browne of the regiment, at the head of their flank companies, united with those of two other corps, commanded the independent flank battalion; and this battalion, the first in the battle and alone, suffered more casualties both in officers and men (I allude particularly to the flankers of the 28th Regiment) than triple that sustained by any other battalion present in that memorable fight. At Albuera the 2nd Battalion of the regiment were led by a gallant officer, Colonel Patterson; and the brigade in which they served, that which with the brigade of the gallant Fusiliers turned the wavering fortunes of the day, were commanded by the gallant Abercrombie, the second lieutenant-colonel of the regiment.

Next morning at parting the light bobs gave me a cheer. I distinguished among them some few of the old ventriloquists of Galicia; but on this occasion their notes were, I

believe, genuine. I bade a mournful farewell to the old
Slashers, and bent my steps towards Badajoz, then about
to be besieged. The next evening (March 15th) I came
before the place; and very opportunely Lieutenant
Huddleston of the 28th Regiment, my brother officer in
the battalion company which I commanded for a short
time, arrived on the same day, being appointed to serve
in the Engineer department. He willingly shared his
tent with me; and Sir Frederick Stovin, also of the 28th
Regiment, then adjutant-general of the 3rd Division, introduced me to General Picton, who did me the honour of
saying that I should always find a cover at his table during
my stay before Badajoz. General Bowes, with whom I had
the pleasure of being acquainted at Gibraltar, gave me a
similar invitation. Thus, finding myself comparatively at
home, I felt in no way inclined to proceed too quickly to
Lisbon.

During the siege I assisted generally in the trenches.
On March 16th everything was finally arranged, and on
the following evening the different divisions and regiments
prepared to occupy their respective posts. All the troops
being assembled, generals and commanding officers inspected their brigades and regiments in review order.
The parade was magnificent and imposing. The colours
of each regiment proudly, though scantily, floated in the
breeze; they displayed but very little embroidery. Scarcely
could the well-earned badges of the regiments be discerned;
yet their lacerated condition, caused by the numberless
wounds which they received in battle, gave martial dignity
to their appearance and animated every British breast
with national pride. The review being terminated, a
signal was given for each corps to proceed to that spot of
ground which they were destined to open. The whole moved

off. All the bands by one accord played the same tune, which was cheered with shouts that bore ominous import and appeared to shake Badajoz to its foundation. The music played was the animating national Irish air, St. Patrick's Day, when the shamrock was proudly clustered with the laurel ; and indeed, though these two shrubs are not reckoned of the same family by proud collectors in the Cabinet, veterans hold them to be closely allied in the field. Never was St. Patrick's day more loudly cheered or by stouter hearts, and never was the music more nobly accompanied nor with more warlike bass ; for all the troops echoed the inspiring national air as proudly they marched to their ground. Phillipon maintained an incessant fire of cannon, roared forth in proud defiance from the destined fortress ; and Badajoz being now invested on both sides of the Guadiana, the operations of the siege were eagerly pressed forward.

On the 19th, during the completion of the 1st parallel, a sortie was made by the besieged soon after mid-day. Fifteen hundred of their infantry, screened by the ravelin San Roque, formed between that opening and the Picurina or small redoubt. They immediately pressed forward and gained the works before our men could seize their arms, while at the same time a party of cavalry, about fifty, the only horsemen in the fortress, got in rear of the parallel. The confusion was great at the first onset. Those on guard and the working men were driven out of the trenches, and the cavalry sabred many in the depôts at the rear ; but the mischief being quickly discovered was soon remedied. The Guards being reinforced immediately rallied and drove the enemy out of the works at the point of the bayonet, when many lives were lost. A part of the embankment was thrown into the trenches, and the enemy carried away

almost all the entrenching tools found in the parallel.
We lost one hundred and fifty men in killed and wounded
during this attack.

The siege was now carried on without interruption,
nothwithstanding the severity of the weather, which
frequently filled the trenches with water ; and so great
was the fall of rain on the 22nd that the pontoon bridge
was carried away by the Guadiana overflowing its banks,
and the flying bridges over that river could scarcely be
worked. This threatened a failure of the siege, from
the difficulty of supplying the troops with provisions and
the impossibility of bringing the guns and ammunition
across. Fortunately for the attack of the fortress however the disaster was remedied by the river falling within
its banks.

The morning of the 25th was ushered in by saluting
the garrison with twenty-eight pieces of cannon, opened
from six different batteries ; and in the evening Fort
Picurina was stormed, gallantly carried and permanently
retained. The enemy made a sortie on the night of the
29th, on the right bank of the Guadiana against General
Hamilton's division, who invested the fortress on that
side ; they were driven back with loss, and on this occasion
the besiegers had no casualties.

On the last day of March twenty-six pieces of ordnance
from the 2nd Parallel opened their fire against Fort
Trinidad and the flank of the protecting bastion, Santa
Maria. This fire continued incessantly, aided by an
additional battery of six guns, which also opened from
the 2nd Parallel on the morning of April 4th against
the ravelin of San Roque. On the evening of the 5th
Trinidad, Santa Maria and the ravelin of San Roque were
breached.

Preparations were made to storm the town that night ; but reports having been made by the engineers that strong works had been erected for the defence of the two breaches, particularly in rear of the large one made in the face of the bastion of Trinidad, where deep retrenchments had been constructed and every means resorted to which art and science could devise to prevent an entrance, the attack was therefore put off. Many hundred lives were spared, but for twenty-four hours only. All the guns in the 2nd Parallel were now directed against the curtain of Trinidad ; and towards the following evening a third breach appeared ; and the storming of Badajoz was arranged in the following order for the night of the 6th. The 4th division under command of Major-General the Honourable C. Colville, and the light division under Lieutenant-Colonel Barnard, were destined to attack the three breaches opened in the bastion of Trinidad, Santa Maria and the connecting curtain. Lieutenant-General Picton, with the 3rd or fighting division, was directed to attack the castle, which, from the great height of its walls and no breach having been attempted there, the enemy considered secure against assault. The ground left vacant by the advance of the 4th and light divisions was to be occupied by the 5th division, commanded by General Leith, with instructions to detach his left brigade, under General Walker, to make a false attack against the works of the fortress near the Guadiana, as also against the detached work the Pardaleras. Brigadier-General Power, commanding a Portuguese brigade on the opposite bank, was ordered to divert by making false attacks upon a newly formed redoubt called Mon Cœur, upon Fort St. Cristoval, upon the *tête du pont* and upon I forget what else. With these instructions the troops moved forward from the entrenchments about

ten o'clock at night to attack the destined town. The
3rd Division, under Picton, preceded the general movement
about a quarter of an hour for the purpose of drawing
away the enemy's attention from the openings in the wall,
since these were considered the only really vulnerable
points of the fortress. The 4th and light divisions pushed
gallantly forward against these breaches, and were not
discovered until they had entered the ditch. During their
advance the town was liberally supplied with shells from
our batteries, and the upper parts of the breaches were
continually fired upon by light troops placed upon the
glacis to disperse the enemy and prevent their repairing
the broken defences. This fire was but slightly answered,
until the two divisions mentioned were discovered entering
the ditch, when they were assailed by an awful cannonade,
accompanied by the sharp and incessant chattering of
musketry. Fireballs were shot forth from the fortress,
which illumined the surrounding space and discovered
every subsequent movement.

The dreadful strife now commenced. The thundering
cheer of the British soldiers as they rushed forward through
the outer ditch, together with the appalling roar of all
arms sent forth in defiance from within, was tremendous.
Whenever an instant pause occurred it was filled by the
heartrending shrieks of the trodden-down wounded and
by the lengthened groans of the dying. Three times were
the breaches cleared of Frenchmen, driven off at the point
of the bayonet by gallant British soldiers to the very
summit, when they were by the no less gallant foe each
time driven back, leaving their bravest officers and foremost soldiers behind, who, whether killed or wounded,
were tossed down headlong to the foot of the breaches.
Throughout this dreadful conflict our bugles were con-

tinually sounding the advance. The cry of "Bravo! bravo!" resounded through the ditches and along the foot of the breaches ; but no British cry was heard from within the walls of Badajoz save that of despair, uttered by the bravest, who despite of all obstacles forced their way into the body of the place, and there through dire necessity abandoned, groaned forth their last stabbed by unnumbered wounds. Again and again were the breaches attacked with redoubled fury and defended with equal pertinacity and stern resolution, seconded by every resource which science could adopt or ingenuity suggest. Bags and barrels of gunpowder with short fuses were rolled down, which, bursting at the bottom or along the face of the breaches, destroyed all who advanced. Thousands of live shells, hand-grenades, fireballs and every species of destructive combustible were thrown down the breaches and over the walls into the ditches, which, lighting and exploding at the same instant, rivalled the lightning and thunder of heaven. This at intervals was succeeded by an impenetrable darkness as of the infernal regions. Gallant foes laughing at death met, fought, bled and rolled upon earth ; and from the very earth destruction burst, for the exploding mines cast up friends and foes together, who in burning torture clashed and shrieked in the air. Partly burned they fell back into the inundating water, continually lighted by the incessant bursting of shells. Thus assailed by opposing elements, they made the horrid scene yet more horrid by shrieks uttered in wild despair, vainly struggling against a watery grave with limbs convulsed and quivering from the consuming fire. The roaring of cannon, the bursting of shells, the rattle of musketry, the awful explosion of mines and the flaring sickly blaze of fireballs seemed not of human invention, but rather as if all the elements of nature had greedily combined in the general havoc, and heaven, earth and hell had united for the destruction alike of devoted Badajoz and of its furious assailants.

In consequence of untoward disasters, which occurred at the very onset by the troops being falsely led, their numbers were seriously diminished and their compact formation disorganised. The third or last opening in the curtain was never attempted, although this breach was the most practicable, as it had been made only a few hours before, and thus there had been no time to strengthen its defences. Owing to this ruinous mistake, the harassed and depressed troops failed in their repeated attacks.

CHAPTER XXIV.

AT BADAJOZ.

AT length the bugles of the 4th and light divisions sounded the recall. At this moment General Bowes, whom I accompanied in the early part of the fight, being severely wounded, and his aide-de-camp, my old comrade and brother officer Captain Johnson, 28th Regiment, being killed, as I had no duty to perform (my regiment not being present), I attended the general as he was borne to his tent. He enquired anxiously about poor Johnson, his relative, not being aware that this gallant officer received his death-shot while he was being carried to the rear in consequence of a wound which he had received when cheering on a column to one of the breaches.

Having seen the general safely lodged, I galloped off to where Lord Wellington had taken his station. This was easily discerned by means of two fireballs shot out from the fortress at the commencement of the attack, which continued to burn brilliantly along the water-cut which divided the 3rd from the other divisions. Near the end of this channel, behind a rising mound, were Lord Wellington and his personal staff, screened from the enemy's direct fire, but within range of shells. One of his staff sat down by his side with a candle to enable the general to read and write all his communications and orders relative to the passing events. I stood not far from his lordship. But due respect prevented any of us bystanders from approaching so near as to enable us to ascertain the import of the reports which he was continually receiving ; yet it was very evident that the information which they conveyed was far from flattering ; and the recall on the bugles was again and again repeated. But about half-past eleven o'clock an officer rode up at full speed on a horse covered with foam, and announced the joyful tidings that General Picton had made a lodgment within the castle by escalade, and had withdrawn the troops from the trenches to enable him to maintain his dearly purchased hold. Lord Wellington was evidently delighted, but exclaimed, " What ! abandon the trenches ? " and ordered two regiments of the 5th Division instantly to replace those withdrawn. I waited to hear no more, but, admiring the prompt genius which immediately provided for every contingency, I mounted my horse. I was immediately surrounded by a host of Spaniards, thousands of whom, of all ages and sexes, had been collecting at this point for some time from the neighbouring towns and villages to witness the storming and enjoy the brilliant spectacle, wherein thousands of men, women and children, including those of their own country, were to be shot, bayoneted or blown to atoms. Notwithstanding the hundreds of beautiful females who closely pressed round and even clung to me for information, I merely exclaimed in a loud voice that Badajoz was taken and then made the best of my way to the walls of the castle ; their height was rather forbidding, and an enfilading fire still continued. The ladders were warm and slippery with blood and brains of many a gallant soldier, who but a few moments previously mounted them with undaunted pride, to be dashed down from their top and lie broken in death at their foot.

As soon as General Picton had arrived at the walls he
instantly ordered them to be escaladed, frightful as was
their height. Ladder after ladder failed to be placed
against the walls, their determined bearers being killed.
But Picton, who never did anything by halves or hesitatingly, instead of parsimoniously sending small parties
forward and waiting to hear of their extinction before
fresh support was furnished, boldly marched his whole
division to the foot of the walls ; and thus, without loss
of time, by immediately supplying the place of the fallen,
he at length succeeded in rearing one ladder. Then having
his reserves close at hand, scarcely was a man shot off
when an equally brave successor filled his place ; and in
this manner those who mounted that one ladder at length
made a lodgment. This being firmly established, the fire
from within slackened ; many ladders were soon reared
and the whole of the 3rd Division entered the castle.
The Connaught Rangers were said to be the first within the
wall.   In consequence of some misconduct, General Picton
had changed the name " Rangers " to " Robbers."   After
the storming of the castle a private of the corps called
out half-drunken to the general, " Are we the ' Connaught
Robbers ' now ? "   " No," answered Picton ; " you are
the ' Connaught Heroes.' "

The confusion in the castle was awful all night long.
All the gates had been built up but one, and that narrowed
to the width of two men. On this straight gate a terrible
fire was directed from outside and in. The 3rd Division
first fired on the French and, when they had gone,
continued to fire on their own comrades of the 5th Division,
who had entered the town on the opposite side by escalading
the bastion of San Vincente. This capture was opposed as
fiercely and made as bravely as that of the castle. The

3rd Division having taken the castle about half-past eleven, Picton received orders to maintain it until break of day, when he was to sally forth with two thousand men and fall on the rear of the breaches, which it was intended should again be attacked by the 4th and light Divisions. The party who carried the ladders of the 5th Division lost their way and did not come up until after eleven o'clock, which necessarily made General Leith an hour late in his attack on the bastion of San Vincente, so that before he entered the town the castle was in possession of the 3rd Division. The enemy who defended the breaches being no longer attacked in front, turned all their force against the 5th Division as they advanced from their captured bastion along the ramparts. As soon as General Walker's brigade of this division gained the interior of the fortress, they moved forward along the ramparts, driving everything before them until they arrived not far from the breach in the Santa Maria bastion ; here the enemy had a gun placed, and as the British troops advanced a French gunner lit a port fire. Startled at the sudden and unexpected light, some of the foremost British soldiers cried out, "A mine, a mine!" These words passing to the rear, the whole of the troops fell into disorder, and such was the panic caused by this ridiculous mistake that the brave example and utmost exertions of the officers could not prevail upon the men to advance. The enemy, perceiving the hesitation, pushed boldly forward to the charge, and drove the British back to the bastion of San Vincente, where they had entered. Here a battalion in reserve had been formed, who, in their turn rushing forward to the charge, bayoneted or made prisoner every Frenchman they met, pursuing those who turned as far as the breaches. The 3rd and 5th Divisions interchanged many shots, each

ignorant of the other's success and consequent position;
and both divisions continued to fire at the breaches, so
that had the 4th and light divisions made another attack
many must have fallen by the fire of both divisions of their
comrades.

From both within and without, as has been said, a
constant fire was kept up at the narrow and only entrance
to the castle. This entrance was defended by a massive
door, nearly two feet thick, which was riddled throughout ;
and had the 3rd Division sallied forth during the confusion
and darkness, they must have come in contact with the
5th Division, when no doubt many more lives would
have been lost before they recognised each other. This
was fortunately prevented by Picton being ordered to
remain in the castle until morning.

The scenes in the castle that night were of a most deplorable and terrific nature : murders, robberies and every
species of debauchery and obscenity were seen, notwithstanding the exertions of the officers to prevent them. Phillipon
expecting that, even though he should lose the town, he
would be able to retain the castle at least for some days,
had had all the live cattle of the garrison driven in there.
The howling of dogs, the crowing of cocks, the penetrating
cackle of thousands of geese, the mournful bleating of
sheep, the furious bellowing of wounded oxen maddened
by being continually goaded and shot at and ferociously
charging through the streets, were mixed with accompani-
ments loudly trumpeted forth by mules and donkeys and
always by the deep and hollow baying of the large
Spanish half-wolves, half-bloodhounds which guarded the
whole. Add to this the shrill screaming of affrighted
children, the piercing shrieks of frantic women, the groans
of the wounded, the savage and discordant yells of

drunkards firing at everything and in all directions, and
the continued roll of musketry kept up in error on the
shattered gateway ; and you may imagine an uproar such
as one would think could issue only from the regions of
Pluto ; and this din was maintained throughout the night.

Towards morning the firing ceased ; and the 4th and
light divisions passed through the breaches over the
broken limbs and dead bodies of their gallant comrades.
A great part of the garrison were made prisoners during
the night by the 5th Division ; but Phillipon, with most
of the officers and a portion of the men, retreated across
the Guadiana into Fort Cristoval.   He demanded terms
of capitulation next morning ; but Lord Wellington gave
him ten minutes to consider and straightway prepared
the guns to batter the place.   However, that was prevented
by Phillipon surrendering at discretion.

As soon as light served and communication between
the castle and the town opened, I bent my way along
the ramparts towards the main opening in the Trinidad
bastion.   The glorious dawn of day, contrasted with the
horrible scenes which I had witnessed, filled the mind
with joy.   The sun rose in majesty and splendour, as
usual in the blooming month of April, which in that
climate is as our May.   The country around was clothed
in luxuriant verdure, refreshed by recent dew, which still
clinging to each green leaf and blade in diamond drops
reflected the verdant hue of the foliage upon which it hung
till diamonds seemed emeralds.   A thousand nameless
flowers, displaying as many lovely colours, were on all
the earth.   Proudly and silently the Guadiana flowed,
exhibiting its white surface to the majestically rising orb
which gave to the ample and gently heaving breast of
the noble stream the appearance of an undulating plain of

burnished silver. On its fertile banks the forward harvest
already promised abundance and contentment even to the
most avaricious husbandman. The fruit trees opened their
rich and perfumed blossoms; the burnished orange borrow-
ing colour of the sun glowed in contrast with the more
delicate gold of lemon; and everywhere grey olive trees
spread ample boughs—but here, alas! they were not the
emblems of peace. Every creeping bramble and humble
shrub made a fair show that morning; birds sang in
heaven; all sensitive and animated nature appeared gay
and seemed with grateful acknowledgments to welcome the
glorious father of light and heat. The lord of creation
alone, " sensible and refined man," turned his back on
the celestial scene to gloat in the savage murders and
degrading obscenity that wantoned in devoted Badajoz.

When I arrived at the great breach the inundation presented an awful contrast to the silvery Guadiana; it was
fairly stained with gore, which through the vivid reflection
of the brilliant sun, whose glowing heat already drew the
watery vapours from its surface, gave it the appearance
of a fiery lake of smoking blood, in which were seen the
bodies of many a gallant British soldier. The ditches were
strewn with killed and wounded; but the approach to the
bottom of the main breach was fairly choked with dead.
A row of *chevaux de frise*, armed with sword-blades,
barred the entrance at the top of the breach and so firmly
fixed that when the 4th and light Divisions marched
through, the greatest exertion was required to make a
sufficient opening for their admittance. Boards fastened
with ropes to plugs driven into the ground within the
ramparts were let down, and covered nearly the whole
surface of the breach; these boards were so thickly studded
with sharp pointed spikes that one could not introduce a

hand between them ; they did not stick out at right angles
to the board, but were all slanting upwards. In rear of
the *chevaux de frise* the ramparts had deep cuts in all
directions, like a tanyard, so that it required light to enable
one to move safely through them, even were there no
opposing enemy. From the number of muskets found
close behind the breach, all the men who could possibly
be brought together in so small a place must have had
at least twenty firelocks each, no doubt kept continually
loaded by persons in the rear. Two British soldiers only
entered the main breach during the assault ; I saw both
their bodies. If any others entered they must have been
thrown back over the walls, for certain it is that at dawn
of the 7th no more than two British bodies were within
the walls near the main breach. In the Santa Maria
breach not one had entered. At the foot of this breach
the same sickening sight appeared as at that of Trinidad :
numberless dead strewed the place. On looking down
these breaches I recognised many old friends, whose society
I had enjoyed a few hours before, now lying stiff in death.

Oppressed by the sight which the dead and dying presented at the breaches, I turned away and re-entered the
town ; but oh ! what scenes of horror did I witness there !
They can never be effaced from my memory. There was
no safety for women even in the churches ; and any who
interfered or offered resistance were sure to get shot. Every
house presented a scene of plunder, debauchery and bloodshed, committed with wanton cruelty on the persons of
the defenceless inhabitants by our soldiery ; and in many
instances I beheld the savages tear the rings from the
ears of beautiful women who were their victims, and when
the rings could not be immediately removed from their
fingers with the hand, they tore them off with their teeth.

18

Firing through the streets and at the windows was incessant, which made it excessively dangerous to move out.
When the savages came to a door which had been locked
or barricaded, they applied what they called the patent
key : this consisted of the muzzles of a dozen firelocks
placed close together against that part of the door where
the lock was fastened, and the whole fired off together into
the house and rooms, regardless of those inside; these
salvos were repeated until the doors were shattered, and in
this way too several inhabitants were killed. Men, women
and children were shot in the streets for no other apparent
reason than pastime ; every species of outrage was publicly
committed in the houses, churches and streets, and in a
manner so brutal that a faithful recital would be too indecent
and too shocking to humanity. Not the slightest shadow
of order or discipline was maintained ; the officers durst
not interfere. The infuriated soldiery resembled rather a
pack of hell-hounds vomited up from the infernal regions
for the extirpation of mankind than what they were but
twelve short hours previously—a well-organised, brave,
disciplined and obedient British army, and burning only
with impatience for what is called glory.

But whatever accounts may be given of the horrors
which attended and immediately followed the storming of
Badajoz, they must fall far short of the truth ; and it is
impossible for any who were not present to imagine them.
I have already mentioned that neither the regiment to
which I was just appointed nor that which I had just left
was at the siege. I therefore could have had but little
influence in controlling the frenzied military mob who
were ferociously employed in indiscriminate carnage, universal plunder and devastation of every kind. Three
times I narrowly escaped with life for endeavouring to

protect some women by conveying them to St. John's Church, where a guard was mounted. On one occasion, as Huddleston and I accompanied two ladies and the brother of one of them to the church mentioned, we were crossed by three drunken soldiers, one of whom, passing to our rear, struck the Spanish gentleman with the butt-end of his firelock on the back of his head, which nearly knocked him down. On my censuring the fellow's daring insolence in striking a person in company with two English officers, another of the men was bringing his firelock to the present, when I holloaed out loudly, " Come on quick with that guard." There was no guard near, but the ruse luckily succeeded, and so quickly did the soldiers run away that I felt convinced that their apparent intoxication was feigned. On another occasion a sergeant struck me with his pike for refusing to join in plundering a family ; I certainly snapped my pistol in his face, but fortunately it missed fire or he would have been killed. However the danger which he so narrowly escaped brought him to his senses ; he made an awkward apology and I considered it prudent to retire. By such means as these, by the risk and humanity of officers, many women were saved. We did not interfere with the plundering ; it would have been useless.

One circumstance, being of a very peculiar nature, I shall relate. During the morning of the 7th, while the excesses, of which I have given but a faint idea, were at their height, Huddleston came running to me and requested that I would accompany him to a house whence he had just fled. The owner was an old acquaintance of all the officers of the 28th Regiment, when a few months previously we were quartered at Albuquerque, where he lived at the time. Huddleston conducted me to the bedroom of this man's

wife. When we entered, a woman who lay upon a
bed uttered a wild cry, which might be considered as
caused either by hope or despair. Here were two British
soldiers stretched on the floor, and so intoxicated that when
Huddleston and I drew them out of the room by the heels
they appeared insensible of the motion. The master of
the house sat in a corner of the room in seeming apathy;
upon recognising me he exclaimed, with a vacant stare,
"And why this, Don Roberto?" Having somewhat
recovered from his stupor, he told me that the woman on
the bed was his wife, who was in momentary expectation
of her *accouchement*. In my life I never saw horror and
despair so strongly depicted as upon the countenances of
this unfortunate couple. Several soldiers came in while
we remained; and our only hope of saving the unfortunate
lady's life was by apparently joining in the plunder of the
apartments, for any attempt at resistance would have
been useless and would perhaps have brought on fatal
consequences. I stood as a kind of warning sentry near
the bedroom door, which was designedly left open; and
whenever any of the men approached it, I pointed
out the female, representing her as a person dying of a
violent fever; and thus we succeeded in preserving her life.
Huddleston and I then set to work most actively to break
tables and chairs, which we strewed about the rooms and
down the stairs. I remained for some hours, when I
considered that all was safe; for although many marauding
parties had entered, yet on perceiving the ruinous appearance of the house, and considering that it must have
already been well visited, they went off immediately in
search of better prey. We even scattered a shopful of
stationery and books all over the apartments, and some of
the articles we held in our hands as if plunder, for the

purpose of deceiving the visitors. I recollect taking up some coloured prints of Paul and Virginia ; these I afterwards presented as a trophy of war to an old friend, Mrs. Blakeney, of Abbert, Co. Galway, as the sole tangible remembrance of the storming of Badajoz. I frequently called at the house during the two following days and was happy to find that no further injuries were suffered. Huddleston's servant and mine slept in the house. We ourselves retired to the camp as darkness approached, for to remain in Badajoz during the night would have been attended with certain danger, neither of our regiments being in the place. The sack continued for three days without intermission ; each day I witnessed its horrid and abominable effects. But I shrink from further description.

On the morning of the fourth day (April 10th) the 9th Regiment were marched regularly into town. A gallows was erected in the principal square and others in different parts of the town. A general order was proclaimed that the first man detected in plundering should be executed ; but no execution took place. The soldiers well knew how far they might proceed, and no farther did they go. The butcheries and horrible scenes of plunder and debauchery ceased in Badajoz ; and it became an orderly British garrison. During the sack the Portuguese troops plundered but little, for as they had not been employed in the storming the British soldiers would have killed them had they interfered with the spoil. But during the three days' transfer of property they lay hid close outside the town, where they awaited the British soldiers, who always came with a sheet or counterpane filled with every species of plunder, carried on their heads and shoulders like so many Atlases ; and as these always left the town drunk and lay down to sleep between it and the camp, the artful Portuguese crept up and carried away everything, and thus they finally possessed all the plunder. I witnessed this mean jackal theft a hundred times; and, without feeling the slightest affection for those second-hand dastard robbers, I enjoyed seeing the British soldiers deprived of their booty, acquired under circumstances too disgusting to be dwelt on.

The storming of Badajoz caused a severe loss to the British army. The 3rd and 5th Divisions, who successfully escaladed the walls, lost either in killed or wounded six hundred men each; and the casualties suffered by the 4th and light Divisions amounted to upwards of five hundred more than the loss of the successful escalading divisions.

The great loss caused in the ranks of those who attacked the breaches was due to their having been erroneously led on to an unfinished ravelin, constructed in front of the centre breach, that of Trinidad. This work had been a good deal raised during the siege, and being mistaken for a breach, which in its unfinished state it much resembled, the 4th Division gallantly mounted and soon reached the top. Here they were severely galled by a destructive fire from the whole front; a deep precipice and wet ditch intervened between the ravelin and the breaches. Astonished and dismayed the men began to return the enemy's fire. At this critical moment the light division, who had been led as much too far to their right as the 4th Division had been to their left, came up; and unfortunately they also mounted the fatal deceptive ravelin. All was now confusion and dreadful carnage was passively suffered by those devoted troops. The officers, having at length discovered the mistake, hurried down the ravelin and gallantly showed the example of mounting the Trinidad and Santa Maria breaches, followed by the bravest of the men ; but the formation as an organised body being broken, only the excessively brave followed the officers. On arriving at the top of the breaches, which were stoutly defended, so weak a force were consequently hurled down to destruction. The utmost disorder followed. Thus the attacks on the three breaches, where alone Badajoz was considered vulnerable, all failed of success ; while those defences which both by the besiegers and besieged were deemed almost impregnable, were gallantly forced. Such are the vicissitudes of war, especially in night attacks. At dawn on the 7th there was no dead body near the last made and most vulnerable breach—a proof that by error it was never attacked.

Immediately after the fall of Badajoz the chief part of the army moved towards the north of Portugal, where Marmont had collected his corps. However, all his exploits consisted in a distant blockade of Ciudad Rodrigo and some romantic attempts against the fortress of Almeida. Failing in his attempts against those two places, he marched upon Castello Branco, threatening to destroy the Bridge of Boats at Villavelha ; but on the advance of Lord Wellington to attack him he retired out of Portugal and thus terminated his inglorious incursion.

Fortunately for the operations carried on against Badajoz, Marmont's jealousy of Soult was such that he ignored all his remonstrances and did not unite with him; he continued obstinate and Badajoz fell.

Marshal Soult arrived with his army at Llerena on April 3rd, and on the 4th Lord Wellington made arrangements to receive him. His plan was to leave ten thousand men in the trenches and fight the marshal with the remainder of his army ; but Soult, either feeling diffident of his strength or still in the hope that Marmont would bend his course southerly, arrived at Villa Franca, but thirty miles from Llerena and the same distance from Badajoz, only on the 7th, thus taking four days to march thirty miles in haste to relieve a beleaguered fortress. On his arrival at Villa Franca on the 7th, he was informed that Badajoz had fallen that morning, or rather the night before, and that Phillipon had surrendered at discretion. He then, like Marmont, retired and moved into Andalusia.

CHAPTER XXV.

ALL the troops, except those left to repair and garrison
Badajoz, having moved off, I proceeded immediately
to Lisbon. Here I remained as short a time as possible, not
from over anxiety to see England, but because, although I
had the horrors of the sacking of Badajoz in painful recollection, I felt greater horror at the idea that I might be taken
for a Belemite. During the splendid campaigns which
took place in the Peninsula from 1808 to 1813 many British
officers were collected at Belem, and with peculiar tact so
contrived as always to remain in the rear of the army.
Some were unwillingly kept back from debility of constitution or through wounds, but a large majority were
inflicted with a disease which, baffling the skill of learned
doctors, loudly called for a remedy far different from that
of medical treatment. This patrician band, amounting to
the incredible number of upwards of a thousand, were
formed into an inefficient depôt at Belem, a suburb of
Lisbon, distant thence about five miles. That this over
prudent body was not exclusively composed of wounded
will appear when it is known that the greater number of
its members had never seen nor heard a shot fired during
the whole of the eventful period mentioned, far more
cautious indeed than the smooth-faced Roman patricians

who fled from the slingers at Pharsalia. This careful band
did not venture so far even as the skirts of the fight; and
it might truthfully be said that the movement of the whole
army was attended with less difficulty than the movement
of a single Belemite to the front. The complaint or disease
of which they complained they invariably attributed to the
liver; but medical men after careful analysis attributed
it to an affection of the heart, founding their conclusions
on the fact that whenever any of those backward patients
came forward, the violent palpitations of that organ clearly
proved that it was much more affected by the artificial fire
in the field than was the liver by the physical heat of
the sun.

A ludicrous scene took place in Lisbon whilst I was
there, in which one of these gentlemen of the rearguard
made a very conspicuous, though not happy figure, and so
caused much merriment. Prevailing upon himself to fancy
that he was deeply in love with a young and beautiful
Portugese lady of noble birth and ample fortune, he was
unwearied in his addresses. These, as it would appear,
were not disagreeable to the amiable fair; but her parents
entertaining quite different sentiments, used every endeavour
to cut off all communication between the lovers. Notwithstanding, our hero, active and persevering in the wars of
Venus as passive and quiescent in those of Mars, was not
to be shaken; and finding that his visits to the lady's
house were no longer desired, he became incessant in his
attendance at a post taken up opposite to a particular
window in the rear of the mansion wherein the lady resided.
Here a telegraphic correspondence was established between
the lovers. This being discovered by the vigilant parents,
means were adopted to prevent the appearance of their
daughter at the propitious window. Finding however

that the hero was not to be diverted from his purpose, and that he continued to attend every evening about dusk in the vicinity of the window, they determined to bring about by stratagem that which neither threat nor remonstrance could effect.

In the meantime the champion, more of love than of war, relaxed not in his dusky visits, although uniformly disappointed. Fancy then his ecstasy one evening, after such continued vexations and as he was about to depart, at again beholding the cherished object of all his solicitude present herself at the accommodating window. His heart bounded at recognising the high bonnet with pink ribbons, so well remembered. Half frantic with delight he rapturously pressed his hands to his heart, then applying them to his lips shot them forward in the direction of the lovely fair. Here his happiness was increased tenfold at perceiving that his angel, who on former occasions but doubtingly countenanced his love, now with fervour apparently equal to his own repeated all his amorous gestures ; this he naturally attributed to pure affection, heightened by long separation. His amorous expressions also were repeated, so far as the distance which separated them allowed him to distinguish words, although as he afterwards related he fancied the intonation of the voice an octave higher than usual and the sudden interruptions rather hysterical ; but this he attributed to the flurried state of her mind at the moment. All tended in his excited imagination to show the great interest she felt at the interview. Urged by these sentiments, he hurried forward ; his charmer hurried from the window. Excited to the highest pitch and considering the retreat from the window, which was left open, rather an invitation than a repulse, he determined to enter ; and fortunately discovering a short ladder in the garden, left as he thought through accident or neglect, with its aid he boldly entered the room. The obscurity here being greater, he could barely see the loved object of his search quickly retire to a large arm-chair ; to this he promptly followed, and throwing himself upon his knees held forth his clasped hands in a suppli-cating manner, when lo and behold! the doors were suddenly thrown open and a numerous concourse of ladies and gentlemen with lights hurried into the room before the lover had time to resume his upright position. Fancy his confusion and amazement at beholding in the first person who entered the object of all his affections, and his horror and consternation when turning round to the object before whom he knelt, he found his closed hands firmly clasped by a large Brazilian monkey! This ape was the particular favourite of the young lady, and on this occasion was dressed by order of her parents in the precise apparel which they had seen their daughter always wear during the balcony interviews. Thunderstruck and abashed as he regarded all the objects round and as the shrill voice and chirping hysterical sounds flashed on his memory now dreadfully explained, he fully represented wild despair and abject humility. Yet he still clung to the hope that the young lady would try to extricate him from his degrading dilemma, when she thus addressed him : "Ah, faithless wretch !—not content with endeavouring to betray me alone, but also to attempt seducing the affections of my favourite, my darling monkey ! Begone, wretch, nor let me ever more behold thy odious presence !" and darting at him a glance of the utmost disdain she flounced out of the room. Now, becoming furious at his ludicrous situation, and scarcely knowing how to vent his rage, he drew forth his sword from under his cloak and in a menacing attitude prepared to attack the innocent object at whose feet he had so lately knelt, and to whom he had so ardently poured forth the fervency of his passion. The imitative animal, instantly snatching up a large fan which lay on the armchair and little knowing his danger, immediately assumed a similar menacing attitude, when a loud cry burst forth from all, " Shame, shame, to enter the lists against a poor defenceless monkey ! " This was too much to be borne, and the beau, the dupe of stratagem, followed the example of the young lady by leaving the room, with this difference—the young lady proudly and slowly went upstairs, but our hero with an entirely opposite feeling rushed hurriedly down. There was thought of remonstrances to the British authorities ; but it being ascertained that this tender man of war was not quartered in Lisbon, but a Belemite who in amorous mood strayed away from his tribe, no military investigation took place. However the affair becoming the topic of general merriment, the gallant gay Lothario could not endure the derision to which he was exposed. But what annoyed him most was the report that he had fought a duel with a monkey. He therefore determined to join the army and resigning the voluptuous court of Venus ranged himself at last under the rigid standard of Mars ; thus what the hero of the Peninsula failed to accomplish was brought about by a Brazilian baboon, the forcing of a Belemite from out his safehold to the field of war.

Having remained but a very few days in Lisbon, I proceeded to England and reporting myself at the Horse Guards was ordered to join the 2nd Battalion of my regiment, quartered at Lewes. Thence I was immediately sent on recruiting service ; but having shortly after procured my recall, I applied to His Royal Highness the Duke of York for leave to join the 1st Battalion of the Regiment then in the Peninsula, although I belonged to the 2nd Battalion at home. His Royal Highness was pleased to grant my request; this was facilitated by there being at the time three captains of the 1st Battalion in England. I now proceeded to Portsmouth to procure a passage to Lisbon. Here I found there was but one transport ready to sail for the Peninsula; this being a horse transport was filled with those animals and dragoon officers, to whom alone the cabin was dedicated. However, Colonel Sir James Douglas, Colonel Belnevis, Majors Leggatt and Arnot, infantry officers, having arrived before me at Portsmouth had contrived to get berths, but there was none left for me; even the floor was portioned off. My application for a passage was therefore negatived; but after repeated entreaties to Captain Patten, Agent of Transports, he permitted me to sail in the vessel, with the proviso however that I should pledge my word of honour not to take that precedence in choice of berths to which my rank entitled me; in a word, not to interfere with the convenience of the cavalry officers, who were all subalterns. From my anxiety to return to Spain and impatience of delay, I hesitated not a moment in agreeing to the proposal.

Our voyage proceeded prosperously until we approached the Bay of Biscay, when entering on its skirts and in very rough weather we fell in with a British man-of-war. Perceiving us alone, she very genteelly undertook to protect us. In pursuance of this disinterested act she made signals for us to follow her movements, in obeying which we entered much deeper into the bay than the master of the transport or any other person on board could account for. While we were steering thus for a considerable time, certainly very wide of our true course, an American privateer

with a prize in tow hove in sight, when our kind and
voluntary protector immediately left us, making his course
for those vessels, which on his approach separated taking
different directions. But the British man-of-war turning
his back on the hostile privateer, allowed her to depart
without any molestation; and considering perhaps that he
best served his country in doing so chose the prize for
chase, by the capture of which salvage would reward his
patriotism. The three vessels were soon out of sight.
The man-of-war and the prize we never saw more; but
towards evening the privateer was again discovered bearing down upon us. Approaching within gunshot she lay
to on our starboard bow. Having four guns aside which
were shotted and everything ready for action, we also
played the bravo, and reefing our mainsail also lay to.
Colonel Douglas, as chief in command, took no particular
station; Colonel Belnevis, Major Leggatt and Major Arnot
commanded the starboard guns; the bow gun, same side,
was allotted to me. When we had silently broadsided
each other for some time, the privateer, seeing our vessel
full of troops and moreover double her size, dared not
hazard an attempt at boarding, and perceiving our four
guns aside did not fire into us; while we, on the other
side, had many reasons for not wishing an action. Perceiving
however the hesitation of the enemy, we put the best face
on the affair and resolved stoutly to bear down direct
upon her. On our approaching the privateer crowded all
sail and to our infinite satisfaction bore away, repeating
the same signals made by our faithful commodore in
the morning—*i.e.*, to follow her movements; and this too
with the English flag flying. To say the truth we were
in miserable fighting trim; for although we had four
guns aside, we dreaded their explosion more than the shot

from our enemy. The locks of these guns were but very
imperfectly fastened on ; and through some extraordinary
oversight no medical officer had been embarked.

The wind having much increased and we being in the
centre of the bay, the vessel rolled awfully. Water-casks,
portmanteaus, hencoops breaking from their lashings
fearfully traversed the decks, and obeying only the rolling
of the vessel threatened broken limbs to all who came
in their way. These obstacles and many others of a minor
kind gave particular annoyance to the cavalry officers,
who being dressed for professional fight and mostly being
but a short time in the Service, wore their spurs uncon-
scionably long and consequently detrimental ; for many
things which otherwise would have crossed the deck,
fastened on the spurs, and their owners in the confusion
of the moment could not account for the closeness with
which they were charged, forgetting that their own weapons
dragged the encumbrances after them. All things considered, we were well pleased at not being obliged to fight ;
our nerves could not have been doubted. The infantry,
four field officers and one captain were veterans often
proved in action ; and the gallantry of the dragoons could
not for a moment be called in question, for they showed
themselves gamecocks even to the heels. The name of
one of these officers I mention from his peculiar and
melancholy fate, Lieutenant Trotter, 4th Dragoon Guards.
At the Battle of Waterloo he gallantly took a French
dragoon officer prisoner in single combat. While conducting
him to the rear (of course on his parole and therefore
permitted to ride), Trotter never thought of being on his
guard ; but the assassin, watching an opportunity when
Trotter turned round, drew out a pistol which he had
concealed in his breast and shot poor Trotter through

the head. He instantly fell dead but the murderer escaped.

When we had succeeded in lashing the water-casks, portmanteaus and coops, and recooping the fugitive poultry, and having fortunately got rid of both our foe and our protector, we, to make use of a military phrase, brought up our left shoulders to resume our proper course, from which we had been diverted, nay, ordered to deviate by the insidious interference of a man-of-war. The master of the transport calculated that by obeying his signals, our voyage was considerably prolonged. Thus was the public Service retarded and British troops placed in a perilous situation by a person whose bounden duty it was to protect them, yet who first led us into danger and then left us to our fate in a comparatively defenceless transport while he himself turned his back on friend and foe and went in search of a prize. Few such instances have occurred or are likely to occur, since such conduct is surely as repugnant to the feelings of our brave sailors as to our own.

During the rest of our voyage we met with no further adventure. After our encounter I told Colonel Douglas that having been now called upon duty I was entitled to a choice of berths according to my rank, in which Douglas fully agreed ; but as I had pledged my word to Captain Patten that I should not interfere with the dragoon officers, I continued my usual dormitory, which was on the hay put on board for the horses.

On our arrival at Lisbon, Colonel Douglas ascertained the name of our convoy and that of the captain. He declared at the time that he would report the whole transaction to the Commander-in-chief. Whether he did so or not I cannot say, as I never after had the pleasure

19

of meeting him but once, and that on the Pyrenees and under circumstances which precluded much conversation : he was bleeding profusely from a gunshot wound which he had just received in the neck. I recollect being told on our arrival at Lisbon by a gallant old naval officer, who was highly indignant at the affair, that we were taken in convoy because our voluntary protector did not belong to the station, and therefore took the opportunity of offering his services as a pretext for trespassing on Sir Richard Keats' cruising ground.

Having remained in Lisbon barely long enough to prepare equipment necessary to take the field, I now marched from that capital for the fourth time ; but although superior in rank I did not feel more happy. On former occasions I proudly fell into the ranks of as fine and gallant a corps as ever moved forth to battle ; I laughed and joked with old comrades whom I sincerely esteemed. Our march was enlivened with martial music, and we enjoyed each other's society when the daily march was over. That was a walk of pleasure ; but now the contrast was woeful. Silent and alone I left Lisbon. I had a dreary march of some hundred miles before me ; heavily therefore I plodded along and always in dread of being taken for a Belemite. At last however I fortunately fell in with an artillery officer, a lieutenant who was proceeding to the army with a relay of mules for the guns. My new acquaintance being also proficient in more languages than one, we could, as occasion required, and without dread of detection, pass as natives of different countries ; and through the general information acquired by the curious traveller who has wandered far, we were enabled to act in many capacities. In some measure therefore to brighten the gloom and break the monotony of our

long and dreary march, we exerted our ingenuity in frequent
varieties of calling.

In our playful frolics we acted many parts; but to
recount all the occurrences which took place during this
extraordinarily long march would be impossible; yet, lest it
should be imagined that I wish to insinuate that fortune
smiled upon all our juvenile and thoughtless freaks and
to show that, as all who adventure much, we also shared
her frowns, I shall relate one anecdote. Approaching the
Ebro, we were billeted in the house of a hidalgo a short
way from the town of Reynosa. In the mansion of our
noble host dwelt two beautiful young ladies, nieces of a
High Church dignitary, then absent at Madrid. With one
of these fair ladies the lieutenant of artillery became
desperately enamoured, and his love seemed to be returned.
A mutual attachment was confessed; a union was mutually
agreed upon; and the fair Iberian heroically determined
to knit her fate with that of her lover and confiding in
his honour resolved on an elopement. That my friend's
intentions were perfectly honourable I had no doubt; but
to induce a Spanish bishop to give the hand of his niece
to a heretic was not to be thought of. Under these circumstances I of course lent my aid, seeing that my companion
was determined at all hazard to carry her off. The elopement was fixed for the morning dawn. The heroine, the
better to elude discovery, determined to travel for a stage
or two in male attire; to this I contributed a new hat.
In this hat were closely crammed a pair of doeskin inex-
pressibles belonging to the great gun officer, which were
privately consigned to the fair lady and by her kept in
her room until required. One of our servants was to
accompany the lady and gentleman, who were to start at
daybreak, each riding in a man's saddle and as men do,

to which the lady made no objection. In truth Spanish ladies see nothing either morally or physically wrong in this mode of travelling. The principal object to be attained was to lull the suspicions of the family, particularly that of the young lady's aunt and of her elder sister, whose vigilance was roused by certain telegraphic glances which passed between the incautious lovers. To forward this we invited the whole family that night and generously supplied them with mulled wine highly spiced and sweetened and qualified with a liberal portion of brandy. This punch royal was plentifully supplied ; and to say the truth the beverage was freely quaffed by all to a very late hour, when at length all retired to rest. The anxiously looked-for dawn having appeared, we beheld the little lady emerging from her room fully equipped for travelling. Her costume certainly caused some mirth. My friend's doeskins not being sufficiently ample, were ripped down the rear ; but for security, as well as to prevent untoward accidents, the young lady had established a communication between the separated parts of the dress by cross-lacing or frogging, such as may be seen across the breast of a hussar's blue frock. My hat was tastefully perched on the crown of her head, rather on one side and made fast to a net or caul in which her hair was confined, an arrangement not unfrequently adopted by men in Spain. Thus, with the addition of a pair of top or jockey-boots (also mine) and a handsome whip, she had all the appearance of a smart and fashionable little postilion. Her white jacket was also slit and frogged, but in front and for a similar reason. Now as we lightly tripped downstairs a confused noise was heard through the house, a violent retching caused by the previous night's dissipation ; all were indeed aroused; and as we were hurrying our little postilion

towards the stables we were overtaken by the ever vigilant
aunt and a host of servants. Protestations of honourable
intentions were vain ; the poor little postilion was made
prisoner and marched back to the house, while we slunk
off crestfallen and abashed.

Moving silently along we arrived that night at Reynosa
and were billeted in different houses. Next day we visited
the interesting little hamlet Fontebro, so called from its
being close to two springs, whence that noble stream the
Ebro derives its waters ; this was three miles distant from
Reynosa. On our return we dined with the gentleman
at whose house I was quartered, a most hospitable person ;
his wife was equally hospitable ; they cordially invited
us to remain some days. We met a large party of ladies
and gentlemen at dinner and were highly entertained, as
is generally the case at all foreign tables where people
meet to eat, drink and be merry, rather than to watch what
others eat and drink and criticise their manner of doing
so. I once heard a fine gentleman ask the person next
him at a dinner-party and in hearing of the person who
caused the remark, "Can you fancy anything so vulgar
and ill-bred as to be helped twice to soup?" The answer
was pungent and laconic, "Yes, remarking it."

In the midst of our hilarity a servant entered with a
parcel directed to the two English officers who had arrived
at Reynosa the previous evening. For some reason or
other I felt no inclination to open it ; but the good couple
of the house insisted that we should stand upon no ceremony,
but examine its contents. When I loosened the string
with a faltering hand, the first object which presented
itself was my hat, with a pair of jockey-boots stuffed into
it, the hat so soaked and squeezed that it appeared more
like a dirty wet sponge than a cover for the head ; next

came the little white frogged jacket, which caused a good deal of laughter. On my showing some reluctance to explore further, the lady of the house, next to whom I sat, put her hand into the little bag and to our confusion drew forth my friend's mutilated buckskins with the hussared rear face ; these she held up to full view, whirling them round and round for the benefit of all eyes. The roars of laughter now became absolutely hysterical ; we endeavoured to join in the general mirth, but I fear our laughter partook somewhat of Milton's grin. Hundreds of questions were now asked in a breath—where did they come from? to whom did they belong? why cut them up? with many other curious enquiries, especially from the ladies. Seeing that any attempt at plausible explanation would most likely be doubted, we considered it better truly to relate the principal circumstances, glossing them over as well as we could. Our account but increased the mirth, especially among the fair, who wondered at our having been at all abashed at what should only cause a hearty laugh. One asked which of us helped to lace up the young lady, as she could not see to do it herself ; and other like questions they asked which I cannot now call to mind. They all pathetically lamented the disappointment of the poor young would-be fugitive who was all ready. The affair certainly created much merriment ; but we could not conceal even from ourselves that the merriment was entirely at our expense. Thus ended our last adventure, with a loss to my friend of a pair of doeskin tights cut up for a lady, and to me of a pair of boots and a new hat, for the water with which it was saturated had ruined it beyond repair.

Next morning before dawn we crossed the Ebro and continued our march towards the army, perfectly cured of our frolics. Passing through Vittoria a few days after

the celebrated battle there fought, I halted for a day to
visit many old comrades, seventeen officers of the 28th,
who had been wounded in the action. After cordially
condoling with them all I went on again ; and after a march
of six hundred miles at length joined the army in the
beginning of July on the great barriers placed by nature
to separate France from Spain. The consequences of
the victory at Vittoria still continued to operate. The
enemy were thrust backwards at all points, and about the 7th
or 8th of the month the entire frontier of Spain, from the
celebrated Roncesvalles to the fortress of San Sebastian
on the Bay of Biscay, was, with the exception of Pampeluna
and one or two minor places, occupied by the victorious
allies. In this position the triumphant army remained
tranquil for a short time, except for the operations carried
on in the investment and siege of San Sebastian and of
Pampeluna.

CHAPTER XXVI.

FIGHTING IN THE PYRENEES.

SOON after the battle of Vittoria the titular king, Joseph, returned to Paris and was replaced in the chief command of the French army of Spain by the Duke of Dalmatia. On July 12th this marshal arrived at Bayonne from Dresden, despatched thence by Napoleon. Soult, inferior to no officer in France (except perhaps the emperor), either in judgment or activity, immediately set about remodelling his army ; and to revive their confidence and rouse their drooping spirits, cast down by repeated disasters, he determined to make an offensive movement against the position maintained by the allies. After ten or twelve days passed in continual preparations for carrying out his plans of relieving Pampeluna and if possible raising the siege of San Sebastian, he on July 25th simultaneously attacked the passes of Roncesvalles and Maya ; and such was the weight of his columns that he broke through those passes, obliging the allies, after hard fighting and disputing every inch of ground, to retire, which movement continued the whole of that day and part of the night. On the 26th the enemy again came on and a good deal of fighting took place. The allies still retreated and directed their course towards Pampeluna. Soult was close at hand. The 4th Division under General Cole had passed Villaba, within three miles of Pampeluna, in full retreat,

early on the morning of the 27th, closely followed by
General Picton with the 3rd Division, and both divisions
closely followed by Soult. This induced the garrison of
Pampeluna to make a fierce sortie ; and General O'Donnel,
who commanded the blockading troops, seeing Soult
rapidly advancing and the two British divisions as rapidly
retreating, and becoming naturally much alarmed, commenced spiking his guns and destroying his magazines,
when fortunately Don Carlos D'Espana with his division
arrived at the critical moment ; he immediately drove back
the garrison and reassured O'Donnel. Soult now fully
expected to relieve Pampeluna in a few hours and appear-
ances were much in favour of his doing so ; in fact it was
all but accomplished.

Picton, now perhaps reflecting that his retreat in the
morning, together with that of Cole whom he commanded,
was more precipitate than need called for, and perceiving
the crisis at hand and all that depended on the affair,
suddenly halted and placed his division across the outlets
from the valleys of Zubiri and Lanz, thus screening
Pampeluna. At the same time he ordered General Cole
to occupy the heights between Oricain and Arletta ; but
that general, observing a hill which stood forward about
a mile in advance and commanded the road to Huarte,
moved forward to possess it, with the concurrence of
Picton who now saw its importance. Soult, who was close
at hand, also saw the importance of possessing this hill,
which as the armies were then situated was the key of
Pampeluna. He immediately pushed forward a strong
detachment with accelerated pace to gain the hill ; and
so exactly simultaneous was the rush of the contending
parties that while the enemy were ascending one side
Cole's advanced guard were mounting the other. Two

Spanish regiments, part of O'Donnel's blockading troops,
already posted on the hill and seeing the hostile troops
approaching the summit, made a furious charge on the
enemy's ascending strong body and gallantly bore them
down the hill. Soult lost the key. His heavy columns
soon came up, flushed with what they considered a victory,
as they had driven before them two British divisions ; but
their career was suddenly checked on seeing the mountains
in their way crowned by ten thousand troops of Cole's
division ; and not two miles further back stood Picton with
a still stronger force, the 3rd Division, resting on Huarte.

Soult having now his troops in hand commenced a
general attack. His first and most vigorous effort was
against the Spanish hill immediately on the right of Cole's
division ; but the gallantry of the Spaniards was repeated
and the enemy thrust down the hill. At this moment Lord
Wellington arrived from the valley of Bastan, where he had
left General Hill to deal with Count D'Erlon. Although
he witnessed the victorious gallantry of the Spaniards, yet
perceiving the great loss they sustained and the importance
of maintaining the hill, he ordered the 4th English Regiment
to their support. A general skirmish now commenced
along the whole front, which continued until one of the
customary Pyrenean visitors, a dense fog, put an end to
the firing for the day. Various movements took place
on both sides and throughout almost all the divisions
during the night and next morning. About noon the
enemy gathered at the foot of the position ; and a cloud
of skirmishers pushed forward and ascended the hill like
the flames and smoke of a volcano that could not be
contained. At the same time Clauzel's division burst forth
from the valley of Lanz, and pushing forward rapidly
turned Cole's division, and were doubling in his rear when

a Portugese brigade of the 6th Division suddenly appearing checked them in good time ; and at the same instant the 6th Division, who came into line that morning, formed in order of battle across the front of the enemy. Thus the French column, who moved forward with intention to turn the left of the allies, now found themselves in a sore predicament ; two brigades of the 4th Division attacked them on the left ; the Portuguese brigade galled their right ; while the whole body of the 6th Division overwhelmed them in front and with a loud cheer and deadly charge sent them headlong off the field, which was strewed with their dead. This part of the fight was thus terminated. But higher up the hills the battle continued with increased fury ; every hill was charged, taken and retaken repeatedly; nor were the French less forward than the British in repeating their charges. The 6th Division, in which I served with the 36th Regiment, after having quitted those in the valley, now climbed the rugged steep and lined with the troops above just becoming victorious ; and a few more charges decided the fate of the day. The enemy withdrew at all points. They stated their loss to be no more than two general officers and eighteen hundred killed and wounded ; but it was generally rated much higher. The allies had upwards of two thousand men killed and wounded.

The 29th was respected as a military sabbath by both armies, neither firing a shot throughout the day ; but this calm was the immediate precursor of a violent storm. On the morning of the 30th a furious attack was commenced against General Hill's corps, which led to a battle at Buenza. D'Erlon had twenty thousand men, the allies scarcely half that number. Hill maintained his ground for a long time ; but, his left being turned, he retired, losing five hundred men. Being joined by Campbell and

Morillo he offered battle ; but Soult, who had come up,
declined the fight. On the same morning at daylight
another combat commenced at Sauroren ; and this combat
lasted much longer and was far more severe than Hill's.
Here the 6th Division suffered severe loss in charging
the enemy, who retired reluctantly, but too far to return.
They were now driven from the whole of their position and
beaten at all points.

In these battles of the 30th the allies suffered a loss
between killed and wounded, including some taken prisoners,
of nearly two thousand men. The loss on the enemy's
part was far greater ; their killed and wounded alone
surpassed that of the allies, besides three thousand made
prisoners. Soult now turned his face towards France. At
ten o'clock on the morning of the 31st General Hill came
up with his rearguard between Lizasso and the Puerto.
Turning round, they halted and made good battle ; but
their position was forced. Fortunately for them a thick
fog prevented an effective pursuit. The allies lost about
four hundred men and the enemy about the same number.
On August 1st and 2nd the enemy were in full retreat for
France ; and although, wherever encountered they suffered
defeat, yet they were never in flight ; and on these two
days we suffered a loss of at least one thousand men put
hors de combat ; and we were on the point of suffering
another and a more severe loss.

On August 2nd, the last day of the fighting, the Duke
of Wellington hurried to Echallar to reconnoitre the
enemy and consult his maps, taking a party of the 43rd
Light Infantry as a guard ; but the enemy unobserved,
discovering the party sent a detachment to cut them off.
A Sergeant Blood of the 43rd with some of the men, being
in front, perceived the enemy coming on at speed ; and

seeing the danger in which the duke was placed, dashed
down from rock to rock roaring out the alarm.   The duke
instantly mounted and galloped off; the French came up,
but only in time to fire a volley after him.

Both armies now reoccupied pretty nearly the same
positions which they held previous to the attack of July
25th ; and thus terminated the fighting commonly called
the battles of the Pyrenees ; and never were battles
more fierce or harassing.   The principal encounters were
at the point of the bayonet.   We and they charged altern-
ately up and down the sides of rugged and rocky mountains,
exposed to the excessive summer heat of July and at the
same time to the cold of winter.   Dripping with perspiration
from hard fighting and scorching sun in the valleys, we
had immediately to clamber up to the tops of high
mountains and face the extreme cold naturally to be
found there and dense fogs, which soaked through us and
are more penetrating and oppressive than heavy rain ; and
this change we suffered more than once in the day, our
constitutions thus undergoing a similar ordeal to that
which I have heard is resorted to in perfecting chrono-
meters, which, to prove their qualities of compensation, are
moved in rapid succession from an oven to an ice-house
and *vice-versâ*.

During these combats we, with the Spaniards and
Portuguese, lost between killed, wounded, and taken
seven thousand three hundred officers and men.   The
enemy on their part lost upwards of thirteen thousand
and about four thousand prisoners.   This short but bloody
campaign lasted but nine days, one of which, the 29th,
was dedicated to rest and peace ; on the other eight days
ten distinct battles were fought and hotly contested.   I
cannot enter into or attempt a full description of those

combats, fought along positions always intersected by lofty
mountains which generally confined the view of regimental
officers to their respective corps. Even staff officers
scarcely knew what was passing beyond the limits of their
brigades or divisions ; and consequently the information
necessary to furnish accurate detail must depend on the
narratives of many, and thus would far exceed the just
limits of these modest Memoirs. Throughout those
combats the Spanish fought with the greatest bravery,
as did the Portuguese. It was remarked at the time
that had Picton with the two divisions under his command
continued to retreat for two hours longer on the morning
of the 27th, Soult would inevitably have gained the double
object which he had in view, the relief of Pampeluna and
the animation of his drooping troops ; for although he
might have been compelled to retreat immediately afterwards, he could have boasted of beating back the allies
and succouring the beleaguered fortress, and averred that
his subsequent retreat was preconcerted to guard the
French frontier. And this renewal of the spirit and confidence of his troops might have been attended with double
disadvantage ; for it may be remarked of opponents
throughout animated nature that as one becomes elated by
success, the other in equal ratio becomes depressed ; and
though physical strength remain intact, moral influence is
shaken.

Some changes in posting the divisions now took place.
General Hill's corps formed on the heights above Roncesvalles ; and the 6th Division lay down in front of the Maya
Pass. The contending armies now again remained tranquil,
although our lines were not far asunder, but in no part
so close as at the Maya Pass, where the advanced sentries
of both lines in many places, particularly at night, were

not ten yards asunder. In this novel mode of campaigning
we continued for upwards of three months. At the commencement some fieldworks were thrown up by us and
soon abandoned ; but during the whole time of our stay
there the enemy were incessant in fortifying their lines
from the base of the mountains to their very summit, upon
which their strong forts and redoubts were constructed.

While we were in this position no acts of hostility took
place save at Pampeluna and San Sebastian, although our
mutual piquets after nightfall were in some parts in the
same field, occasionally separated by a partial wall or small
stream and frequently by nothing which might show a line
of demarcation. Slight or, as they were termed, china walls
were the most frequent barriers. In many instances the
advanced sentries were almost in contact ; yet so well
was civilised warfare understood that they never interfered
with each other and scarcely ever spoke. The usual words,
" All's well, " were never cried out. This monotonous roar
was superseded by " stone chatters "—white polished stones,
about two pounds' weight each, were placed on the spot
where each sentry was usually posted at night, and he
struck them against each other twice in slow time. This
was repeated along the chain of sentries. Should any sentry
neglect this for more than five minutes, the next sentry
instantly struck the stones three times and quickly ; this
rapidly passed along the line and a visit from the piquet
immediately followed. By these means we were sure that
a sentry could not sleep nor be negligent on his post for
more than five minutes at a time. It was rather remarkable
that whatever signals our sentries made were immediately
repeated by those of the enemy. In visiting these advanced
sentries, I sometimes spoke to French officers performing
a similar duty, although this, strictly speaking, was not

sanctioned. On those occasions I often got a small flask of French wine ; the manner in which this was procured was rather curious. The French officer put down his flask and retired a few paces, when I advanced and emptied it into my wooden canteen ; I then replaced the flask and my friendly foe took it up after I had retired. This may appear strange to the civil reader and upon reflection so it did to ourselves ; nor could we well explain how it was that two officers familiarly conversing within a few yards should entertain such absolute horror of coming within touch, as if it were equal to high treason ; but such was the case. It would seem that warfare bore close affinity to the plague ; so long as you avoided contact all was safe. It was prohibited under the heaviest penalty that soldiers should ever exchange a word with the enemy. At this time the army was very scantily provisioned ; and many disgraceful desertions took place to the French who were well supplied.

On one of my visits to the sentries, when I had got my flask of wine, the French officer asked me, apparently as a commonplace question, when we intended to attack them, adding, " You need have no hesitation in telling us, for we know you intend it, and we are prepared night and day to receive you." I replied that as to his preparation to receive us his present generosity gave earnest ; but as to the time when the attack should take place, I was totally ignorant. I added that Lord Wellington was too well acquainted with natural consequences not to know that he who betrays himself by divulging his secrets cannot reasonably depend on another for fidelity ; and that he who threatens openly will be counteracted secretly ; that in either case defeat is generally the result. After this I never entered into conversation with any French officer.

Whilst our right and centre were in this state of tranquillity, towards our left, especially near San Sebastian, the war was carried on with the greatest activity. This fortress, after one or two failures and very severe losses on our part, was at length taken by storm on August 31st. The small castle which crowned Monte Orgullo held out until September 9th, when it capitulated, the gallant governor having obtained honourable terms. Immediately after the storming the town was set fire to in all quarters; and the most shocking barbarities, such as are scarcely credible, were perpetrated by the British soldiers on the unfortunate inhabitants of all ages and sexes.

Early in August Soult had meditated a strenuous attack to relieve San Sebastian, but the scattered and disorganised state of his army caused much delay. At last, when all was ready, he was about to assault the allies on August 30th, but something prevented which induced him to defer the attack until next morning. On August 31st therefore at daylight, the enemy rushed forward with the usual impetuosity attending their first attack, bearing down all before them. Their front column, directed by General Reille, made great progress up the heights to San Marcial, while Lamartiniere's division assailed to the right; and when their skirmishers had gained two-thirds of the hill and were checked, their dense column were moved forward. Then the Spaniards, who were posted there, undauntedly coming forward, vigorously charged the French column and sent them headlong down the hill.

During this time the head of Villatte's column, having crossed the fords at the foot of the hill on rafts and boats, ascended the ridge and more vigorously renewed the fight, and gained the left of the Spanish line. The 82nd English

Regiment moved forward a short distance to maintain the post. At this moment Lord Wellington appeared, when the Spaniards, scarcely kept steady by their own officers, now shouting forth a cheer of recognition rushed forward to the charge with such impetuosity that these opponents too were swept down the hill as if by a torrent. Some pontoon boats which came to their rescue, becoming overloaded by the fugitives in their hurry to get away, were sunk, when many were drowned; and the breaking of the bridges to allow the boats to come to the rescue decided the combat at that point, with the loss of many hundreds of the enemy. Soult, who beheld this defeat from the mountain called "Louis XIV.," determined to try in another quarter; but it was several hours before the scattered masses could be collected and the bridges repaired. This effected, he sent the remainder of Villatte's reserve over the river, and uniting it with Foy's division urged on a more formidable attack at Vera. In this combat he was not more successful; but although beaten at all points, still he hesitated not. He determined to make a third attack, for he had plenty of troops still left. He had forty thousand men collected in the morning; he attacked with thirty thousand; and the allies in action amounted to only ten thousand. But the heavy cannonade clearly heard from San Sebastian during the morning now ceased, for during the combats above mentioned, San Sebastian had been stormed and taken without any interruption from without. The movements of Soult previous to his attack were in appearance confused, but they were designedly so, with a view of deceiving Wellington; but the latter was well informed on the night of the 29th what Soult's plan was; and he consequently sent orders to the Maya Pass to move the troops there stationed forward on the morning of the 31st to keep D'Erlon's corps occupied, and prevent his sending any reinforcement to aid Soult's attack. Sir Charles Colville therefore moved out with the 6th Division. We had a sharp affair and lost some fifty or sixty men ; no other part of the right or centre of our line was disturbed. Wellington felt perfectly secure in the strength of his position. A brigade of Guards had come up from Oporto ; and three fresh regiments had just arrived from England and formed a brigade for Lord Aylmer. Soult, having received in the course of the day (31st) a report of the storming and capture of San Sebastian, no longer hesitated ; he retired, determined to assemble his forces and prepare for a more general action. In these latter combats the enemy lost three thousand five hundred men, the English and Portuguese one thousand, the Spaniards sixteen hundred, all in the field; but the whole loss of the allies on this day, including the storming of San Sebastian, exceeded five thousand. Both armies now fell into their former positions, and for some time tranquillity was observed.

CHAPTER XXVII.

IN THE BATTLE OF NIVELLE.

EARLY in October the Duke of Wellington, having San Sebastian now secure in his rear and foreseeing that a great battle must soon be fought, determined to push forward his left wing, gain the lower Bidassoa and the great Rhune mountain and thus establish a part of his army within the French frontier. The better to conceal his design, which was rather hazardous, continual manœuvring took place from right to left of the allied lines, which completely succeeded in deceiving the enemy. Everything was so well arranged that not the slightest appearance of an attack was discovered. On the morning of October 7th the 5th Division and Lord Aylmer's brigade proceeded to the fords ; and still the enemy perceived no change, the tents in the allied camp being left standing. The 5th Division soon crossed the stream, and had formed on the opposite bank without firing a shot or a shot being fired at them, so completely were the enemy taken by surprise. A signal rocket was now fired from Fontarabia, when the batteries along the whole line of our attack opened against the enemy, who were driven from their different posts before they well knew what was passing ; and so little did Soult contemplate an attack in that quarter, always expecting it from Roncesvalles, that on the 6th he reviewed D'Erlon's division at Ainhoa, and remained that night at Espelette. Next morning, although a false attack was made against D'Erlon's position, yet Soult having heard the cannonade from San Marcial, instantly discovered the true point of attack and hurried thither ; but before he arrived at the scene of action all his positions on the Bidassoa were carried ; and although his presence corrected many errors and gave surprising confidence to his troops, yet he never could regain what was lost during his early absence. He loudly complained of want of vigilance in his generals ; and not without just cause, for they were nowhere prepared.

Meanwhile the 6th Division continued the false attack on D'Erlon. Colonel Douglas with a Portuguese brigade was sent further on to the left, and the 36th Regiment were ordered to be in readiness for his support. Colonel Leggatt, who commanded us, sent me to find Douglas and inform him that the regiment were ready when required. Douglas had attacked and gallantly carried a post strongly occupied on the crown of a hill, at the foot of which I arrived just as he was led down, having been severely wounded in the neck. After the usual congratulations of old friends I delivered my message. He requested me to ride up the hill and see what was going forward, adding that the position was gallantly carried and it would be a pity to lose it. Topping the hill I found the Portuguese warmly engaged ; but the enemy were advancing in force on two sides of the hill. I rode back to Douglas, who was slowly moving to the rear, and he asked me to go as fast as possible and report ; there was no time to be lost. Taking the nearest direction towards the regiment, I was compelled to pass in front of a line of

the enemy's skirmishers, who had been winding round the
hill. They displayed the courtesy of their nation by dis-
charging a general salute ; its only result was a shot
through my great coat and one in my saddle-bow. Having
safely run the gauntlet and though in great haste, yet
resolving to show the polite nation that we yielded as
little in courtesy as in arms, I turned round and taking
off my hat bowed low. The firing ceased and they gave
me a loud cheer. Hurrying forward, I soon joined the
regiment who were already in motion. Pushing on with
the light company, to whom I acted as guide, and arriving
at the point where I had saluted the skirmishers, we fully
expected to be engaged ; but to our surprise the French
were retreating, leaving the hill in possession of the
Portuguese. It appeared that as soon as our regiment
began to descend from the lofty hill upon which they were
formed, they were perceived by the enemy, who, taking them
no doubt for the head of a strong column, considered
it prudent to retire. The regiment having come up,
ascended the hill, where we remained until towards dark,
and then retired, leaving the post to the Portuguese.
The loss of the Portuguese was rather severe, upwards
of a hundred and fifty men *hors de combat*. But the
spirited attack made by Douglas, the British regiment
moved up to his aid, and the false attack of the whole
6th Division completely succeeded in deterring D'Erlon
from making any attempt to succour the French right wing,
where the true attack was raging and where his support
was most necessary.

During all these movements and combats, which lasted
nearly three days, the allies were invariably successful ; and
all the objects proposed were fully attained. The fighting
was desperate and well maintained on either side. On

fording the Bidassoa, Halket's light Germans drove up all
the enemy's advanced parties close to the summit of the
Croix des Bouquets; but this being the key of the position,
the enemy were strengthening it continually from the first
onset both with guns and troops: so that when the
Germans approached, the position had become so strong
that Halket, having lost many men during his ascent, was
brought to a stand. At this critical moment Colonel
Cameron with the 9th Regiment, having arrived just as the
Germans were checked, put them aside and making a
desperate charge gained the summit. The enemy's guns
had just time to retire through their infantry, who also
quickly retreated to a second ridge. The approach to this
was narrow ; but Cameron reducing his front quickly
followed. However, the enemy having the start were soon
formed, and the approach being winding with sharp turns,
they poured a destructive fire both in front and flank into
the regiment. Yet this did not retard their quick advance
for a moment ; while the enemy seemed no way moved by
the vehement advance of Cameron until the regiment
approached within a few yards, when a loud cheer and
rapid charge so astonished them that they scarcely knew
what they were about until they found themselves borne
off the hill. Thus the 9th Regiment gallantly carried the
key of the position, but with a heavy loss both in officers
and men, the usual result of unswerving bravery. But
were I to relate the gallant deeds of all throughout the
whole of these operations, it would be necessary to enumerate all the British corps employed ; nor was the bravery
displayed by the Spaniards less daring. Courage was never
wanting to the Spanish soldiers ; but confidence in their
chiefs was rare. Through the battles of the Pyrenees
their divisions were intermixed with those of the British,

not formed aloof in a separate corps, as at Talavera and
Barossa, nor depressed and held back by such paralysing
commanders as Cuesta and La Peña. They now, conjointly
with their brave allies, fought forward ; and well did they
maintain their line. On the 8th, after General Giron with
a body of Spaniards had driven off the French outposts
on the road from Vera to Sarre and was charging up a
hill near Puerto and pressing on abreast with the British
troops, he was suddenly checked by a strong line of
abattis, defended by two French regiments sending forth
a heavy fire. The Spaniards became irresolute, but maintained their ranks. At the moment Lieutenant Havelock,
of the 43rd Regiment, who was on the staff, witnessing the
check and unable to curb his excitement, taking off his
hat and holloaing to the Spaniards, applied his spurs and
dashed over the defence in among the enemy. At this the
whole line of Spaniards broke into cries—" The little fair
boy !—Forward with the little fair boy !" and they tore
through the abattis, and furiously charging the two French
regiments drove them up the hill and over and hurried
them into the embrace of General Kemp's ascending
brigade, who sent them waltzing with graceful velocity
round the base of the hill. But although gallant example
will almost always fix wavering resolve and give impetus
and immediate decision to calculating courage, yet it but
seldom succeeds in eliciting bravery out of cowardice. The
surest criterion by which to judge of the gallantry and
steadiness of the Spaniards during those operations is by
reference to the casualties they suffered. It is true that
a body of men may suffer great loss even in running away,
but in the present instance there was no retreating ; all was
fighting forward ; and when men advancing or standing
still suffer severe loss, it is a certain proof of bravery and

firmness. The loss of the enemy during these last combats was fourteen hundred men ; and that of the allies, British, Portuguese and Spaniards, sixteen hundred ; and of this number eight hundred were Spaniards.

Most persons who have written on the campaigns in the Peninsula represent the Spanish army as ragged, half-famished wretches ; nor did I refrain from such epithets on seeing the miserable troops commanded by the Marquis Romana in the campaign of Sir John Moore ; but on reflection no blame could be attached either to their immediate commanders or to the soldiers for their motley appearance. The scandal and disgrace were the legitimate attributes of the Spanish Government. The members of the Cortez and Juntas were entirely occupied in peculation, amassing wealth for themselves and appointing their relatives and dependents to all places of power and emolument, however unworthy and unqualified ; and although it was notorious that shiploads of arms, equipments, clothing and millions of dollars were sent from England for the use and maintenance of the Spanish troops, yet all was appropriated to themselves by the members of the general or local governments or their rapacious satellites, while their armies were left barefoot, ragged and half-starved. In this deplorable state they were brought into the field under leaders many of whom were scarcely competent to command a sergeant's outlying piquet ; for in the Spanish army, as elsewhere, such was the undue influence of a jealous and covetous aristocracy, that, unsupported by their influence, personal gallantry and distinction, however conspicuous, were but rarely rewarded. This is a pernicious system, especially with an army in the field ; for injustice and neglect powerfully tend to damp and dispirit the ardour even of the most zealous and devoted, and discourage that

landable ambition which is the lifespring in the breast of
a true soldier.

Again the armies became tranquil except at Pampeluna.
Shortly before its surrender it was ascertained that the
Governor-General was in the habit of sending despatches
to Soult by a woman. A general order was therefore
issued to the covering divisions to have all women
coming from the rear and going to the front searched.
Soon after this order was received, a woman who
passed into the camp of the regiment came howling to
the commanding officer, who, not comprehending a word
she said, sent for me to interpret. This was attended
with some difficulty, the Basque dialect being but imperfectly known and the woman totally ignorant of any other.
However it appeared that this woman, suspected of carrying
despatches clandestinely, came simply to dispose of a
pannier of bread and a small basket of eggs. In passing
the quarter-guard she was stopped and searched, during
which search all her bread and eggs were taken away by
the men of the guard, commanded by a lieutenant of
the regiment. Payment was not forthcoming, for the simple
reason that the troops, being six months in arrear of pay,
not a sixpenny piece was to be found amongst the men.
On my reporting the affair as it occurred, the colonel
ordered the officer to pay for the bread and eggs out of
his private finances, at the same time giving him and the
whole guard a severe but well-merited reprimand ; for
besides the plundering of the woman, which might have
been attended with serious inconvenience by deterring
others from bringing supplies to the camp, the woman
came from the front ; and this must have been seen by the
whole guard. On my paying the woman for her bread
and eggs as directed, she loudly demanded remuneration

on other accounts—loss of time, torn garments, etc. ; but
strictly confining myself to the colonel's instructions I
declined entering into her others affairs, at which she
appeared much disappointed.   There were at that period
many females searched with scant ceremony, but whether
or not any despatches of the nature expected were ever
seized I never heard.

Soult having failed in every attempt to throw succour
into Pampeluna, it surrendered on October 31st, after a
gallant defence of a few months, during which many
successful sallies were made.   The covering divisions being
now at liberty, a forward movement was decided upon ;
but the first days of November were excessively boisterous
and rainy.   On the 6th and 7th, the earliest period when
a movement could take place, the right wing under Sir
Rowland Hill were pushed into the valley of Bastan, preparatory to a general attack which was intended for next
day ; but the heavy rain which fell on the evening of the
7th and next day rendered the roads again impassable,
and so the battle of the Nivelle was delayed for two days.

On the evening of the 9th the 6th Division descended
through the Pass of Maya, which we had guarded with
such anxious care for upwards of three months ; and
marching the whole of that night we found ourselves on
the memorable morning of November 10th close in front
of the enemy's position, which they had been incessantly
strengthening during the whole of that period.   It was
still dark ; and here we halted in columns, awaiting the
progress of our left and left centre, who were pushed
forward before daybreak.   At length the auspicious dawn
appeared, cheering and renovating after a harassing night
march over deep and slobbery roads.   Although in our
present position we appeared to be well sheltered by forest

trees, yet as soon as the misty haze of dawn was dispelled
by clearer light our columns were discovered by the enemy's
redoubts, which frowningly looked down from the heights
above. After a short cannonade, which they immediately
opened, their range became so accurate that their shells
were falling amongst us rather quickly, causing many
casualties. I saw one shell drop in the midst of a Portuguese regiment in close column immediately in our rear ;
it blew up twelve men, who became so scorched and
blackened that on their fall they resembled a group of
mutilated chimney-sweeps. The 36th Regiment lost
several men by the bursting of shells. Sir H. Clinton,
who commanded the division, perceived that although the
huge trunks of the trees amid which we were formed
might stop a solid round-shot propelled horizontally, yet
their open branches afforded no protection against shells
descending from a height above us. Considering therefore
the place no longer tenable, he marched us out of the wood
and drew up in line on its skirts in full view of the enemy's
redoubts, judging that even this open exposure would not
be attended with so severe a loss as continuing to be
shelled in column.

We now had a full view of the splendid scenery in front
and the active warfare on our left ; and I had an opportunity
of witnessing a good deal of what was passing. A long
narrow strip of ground, flanked with a wall on either side,
not far from us, separated the combatants on our left.
The British troops frequently advanced and were driven
back ; so did the enemy, and so they fared. Often did
French officers advance into the field bearing their standards
to animate their followers ; but they instantly fell and were
as instantly replaced. At last the British troops, disdaining
the protection of the wall, rushed in a body into the field

and carried it.   I can see plainly before me now Colonel
Lloyd, who commanded the 94th Regiment, mounted on a
large jet black charger, waving his hat to cheer on his men
and riding up to the bayonets of the enemy close behind
their wall.   I saw him fall.   His men were up at the
instant and dearly avenged their commander's death.   I
felt double regret at his fate, having had the pleasure of
being intimately acquainted with him when he was in the
43rd Regiment.

The order at length arrived about ten o'clock for the
6th Division to advance.   Wrought up to the greatest
excitement from being so many hours without moving,
exposed to a fire of shot and shell and musketry from the
breastworks of enemies partly concealed, and seeing the
battle advancing upwards on our left, we now eagerly
rushed forward.   Proceeding rapidly we soon waded the
Nivelle immersed above our middle, the men carrying their
pouches above their heads, and immediately drove back
all the enemy's piquets and outposts on both banks of the
river without deigning to fire a shot.   Some few we
bayoneted who were too obstinate to get out of our way in
time.   Thus far advanced, the glorious scene became more
developed.   High up the mountains the blaze from their
forts and redoubts was broad and glaring, while the mountain
sides presented a brilliant surface of sparkling vivid fire,
never ceasing but always ascending as our gallant troops
rushed forward ; and nearly two hundred pieces of artillery
angrily roaring forth mutual response, echoed from
mountain to mountain, rendering the whole scene truly
magnificent.

Having crossed the Nivelle, we rapidly advanced towards the forts and redoubts above Ainhoa, destined
to be carried by the 6th Division.   The hill which

we, the 36th Regiment, faced was the steepest I ever climbed. The ground over which we had to pass had been intersected for months with incessant labour and French resource; every five yards exposed us to a new cross-fire and deep cuts, which furnished graves for many a gallant British soldier. The brambles all through were so high and thickly interwoven and the inequalities of the ground so great as to prevent those who were not ten yards asunder from seeing each other. We moved forward in line; there was no road. Under such circumstances but little order could be preserved; and, as must be expected where all were anxious to advance, the strongest and most active gained the front. In this disordered order of battle the regiment advanced against the heavy-armed battery and principal redoubt. This was the goal which we kept in view, the prize, to obtain which the regiment unswervingly and rapidly ascended the mountain, from whose summit it thundered destruction all around. Between us and the base of this battery, to which we at length drew near, a small and rather clear space intervened. I shot forward alone with all the velocity I could command after so rapid an ascent, and arriving immediately under the fort I perceived the enemy regularly drawn up behind trees cut down to the height of about five feet, the branches pointing forward, forming an abattis. I immediately turned about, and after receiving an appropriate salute retraced my steps with redoubled speed. I seized the king's colour carried by Ensign Montgomery, which I immediately halted; and called for the regimental Colour Ensign, McPherson, who answered, "Here am I." Having halted both colours in front of the foremost men, I prevented any from going forward. By these means we shortly presented a tolerably good

front, and gave the men a few moments' breathing time.
The whole operation did not take above ten minutes; but
the men coming up every instant, each minute strengthened
the front. At this exciting moment my gallant comrades,
Lieutenants Vincent and L'Estrange, who stood by my
side, remarked that if I did not allow the regiment to
advance, the 61st Regiment would arrive at the redoubt
as soon as we should. I immediately placed my cap on
the point of my sword and passing to the front of the
colours gave the word, "Quick march. Charge!" We
all rushed forward, excited by the old British cheer. But
my personal advance was momentary; being struck by a
shot which shattered both bones of my left leg, I came
down. Vincent instantly asked what was the matter.
I told him that my leg was broken, and that was all.
I asked him to put the limb into a straight position,
and to place me against a tree which stood close by; in
this position I asked for my cap and sword, which had
been struck from my hand in the fall; and then I cheered
on the regiment as they gallantly charged into the redoubt.

The fort being carried, the regiment pursued the enemy
down the opposite side of the hill, whilst I remained
behind idly to look around me. The scene was beautifully
romantic and heroically sublime. Groups of cavalry were
seen judiciously, although apparently without regularity,
dotted along the sides of every hill, watching an opportunity
of falling on the discomfited foe. Our troops gallantly
bore on over an unbroken series of intrenchments, thickly
crowded with bayonets and kept lively by incessant fire.
The awful passing events lay beneath my view; nor was
there aught to interrupt my observation save a few bodily
twitches, the pangs of prostrated ambition, and the shot and
shells which burst close, or nearly cut the ground from

under me. Alone I lay reclined, being unable to maintain
an upright position ; and thus I had a good opportunity for
melancholy contemplation, not unmixed with patriotic joy
as I reviewed the battle which tended slowly upwards.
The deadly strife was surprisingly grand ; yet the sublimity
of the scene defied all attempt at description. The wreck
and destruction of men and matter was strewn around ;
the piteous life-ending moans of the wounded writhing in
torture, and the loud yelling fury of the maddened combatants, repeated by a thousand discordant echoes, were
truly appalling, especially to a person who being put out
of the fight could be only a spectator of the tumult. The
fierce and continued charge of the British was irresistible,
nor could they be checked ; onward they bore, nor stopped
to breathe, rushing forward through glen, dale and forest,
where vivid flashed the fire and bright gleamed the steel.
Yet they seemed to chase only the startled red deer,
prowling wolf or savage wild-boar, until they arrived at the
steel-bristling strongholds of the foe. Now they occupied
the same level upon which I lay. Here the battle raged
in its utmost fury ; and for a short time it became
stationary. The contending foes were the soldiers of the
two most warlike nations of Europe and the most steadfast
in mutual jealousy and aversion. The British legions
impetuously rushed forward on the native soil of France,
resolved to uphold till death the honour and glory of their
country. Those of France with equal bravery and resolution
determined to resist to the last this insulting intrusion
on their soil. Thus mutually stimulated to madness, they
met with a shock tremendous. France nobly maintained
her well-earned military fame ; but her surprisingly valiant
deeds proved vain in this bloody border strife, where noble
emulation wrought up to the highest pitch the Percy and

Douglas and a third not nerveless arm, all now dealing forth deadly blows under one and the same banner. What foe could resist their united attack or penetrate the shield formed of the Rose, Shamrock and Thistle when closely bound together in a union strong as lasting? What foe could triumph over Wellington, who, born in Ireland, with the keen policy of Scotland, adopting England and combining the genius of all three, was the one appropriate chief to wield their united strength in the field? A force constituted of such moral and physical strength, and led by such a man could not long be withstood. The star of the three united nations shone victorious on the summits of the lofty Pyrenees, gilding the tall pines which capped their heads for miles and foreboding downfall to Imperial France, since it was the star of true liberty and national independence. The French on their side with broken brand and fallen crest reluctantly gave way, sullenly retiring within their national boundary, no longer invulnerable.

CHAPTER XXVIII.

I RETURN WOUNDED TO IRELAND, AND TRAVEL IN A COACH
OF THAT COUNTRY.

THIS memorable battle, which introduced the victorious
British army and their allies into France, commenced
before daybreak and continued until after dark. The enemy
were beaten back from their strong frontier position, losing
fifty-one guns, two thousand prisoners, stores incalculable and
some thousands killed and wounded ; the nature of the ground
prevented the number of these from being ascertained,—
it must have been immense. As to our regiment's advance
up the hill to the attack, it may perhaps be alleged that
I should not have urged forward the colours so rapidly nor
have been so far in front. Our advance, considering the
steepness of the hill, was certainly rather rapid ; but had
we not thus rapidly advanced, as in a continued charge
through breastworks, we should have lost double the
number of men ; and it certainly would not have fallen to
the proud lot of our regiment *alone* to have stormed and
carried the enemy's great redoubt ; and this we did, as
may be gathered from the remark made by Vincent and
L'Estrange about the 61st Regiment. But it is of little
consequence whether I kept up with the colours or the
colours came on at my pace ; anyway it affords proud
consolation to reflect that it was in front of them I fell.

Immediately before entering the redoubt, Montgomery,

who carried the king's colour, furled the sheet round the staff, which he used as a lance, and thus armed gallantly charged in amongst the foremost bayonets. Being a powerful and athletic person (afterwards lieutenant of Grenadiers), he made good use of his silk-bound weapon, and never did blood-stained royal banner bear more honourable testimony of personal prowess in war. I know not what became of the staff ; it should ever be kept with the regiment and accompany it into action. Besides common promotion arising from casualties, one captain of the regiment got the brevet rank of major ; he was *not* in the action, but I, who was serving voluntarily and had a leg shattered while charging at the head of the regiment, was neglected. Being subsequently asked if I did not get the brevet step for my voluntary services and wound, I answered no, but that I got a permanent step and that was a lame one.

From the Duke of Wellington's despatch relative to the battle of the Nivelle the following extract is copied : " While these operations were going on in the centre, I had the pleasure of seeing the 6th Division, under Lieutenant-General Sir Henry Clinton, after having crossed the Nivelle and having driven in the enemy's piquets on both banks, and having covered the passage of the Portuguese division under Lieutenant-General Sir John Hamilton on its right, make a most handsome attack upon the right of the Nivelle, carrying all the intrenchments and the redoubt on that flank." In justice to the regiment I beg to remark that if the attack of the division was most handsome, that of the 36th Regiment must have been most beautiful, for it was this regiment which managed to take the lead and single-handed carried the redoubt.

Immediately after the redoubt was taken, under which

I fell, another fort on our right, not yet attacked, turned some of its guns against the one just captured ; and their shot and shell ploughing the ground all around me nearly suffocated me with dust and rubbish. Those who were not very severely wounded scrambled their way down the hill ; but I might as well have attempted to carry a millstone as to drag my shattered leg after me. I therefore remained among the dead and dying, who were not few. My situation was not enviable. After some hours Assistant-Surgeon Simpson of the regiment appeared. I then got what is termed a field dressing ; but unfortunately there were no leg splints ; and so arm splints were substituted. Through this makeshift I suffered most severely during my descent. Some of the band coming up, I was put into a blanket and carried down the hill ; but as we proceeded down this almost perpendicular descent, the blanket contracted from my weight in the middle, and then owing to the want of the proper long splints the foot drooped beyond the blanket's edge ; it is almost impossible to imagine the torture which I suffered. Having gained the base of the hill towards dark, a cottage was fortunately discovered and into this I was carried.

Up to the noon of this day I congratulated myself on my good fortune in having served in the first and last battle fought in Spain, and proudly contemplated marching victoriously through France. I recalled too with pleasure and as if it were a propitious omen, that on this day five years ago I first trod Spanish ground. On November 16th, 1808, we marched into Fuentes de Oñoro, under the command of Sir John Moore. Then I was strong hale and joyous, with the glorious prospects of war favourably presented to view ; but the afternoon of this, the fifth anniversary, proved a sad reverse. On this day I was carried out of

Spain, borne in a blanket, broken in body and depressed
in mind, with all my brilliant prospects like myself fallen
to the ground.   Such is glorious war.

After the field dressing Simpson departed in search of
other wounded persons ; and on his report of my wound
two or three other medical officers sought me, fortunately
in vain, that they might remove the limb.   On the 4th
day I was conveyed to a place where a hospital was
established ; but the inflammation of the leg was then so
great (it was as big as my body) that no amputation could
be attempted.   A dressing took place which was long and
painful, for I had bled so profusely while in the cottage
that a cement hard as iron was formed round the limb, and
before my removal it was absolutely necessary to cut me
out of the bed on which I lay.   After a considerable time
passed in steeping with tepid water, the piece of mattress
and sheet which I carried away from the cottage were
removed ; and now began the more painful operation of
setting the leg.   Staff-Surgeon Mathews and Assistant-
Surgeon Graham, 31st Regiment, were the operators.
Graham seized me by the knee and Mathews by the foot.
They proposed that four soldiers should hold me during
the operation ; to this I objected, saying with a kind of
boast that I was always master of my nerves.   They now
twisted and turned and extended my leg, aiming along it
like a spirit level.   The torture was dreadful ; but though I
ground my teeth and the big drops of burning perspiration
rapidly chased each other, still I remained firm, and stifled
every rising groan.   After all was concluded I politely
thanked Mathews, carelessly remarking that it was quite
a pleasure to get wounded to be so comfortably dressed.
This was mock heroism, for at the moment I trembled as
if just taken from the rack ; however, it had a strange effect

upon Mathews, who told Lavens that he feared I was somewhat deranged from the great loss of blood and agonising pain which I suffered. Lavens, Assistant-Surgeon of the 28th Regiment and an old messmate, only laughed and offered to be responsible for the soundness of my intellect if no other cause than bodily pain interfered. Some time afterwards Mathews told him that the inflammation had much subsided and he thought that amputation might safely be performed; yet I appeared so strong, doing so well and in such good spirits, he felt some little inclination to give the limb a chance, if he could believe that my good spirits would continue. Lavens, whom I saw every day, replied that he need not dread low spirits on my part under any circumstance, and as to the difference between the loss of life and that of a limb he felt convinced it would be no great matter to me. If therefore he thought the preservation of the limb depended on corporeal or mental constitution, he recommended the trial. Mathews told all this to me, when I willingly concurred in the attempt to save the leg. It had served me well during many a long and weary march, in many a lively skirmish and some hard-fought battles, particularly whilst in the 28th Light Company; I therefore felt extremely unwilling to part with it. One feels regret at losing even a favourite walking-stick; what then must the feeling be at losing a faithful leg? The trial was decided on; but in justice to Dr. Mathews I feel called upon to declare that he most fully pointed out the imminent danger attending the experiment. Thus far I have entered into detail in consequence of a remark made to the General Medical Board, Drs. Weir, Franklin and Car, who said, when I appeared before them in London, that the medical officer who saved my leg was in no way borne out in making the attempt, for there were ninety-nine chances to one against my life. It is true that the wound was as severe as could possibly be inflicted ; the tibia and fibula were both shattered, and the orifice made seemed the entrance to a quarry of bones, five-and-thirty pieces of which exfoliated and kept the wound open for several years.

When I was carried out of the field my whole fortune consisted of one crusado novo, a Portuguese silver coin value three shillings. This I had much difficulty in persuading the poor cottagers to accept, not from a consideration that the sum was an inadequate remuneration for the mutilation of their mattress and whatever food they supplied, but solely from pure motives of generosity. They wept at my parting, and prayed to every saint in heaven or elsewhere for my speedy and perfect recovery. On my arrival therefore in hospital, I possessed not a single farthing ; and in my situation other nourishment was required than that of a ration pound of bread and beef. My host, Don Martin D'Echiparre, continually sat by my bedside. Looking upon him as a generous and liberal person, I, after a few evenings, candidly confessed my pecuniary embarrassments, requesting him to lend me a few dollars and offering him my gold watch until I should receive a remittance from the pay-master. He replied, " Do you take me for a Jew? I never lend less than a hundred guineas ; these you may have when you please." This I considered a bombastical evasion and declined his offer. Next morning he made his usual visit and approaching close said in a low voice, " You refused last night to take a hundred guineas ; take at least these fifty," and he held them forth. I told him that so large a sum was both superfluous and useless ; however, after a good deal of controversy, he consented to lend me so small a sum as ten guineas.

After a lapse of three months an order was received to remove the hospital depôt to St. Jean de Luz. What was to be done ? I had received no remittance ; consequently I had no means of repaying the ten guineas, six of which were already spent—one more was absolutely necessary to defray the cost of my removal to St. Jean de Luz, which would take four days. I was to be carried in a litter borne by inhabitants, to pay whom would require the greater part of the guinea. To pay back the remaining three would be but a poor return ; but my truly noble and generous host having entered the room, relieved me from my unpleasant dilemma. After expressing his deep regret at my departure, he thus addressed me : " Being aware that you have had no remittance from the army ; and knowing from the hospitable and generous manner in which you have entertained the many officers who continually came to see you, in which hospitality I nightly participated with pleasure, that you must want money, I put these four farthings in my pocket for you," presenting four Spanish doubloons. " I offer you," continued he, " this small sum because of your obstinacy in refusing the hundred guineas ; but if you will accept that sum and another hundred in addition, you would please me much more. Do not pay me from St. Jean de Luz nor from England, but only when you get home to your friends in Ireland ; and if you never pay, it will be of no consequence whatever." However I declined to accept either hundreds or doubloons : and after mutual protestations of sincere friendship and regard, we bade each other a final farewell and parted with unfeigned regret. This anecdote I relate as highly honourable to the country in which it occurred. D'Echiparre was a Frenchman by birth, but a Spaniard by adoption, and in the Spanish language we always conversed. He

was a Valladolid merchant and had realised upwards of
ten thousand pounds, which in that part of the country
was considered a handsome fortune.

On my arrival at St. Jean de Luz I was so fortunate
as to procure two months' pay (not in advance for we were
seven months in arrear), when I immediately sent the ten
guineas to my generous host.

The time having arrived to get rid of the cumbrous sick
and wounded officers, we were removed to los Pasages and
there embarked in a transport bound for Portsmouth ; but
the wind proving contrary prevented our entering the
channel and we were compelled to put into Bantry Bay
in Ireland. Here we anchored close to a village, if I
recollect right, called Castletown, and put up at an inn
kept by the widow Martin. The wind continuing very
boisterous and contrary, we resolved to travel overland
through Ireland. Enquiring for a postchaise, we were
informed that there was a postchaise, but that some miles
of the road were as yet unfinished, and consequently not
carriageable. Upon this we dropped down to the village
bearing the name of the bay. Here having learned that
the road was perfectly good, we landed our baggage and
went ashore ; but now to our great dismay we found that
this village had no postchaise. In this dilemma we
decided to place our baggage on pack-saddles and to travel
as in Spain. The operation of packing had commenced,
when looking into the courtyard I discovered a hearse.
Upon enquiry the waiter said : " Please, your honour, it is
an ould lady who died here lately, and her friends thought
they would bury her proudly ; so they sent to Cork for
the hearse and it is going back to-day to Bandon." I
sent for the driver and immediately concluded a bargain ;
he engaged to carry us to Bandon in the hearse ; and thence

we were to have two postchaises to take us to Cork for
a sum agreed upon. The pack-saddling was relinquished ;
and the whole party, consisting of Captain Taylor, 28th,
with a broken thigh, Captain Girlston, 31st, a broken arm,
Captains Bryan and Cone, 39th, sick leaves, and Captain
Blakeney, 36th, a broken leg, entered the hearse. Our
first stage was Dunmanway, where we made a tremendous
meal ; the innkeeper complimented us by saying that he
never saw travellers in a hearse make so hearty a breakfast. Our appearance must have been extraordinary ; for
as we moved along in the carriage of death, but not with
its usual pace, the country folk, abandoning their legitimate
avocations, ran after us for miles.

On our arrival at Bandon thousands of the inhabitants
followed and impeded our way. I recollect that a regiment
of militia quartered there ran like others to see the novel
show, when hundreds of the runabout crowd cried out to
them : " Get ye out of the way ! What have ye to do with
the honours of war ? Look there ! " and they pointed to
our crutches, which stuck out from the open hearse in
all directions, like escutcheons emblasoning the vehicle
of death. At length we got safe to our inn, attended as
numerously as if the hero of the Peninsula himself had
been present. Here I called upon a lady who lived close
to our inn—a Mrs. Clarke. She had two sons in the army,
with both of whom I was intimately acquainted, particularly
the eldest ; he was a brother officer of mine in the 28th
Regiment and was afterwards removed to the 5th Regiment,
in which he lost a leg. To him we are indebted for that
valuable publication, *The United Service Journal.* The
other I knew in the 77th Regiment ; he also had been
severely wounded in the leg, so that the lady had seen both
her sons on crutches. When she saw the rough crutches

which I carried, or rather which carried me, she offered me a pair more highly finished, belonging to one of her sons ; but since mine were made of the halberts of two sergeants who lost their lives charging into the redoubt under which I fell, I declined the lady's very polite offer.

Next morning we set out for Cork ; and being actually enclosed within postchaises we contrived to screen our honours of war from public notice and therefore were not cheered to our hotel. At Cork the party separated, each making his way to England as best he could. On my arrival in London, I waited on Sir Henry Torrens, military secretary to His Royal Highness the Commander-in-chief. I mentioned to the secretary my intention of memorialising the Duke of York for promotion by brevet, in consideration of my voluntary services and severe wounds received whilst so serving. Sir Henry after hearing my statement said that I was perfectly right, but at the same time advised me to procure testimonials of my services from my different commanding officers in support of my memorial. With this advice I willingly complied, conscious of my having on every occasion endeavoured to perform my duties to the fullest extent of my abilities. After such encouragement from so high an authority as the Commander-in-chief's secretary and firmly relying on the nature of the testimonials which I should receive, I considered my promotion certain. I immediately wrote to Colonel Cross, commanding 28th Regiment at Fermoy, and to Colonel Browne (late 28th), commanding 56th Regiment at Sheerness. With their replies and a memorial to His Royal Highness, I waited on the secretary ; but on presenting them, he, without even opening them, said : " Recollect, Captain Blakeney, that I did not promise you promotion. I cannot give away majorities." I replied that I did not apply for a majority ;

I only asked for the rank by brevet, which was throughout the army considered as a reward for meritorious officers when regimental promotion might be attended with difficulty. I received no answer. Chagrined and disappointed because, when the secretary had told me that I was right in making a memorial and had advised me to get my commanding officer's testimonials, he now opposed that memorial before he even submitted it to the Commander-in-chief, I retired with strong impressions, which I now decline to state. In a short time I received an answer to my memorial stating that I could not at the present moment be promoted by brevet, but that I should get a majority when a favourable opportunity offered. Unbounded confidence was not inspired by this promise from the Horse Guards, particularly after what had passed on the subject. How far this diffidence was justified may be seen in the sequel.

The above statement may appear extraordinary; but between the time of my first interview with Sir Henry Torrens and the arrival of those testimonials from my various commanding officers, which the secretary had suggested, the star of Napoleon had begun to set. His abdication soon followed ; war was no longer contemplated ; and the claims of officers, of whatever nature, were abandoned to a heartless neglect.

CHAPTER XXIX.

A FTER remaining in London at a heavy expense while
I awaited the answers of my commanding officers
and the result of my memorial, I left town and joined the
2nd Battalion of the regiment, then quartered at Lewes.
Here I remained for some time ; and then being still on
sick, or rather wounded, leave, I visited my old acquaintance,
the Prince d'Arenberg, from whom I had received repeated
and pressing invitations. Arriving in Brussels, I found
that unfortunately he was then in Italy. When I was
rather weary of Brussels but unwilling so soon to go
back to England, especially as the prince was shortly
expected to return, some particular friends, Sir John
Burke of Glenesk, Sir William Elliot and Lord Bury,
aide-de-camp to the Prince of Orange, determined on an
excursion to Paris, and I was prevailed upon to accompany them. We travelled in Burke's private carriage.
The early part of our journey was excessively agreeable ;
but on drawing near the capital we encountered an extraordinary number of vehicles of every description and on
approaching a small town within a post or two of Paris
towards dark, we met a train of from thirty to forty carriages.
Upon asking the cause of this great concourse, a Mrs.
Atchison, whom with her two amiable daughters we had
known at Brussels, exclaimed from one of the carriages,

" What, are you not aware that Napoleon will be in Paris to-morrow ? " and she added that every British subject there was hastening away as fast as post-horses could be procured, which was attended with much difficulty and delay. Thunderstruck at this information, for not a word even of Napoleon's escape from Elba was known two days before at Brussels, we immediately stopped ; and as soon as we could procure change of horses we proceeded to Cambray. Here the party separated : Mrs. and the Misses Atchison escorted by the two baronets leisurely proceeded to Brussels ; Lord Bury and I shaped our course with all speed for Ostend, on our way to England. We were detained at Cambray until towards dark by the difficulty of procuring post-horses ; but just as we were about to set forward, a French officer carrying, as he stated, despatches of utmost importance, galloped into the yard, his steed covered with foam. He immediately demanded a horse, and the authority which he carried left the postmaster no choice ; he immediately provided one. I asked the officer a few questions as to the sentiments entertained in the capital and of the nature of his despatches, but I could procure no direct reply. As I was getting into Lord Bury's cabriolet, with his lordship and his private servant, I chanced to mention that our route lay through Lisle, when the man of despatch at length opened his mouth, saying that he also was bound for Lisle, and that if we would take him into our carriage and let the servant ride his horse, he would engage to pass us through the different enclosed towns which lay in our route, at which without his intervention we should be detained if arriving after dark. This proposal was made in consequence of the inclemency of the weather, which was tremendous, incessant heavy rain, accompanied with high winds,

thunder and awful lightning. Though Bury felt reluctant
to expose his servant to the raging elements, yet our great
anxiety to get clear of the French territory overcame every
other consideration.

During our progress I asked our new companion many
questions, but he would appear much fatigued and slept, or
feigned to sleep, the greater part of the time ; however,
he kept his word in passing us through the towns. On
presenting his credentials the drawbridges were dropped,
we entered, changed horses and passed on without our
passports being looked at until we arrived at Lisle. Here
our companion left us with scant ceremony. Being no
longer under the protection of the man of despatch and
having arrived after dark, we were not permitted to leave
the fortress until morning. We afterwards learned that
this officer, who sat so very comfortably in Lord Bury's
carriage between two British officers, was at the time the
bearer of disaffected despatches to induce the two Generals
Lallemande to declare in favour of Napoleon.

Our night at Lisle was restless ; but fortunately we got
off next morning without meeting any obstruction, and
having soon entered the Belgian territory felt a degree of
security which previously we considered very doubtful.
Our feelings somewhat resembled those experienced by
the Prince d'Arenberg after crossing the Spanish frontier
into Portugal.

Although now freed from dread of detention, yet we
relaxed not in posting forward to Ostend. On arrival Lord
Bury waited on General Vandeleur, commanding the British
troops there, and related the circumstances attending our
journey. The general was excessively astonished and
appeared somewhat startled, not having had the slightest
knowledge of Napoleon having left his island ; indeed he

seemed rather incredulous. Bury requested that I should
be sent for to the hotel, where I was making hasty preparations for our departure to England. On appearing, I
confirmed Lord Bury's statement, adding that from all I
could collect along our route, or rather flight, I felt
perfectly convinced that Napoleon was at that moment in
Paris. Courtesy, and I believe courtesy alone, induced the
general no longer to appear incredulous. At the same
time he begged us to be very cautious as to what we
should say, for if what we had heard were true he would
find himself in rather an embarrassing position among
the Belgians, who seemed much inclined towards the
government and person of Napoleon.

Being politely dismissed by the general we proceeded
to England, and landing at Ramsgate pushed forward to
Canterbury. Here we halted for breakfast, when hundreds
collected round the hotel since a report was spread that the
Duc de Berri had just arrived from France, whom they
were anxious to behold ; but upon learning that it was the
English Lord Bury, not His Royal Highness the French
Duc de Berri who had arrived, they retired rather disappointed. That night we arrived in London, but not a
soul would give credence to our account ; and Napoleon
was victoriously sitting on the throne of France and in the
heart of the capital some days before even his departure
from Elba was known in London.

Immediately on my return I applied to Sir Henry
Torrens for a staff appointment in the army of Belgium ;
and I asked that, should His Royal Highness not have
an opportunity of appointing me at present, he would be
pleased to permit my proceeding there, as from my acquaintance with many general officers under whom I had had the
honour of serving, I felt emboldened to think that I should

be employed. This letter was written to Sir Henry Torrens at his own request ; but as he was a few days afterwards sent to Brussels to confer with the Duke of Wellington, I repeated my request to Lieutenant-Colonel Shaw, Military Secretary *ad interim*. To this application I received an answer to the effect that the commander-in-chief was sensible of my zeal for active service, but had no present opportunity of employing me on the staff, nor could he comply with my request for leave of absence. It may be necessary here to state that at that period a general order had been issued strictly prohibiting all officers on leave of absence from leaving the kingdom without the special permission of the commander-in-chief. My leave of absence which terminated on the 24th of the month was renewed as a matter of course, but not without the pro- hibition mentioned.

My regiment being in Ireland and not ordered to the Netherlands, I still remained in London urging my request, but to no purpose. In the meantime the battle of Waterloo was fought ; and the 36th were ordered to reinforce the duke's army. I now procured permission to proceed direct from London. Major-General Sir William O'Callaghan was ordered out at the same time ; and as we had been intimately acquainted in the Peninsula, I now acted as his aide-de-camp. In this way I anticipated the arrival of the regiment in Paris by at least a month, which gave me full opportunity, uninterrupted by regimental duties, of examining the discipline, dress and movements of the different armies then in Paris, particularly as they passed in review order.

This review was a splendid spectacle. Each crowned head of the powers engaged had nominally a regiment in the army of each brother sovereign ; and each in his turn

marched past as colonel of his regiment, saluting with due
military discipline the crowned head to whose army the
regiment belonged. The Emperor Alexander wore his
cocked hat square to the front, kept firm on his head by
a black ribbon tied under his chin. When he saluted in
marching past his chosen master, he shot his right arm
at full length horizontally from his right shoulder, and
then curving the arm with tolerable grace to the front
he touched the upper part of his forehead with his hand,
the fingers closed together and the palm turned downwards.
His appearance was soldier-like ; yet he seemed not a hardy
veteran, but rather a good-humoured, well-conditioned
English yeoman than the representative of Peter the Great.
Contentment, apparently uninterrupted by thought or reflection, seemed to sit on his unruffled brow. The King of
Prussia wore his hat fore and aft. In saluting he sent
his right hand perpendicularly upwards, the palm turned
towards his face, his fingers stiff and their tips brought
suddenly against the point of his hat. Sullenness was
portrayed on his countenance. His figure was tall ; but
I saw nothing lofty about him save his station, which, had
it not been hereditary, would never have been his. He
was what we call in a horse wall-eyed. Nothing indicated
the determined warrior, polished courtier or profound
statesman ; and during the whole time in which I presumed
to regard him I do not recollect that a single thought of
the Great Frederick flashed on my mind. The Emperor
Francis wore his hat neither square nor fore and aft ; the
right cock was brought rather forward. In saluting, his
right arm was slowly brought up to meet the fore part of
his hat, to touch which his fingers were bent into a bunch.
His stature was scarcely above the middle size, his face
melancholy and overcast ; it did not appear to be that

sullen melancholy which indicates disappointed ambition
—it seemed rather to be produced by painful recollections of happy scenes and feelings which, like blooming
youth gone by, can never return. His deportment was
that of an over-thoughtful, but an affable gentleman ;
dejection he combated, but could not shake off; he would
appear happy, but failed in the endeavour. His former
deadly foe and conqueror (a fortunate revolutionist emerged
from obscurity) was now united to the child of his affections, the descendant of the Cæsars. The overthrow of
the one must drag down the other. Unwillingly then
he drew his sword, for whatever he might have previously
suffered he now made war against his daughter and her
husband. These conflicting feelings must have harassed
his very soul ; his position was cruelly embarrassing ;
and it was impossible to witness his distress and not
participate in his feelings. His appearance throughout
proclaimed him an unwilling actor in the gorgeous show.
He alone seemed to reflect that players sometimes act the
part of kings, but that here the farce was reversed.

It struck me as rather singular and wanting in delicacy
that every band of music in the Austrian, Russian and
Prussian armies, while they marched past the group of
kings, played the tune by us called *The Downfall of Paris* ;
but I subsequently learned that among the nations mentioned,
as also in France, the music bore a quite different name
and meaning.

During these reviews the troops of the foreign nations
marched from Paris through the Place Louis Quinze ; and
passing through the Champs Elysées filed off into the
suburbs. The last review, or rather march past, was by
the British troops. The line of route was now reversed.
Our troops, proudly following the tattered flags but upright

standards of Britain, debouched from the Champs Elysées, and after marching past filed through Paris. The music played at the head of every regiment was the inspiring tune "The British Grenadiers." The duke took his station close to the Place Louis Quinze, towards the entrance from the Champs Elysées. He was dressed in the uniform of a British field-marshal ; he grasped a mamaluke sabre, the hand which held it resting on the pommel of his saddle. In this position he remained for some hours during the marching past of the troops ; and although he evidently saw all, yet he moved not at all ; and during the whole time (for I was near) even his sword moved not an inch from its original position. All the working was in his mind ; his body was absolutely still.

As the British troops moved forward they called forth general admiration; and, candidly speaking, their appearance was splendid in the extreme. This opinion is not prompted by either partiality or prejudice ; but having had the opportunity of previously beholding the parade of the allied troops, all showing stage effect rather than the free use of the limbs, I could not avoid noticing the contrast between them and the British soldiers, whose movements were in strict conformity with the intention of Providence in providing joints to be freely used for the easy carriage of the body. It was this manly, free and firm step which induced the Emperor Alexander after the reviews were over to declare that he would introduce the British discipline and system of drill into his army, since the English movements were more in conformity with the natural structure of man. Even the dress of the British soldier was calculated more for comfort and use than for mere outward appearance, and yet was far from being unseemly.

The Russian troops appeared like rampant bears ; the

Prussians like stuffed turkeys ; the slow-going Austrians
were in figure, countenance and appearance altogether
characteristically Germanic ; the French, from their being
well inured to fire and moving with such little up-and-
down steps making but little progress to the front, brought
to mind that species of animal called turnspit in the active
performance of his duty.   But the object of general regard,
and that which attracted the attention of all, was the hero
who led the British troops through an unparalleled series
of brilliant campaigns and victorious battles.   The all-
seeing eagle eye which illumined his countenance, the
aquiline nose which stamps talent on the countenance of
man, together with the peculiar length of upper lip, marked
him apart.   In all he seemed the Roman of old—save
in pomp.

Shortly after the reviews the 36th Regiment arrived
in Paris, and on the same day Sir William O'Callaghan's
aide-de-camp, his nephew, Captain Colthurst, made his
appearance.   The general being thus provided, I joined
my regiment.   We were quartered at Montmartre, the
theatre of Marmont's fidelity.   Subsequently we encamped
in the Bois de Boulogne ; thence we moved into cantonments
not far distant from Versailles.   A part of the regiment were
quartered in the Chateau of the Postmaster-General of
France.   His history so far as it relates to his attachment
to Napoleon, his imprisonment and the mode of his escape
aided by a British general officer lately reinstated in rank,
is already well known.

Towards the close of December 1815 the regiment was
ordered home.   We passed through Paris on the day that
Marshal Ney was shot ; whether our presence there during
that melancholy occasion was accidental or designed I
cannot say, but it was probably designed.   His death was

worthy of his former undaunted character, which gained
him the title of "Le brave des braves." Disdaining to
have his eyes bandaged he commanded the soldiers
appointed for his execution to fire ; and shedding bitter
tears they obeyed his order, by which France was deprived
of the bravest and brightest genius who ever led her armies
to victory. On the second restoration of Louis XVIII. a
general pardon was granted by proclamation in his name
to all French subjects then residing in Paris ; but by a
strange construction of words it was argued that Ney was
not included, although at the time he did reside in Paris,
if a soldier be considered as ever residing anywhere.

Soult, although he fought in the ranks of Napoleon at
Waterloo, yet made so noble a defence that the Duc de
Richelieu durst not push the prosecution ; yet His Grace
declared that it would be an abuse of mercy to pardon Ney.
He was found guilty of high treason, upon which verdict
he was executed. But against whom or what was the
treason ? Not against France, in whose defence or for
whose aggrandisement he fought five hundred battles, and
never drew his sword against her. His treason then
consisted in his unfortunate choice of allegiance between
two individuals : one, the Emperor selected by the French
nation and under whose standard all the armies of France
were ranged ; the other a king indeed but a nominal one,
a king who fled his country on the approach of a foreign
invader, as Napoleon actually was on coming from the
Island of Elba. This king too was opposed by the nation
upon whom he was foisted, as he himself gratefully but
imprudently proclaimed by declaring that next to God
he owed his crown to the Prince Regent of England. This
insult to his countrymen was deeply felt all through France,
and cannot be more forcibly expressed than by the manner

in which the French at the time proclaimed him as " Louis XVIII., King of France and Navarre, by the grace of three hundred thousand foreign bayonets."   As traitor against this king, Ney was executed ; but, had he been spared, the monarch's crown would have been the brighter, and the bravest of the brave have been spared to his country.

In our route to Calais the detachment of the regiment to which I belonged passed through the village of Creçy, where we halted for a day.   Natural curiosity, not unmixed with national pride, induced some of us to visit the plains glorious to Edward III. and the Black Prince.   Our guide pointed out the little tower in which the victorious Edward is stated to have taken post during the battle ; it had all the appearance of having been a windmill.   The glorious days of the Edwards and Henrys flashed on our imaginations : days when the warlike monarchs led their gallant troops in person and by their heroic example fired them to deeds of glory ; days when personal merit was promptly and impartially rewarded.   Rewards for gallant deeds of arms did not *then* depend upon a county election.   The chief who witnessed and who consequently could best judge possessed the power to reward without reference to the jarring interests of voters at home.

On surveying the extensive plain, our guide pointed out a mound, distant from the windmill about two miles.   Here it was, he said, that the French army made their last desperate effort.   A small chapel is built on the site, called " La Chapelle des Trois Cents Corps Nobles," to commemorate the fact that where the chapel stands three hundred nobles of the contending armies fighting fell.   On returning to our billets I signified to the man of the house my wish to visit the hallowed spot next morning, as it was then too late in the day.   Upon this our good host entertained us with many legendary tales of the chapel, and said amongst other things that the door could never be kept shut. My evident incredulity rather displeasing him, he protested most solemnly that bolts and locks had been repeatedly put on the door to endeavour to keep it shut, but to no purpose : it was always found wide open in the morning ; and as to watching it, none could be found sufficiently daring to make the attempt. Notwithstanding the solemn assertions of our good host, I told him that I was determined to proceed to the chapel next morning and shut myself within its mysterious walls. When he had used many arguments to dissuade me from my purpose but found me still determined, he remarked that there was one difficulty in my shutting myself up there, since, in in consequence of the fact that the chapel could never be kept closed, it had been without a door for more than a century. Much disappointed, but still perceiving by the solemn manner of my host that his account of the chapel was not intended as a jest, I told him that I should certainly go there next morning and nail a blanket against the doorway, to witness the consequence of closing the chapel ; and this foolish act I was determined to carry into execution, but as we received orders that night to continue our march at daybreak next morning, my quixotic enterprise was frustrated. The impossibility of closing the chapel was religiously believed by every inhabitant of the place, not excluding the parish priest.

We embarked at Calais and descended at Ramsgate and Dover, and thence proceeded overland to Portsmouth, which we garrisoned until the year 1817, when we embarked for the Island of Malta.

CHAPTER XXX.

AT BRUSSELS WITH DUKE D'ARENBERG.

IN 1819 I procured leave of absence to proceed to England; and in this year I repeated my visit to Brussels. I found Prince Prosper at home and received the most marked attention from the old duke, his father. Here it may not be irrelevant to mention that Napoleon, as contributing to fortify his unwieldy empire, insisted on the Prince Prosper marrying a Miss Tacher, a niece of Josephine, and transferred to him his father's title, Duke d'Arenberg, at the same time by a similar arbitrary act compelling the old unduked duke to assume the title of a baron of the French empire. This was one of Napoleon's master strokes of policy. Prince Prosper was now married to his second wife having been previously divorced from his first duchess, Miss Tacher that was, to whom the mustachios had been sent from Lisbon.

At the old duke's table I had always a cover; and a groom and a pair of horses were exclusively at my service. The duke was a remarkably fine old man, but had been blind for many years when I had the honour of making his acquaintance. The calamity occurred through the following lamentable circumstance. At his father's house, celebrated for hospitality, a large party of friends were entertained, for whose greater amusement rural sports were resorted

to. The wild-boar hunt was generally selected, .in which
the duke, then a young man, took great delight; but as
one of the guests, who was *chargé d'affaires* of the British
Court, expressed an unwillingness to join in the boar hunt,
preferring partridge-shooting, the young duke in courtesy
gave up his favourite amusement and joined his friend,
for whom he entertained the greatest esteem. All being
arranged, the parties set forth, and on their arrival at
Enghien, a considerable estate belonging to the duke about
five-and-twenty miles from Brussels, the sport began. The
duke took his station behind a hedge ; and his English
friend screened himself behind a neighbouring fence. The
cover being very close, beaters were sent in to drive out
the birds, as in woodcock-shooting in England. A rustling
sound being heard by the Englishman, who had the boar
hunt, which took place in the same parts, still in his mind,
he fired through the fence and lodged the contents of
his gun in the face of his friend. At a cry of distress from
the duke, the Englishman broke his way through the
fence, when fancy his horror at perceiving his dear friend
prostrate on the ground, his figure recognised, but all
his features disguised by blood and his eyes incapable of
seeing his agonised friend. Nearly frantic at witnessing
the dreadful result of his incautious fire, he holloaed out
for assistance ; and on the arrival of some domestics he
instantly ran into the town of Enghien, and ordering a
postchaise drove off to Brussels, nor stopped he, except
to change horses, until he arrived at Ostend, where he
instantly embarked for England, never again to return
to the Netherlands. The two faithful friends never more
beheld each other, one because he was blind, the other on
account of a horror which he could never overcome. The
duke was carried to Brussels and the first medical aid

which the Netherlands could produce immediately consulted. The most eminent physicians and surgeons of France and England were sent for, but to no purpose—the vision was for ever destroyed.

During my visit at Brussels, by the duke's desire, I passed a few days at Enghien. Being alone, I was entertained by an old family steward, who always resided there. The family mansion having been burnt, its place was supplied by two handsome pavilions. The old domestic, who had been previously advised of my visit, was the most respectable person for his station whom I over met; in truth, he appeared a perfect gentleman of the old school, as well in dress as in address. Nearly seventy chill winters must have passed over his head, but although those rigid seasons left many a rough stamp behind, his sympathy and warm heart gave ample testimony that an equal number of genial summers had done their part. His white hair was bound with black ribbons and formed a massy queue, extending some way down his shoulders; yet, silvered as were his venerable locks, he was highly powdered too,—this always gives a peculiarly dressy appearance. His coat was of the old-fashioned cut, sloping backwards from the lower part of the breast to the extremity of the skirts and bearing large steel buttons. His waistcoat was of a similar cut, having long low-flapped pockets, below which were short velvet breeches, black silk stockings and polished shoes with large silver buckles. To be attended by such a personage during dinner distressed me very much. I should have felt more easy if in place of serving he had sat down and borne me company; this I proposed, but no remonstrance of mine could prevail upon him to acquiesce. He remarked that he could never so far forget his duty and respect as to sit at the same table with his lord's guest, and moreover that I should be without the attendance which he had received orders to give. I then proposed that the young lad who always rode after me should wait. To this he objected, unless I ordered it, which I declined to do, perceiving by a half-muttered expression that it would be indecorous to introduce a stable groom into the dining-room. After dinner, which I hurried over, I insisted on his placing a second wineglass and obliged him to sit down, stating that there were many circumstances relative to his lord with which I wished to become acquainted, and for which I had the duke's authority. This he considered as a mandate and sat down ; yet such was the distance at which he placed his chair from the table that he imposed upon himself the obligation of standing up whenever I prevailed upon him to take his glass of the good wine, which I had always to pour out for him.

During my stay at Enghien this respectable gentleman-butler related many anecdotes of gallant deeds performed by the Dukes d'Arenberg, but as was natural dwelt most upon those scenes which took place in his own time. Next morning he conducted me to the spot where the fatal accident deprived his lord of sight. The old man was of the shooting party ; and with tears in his eyes he described the whole scene most minutely and pathetically. Having seen all the grounds, I returned to the pavilion ; but on that day too I could not prevail on the old man to sit down to dinner, and finding him inflexible and being hurt at seeing so old and so respectable a person on his legs whilst I sat at dinner, I determined to depart next morning. On coming away I cordially shook the good old man by the hand, and would most willingly have made some donation, but I could not presume to offer him money, knowing how much it would hurt him; I should as soon have offered such an affront to the duke.

When I returned to Brussels the good old duke asked me with the greatest coolness if I had seen the spot where he was deprived of sight. He seemed to treat the circumstance with perfect indifference ; but he evidently felt great emotion whenever the name of his unhappy friend was mentioned, and I repeatedly heard him say, "My poor friend ! he suffers more than I do." Some years after the accident took place the duke visited England, and calling upon his friend, who happened to be out, left his name and address. When the other returned and saw the duke's card, he instantly ordered post-horses and departed for Italy, not being able to summon fortitude sufficient to encounter that friend whom he so highly prized. The duke suffered much by this disappointment ; for although deprived of the power of seeing him, still it would have afforded him the greatest consolation to press to his bosom the friend whom he now more than ever esteemed. Not long after the duke travelled into Italy, where he was doomed to experience a similar disappointment. Happening to visit the same town in which his friend was living for a time, he paid him a visit, but not finding him at home did not leave his card, as he hoped to meet him another time ; but when the friend returned and heard from his servant a description of the caller, he instantly set out for England. They never met after the sad accident ; and they both departed this life nearly at the same moment.

During the duke's sojourn in England he ordered a machine to be made entirely imagined by himself, which in his lamentable state enabled him to play at whist, a game to which he was very partial and which afterwards

principally contributed to his amusement. It was a small
mahogany box about eighteen inches long, six inches deep,
and the same in breadth ; it screwed under the leaf of
the table in front of where the duke sat to play ; in its
side were four rows or little channels, and in each channel
were thirteen holes corresponding with the number of cards
in each suit ; in each of these holes was a movable peg,
which could be pushed in or pulled out. The pack being
dealt out, a page, who sat close to the duke, sorted his
cards, placing them in suits and in order of value from
left to right, each suit being separated from the others
by the duke's fingers, between which they were placed
by the page. Beginning from the left with spades, hearts,
diamonds and clubs in order, the peg corresponding with
each card in the duke's hand was drawn out, so that the
duke passing his fingers over the machine learned each
card in his hand by means of the corresponding peg.
Each of the other players named the card which he played.
For instance, the person sitting on the left of the duke said,
" I play the seven of hearts " ; the next, " I play the ten " ;
the third, " I play the queen," when the duke exclaimed,
" And I play the king," and infallibly down came the
king. I never saw him make a mistake. When he had
played a card he pushed in the peg corresponding to that
card. On one occasion having had the honour of being
his partner against the Marquis de Grimelle and another,
I won a napoleon, which I bored and kept in memory of
having won it with a partner totally deprived of sight.
The duke was much pleased at my doing so.

The duke entertained in princely style. His table
displayed the choicest viands, the rarest productions of
the seasons and the most exquisite wines. I remarked
that on fast-days there was a particular kind of white soup

always placed before the abbé who was attached to the family. Curiosity induced me to ask Prince Prosper, next to whom I always sat, of what this select soup consisted. The prince replied in a suppressed tone of voice that it was extracted from frogs; "For," said he, "the Church has decided that those animals are not to be considered as flesh : but yet, since the soup thus produced is not sufficiently rich, a couple of pounds of veal are added ; and although he is fully aware of the deception practised, the abbé is so good a person that he pardons the cook and absolves him from all sin."

My leave of absence allowing me to remain no longer at Brussels, I returned to England. At parting, the good, the truly noble old duke presented me with a letter of introduction recommending me to the protection of H.R.H. the Duke of Kent; and although, as I have stated, he had been blind for many years, yet I saw him write the concluding one or two lines and subscribe his name to this letter.

On my arrival in London, finding that the Duke of Kent was then at Sidmouth, I presumed to write to him, enclosing Duke d'Arenberg's letter. In my letter to His Royal Highness I gave a short summary of my services, at the same time stating that an introductory letter from so humble an individual as myself to a personage of such exalted rank could have no other object than that of soliciting His Royal Highness's protection in forwarding my military promotion. By return of post I was honoured with the following reply :

"SIDMOUTH, *January 8th*, 1820.

"The Duke of Kent was favoured last night with Captain Blakeney's letter of the 6th instant, including one from his esteemed and illustrious friend the Duke d'Arenberg, and he feels anxious not to lose a moment in assuring Captain Blakeney that if he possessed the means or influence necessary to expedite his promotion they should *instantly* be exerted to the *utmost* in his behalf both from the friendship and esteem he bears the good duke through whom he has been introduced to him, and from conceiving Captain Blakeney's statement of his services to warrant his friendly interference in his behalf; but the fact is that the duke cannot interfere with any point regarding army promotion beyond the limits of his own corps, the Royal Scots, in which, from the circumstance of its having been during the whole war double the strength of any other regiment, there are too many claimants upon him for long and faithful services for it to be in his power to hold out the slightest expectation to Captain Blakeney of being able to bring him into that corps. This he can assure the captain is a matter of real regret to him, and he trusts when he says so that Captain Blakeney will give him credit for his sincerity. In concluding this letter, the duke feels it an act of justice to the good Duke d'Arenberg to observe that it is impossible for any gentleman to plead more warmly the cause of another than His Serene Highness has that of Captain Blakeney, or to state more strongly the obligations he owes him for his liberal and friendly conduct towards the Prince Prosper whilst that nobleman was a prisoner of war under his charge. If Captain Blakeney should happen to be in town when the duke returns to Kensington, which will probably be the end of March or beginning of April, the duke will have great pleasure in receiving him and in explaining the matter more fully to him *viva voce* than it is possible for him to do in a letter, however extended the length of it might be. Should Captain Blakeney have occasion to address the duke again previous to his arrival, he is requested to leave his letter at Messrs. Kirklands, No. 88, Bennet Street, St. James's.

"CAPTAIN BLAKENEY, 36*th Regiment.*"

I scarcely need say that such a letter as this from the son of my Sovereign was to me most highly flattering, and on it was founded the delusive expectation of presenting myself before His Royal Highness and verifying the statement of my services as advanced in my letter. I applied at the Horse Guards for copies of the different recommendations forwarded from time to time in my favour by general and other officers, as well as of those which accompanied my memorial presented to H.R.H. the Duke of York in 1814. These were very liberally given to me, and are as follows :

From the Right Honourable General Lord Lynedoch, G.C.B.

"Isla de Leon, *March 30th*, 1811.

"Sir,—I have the honour to state to you that I have just received a report from Lieutenant-Colonel Browne of the 28th Regiment, who commanded the flank battalion which so greatly distinguished itself in the action of the 5th instant (*i.e.*, at Barossa), of the eminent services of this officer. All the other officers of the regiment left wounded, and himself severely hurt by a contusion, he continued to animate and keep the men of those companies together during the hottest fire, giving the lieutenant-colonel the most essential assistance. As Lieutenant Blakeney is a lieutenant of July 1805, I trust this statement will be most favourably considered by the commander-in-chief, and that this officer will soon reap the reward of such distinguished conduct.

"I have the honour, etc., etc., etc.,

"Thomas Graham,

"*Lieutenant-General.*

"Colonel Torrens, *Military Secretary.*"

From the Honourable Colonel Abercrombie, C.B.

"Albuquerque, *November 20th*, 1811.

"Sir,—I have the honour to enclose to you herewith a memorial which has been transmitted to me by Lieutenant Blakeney belonging to the battalion under my command, and

23

which I request you will be good enough to forward to Major-General Howard.

" As far as I had an opportunity of judging of the merits of Lieutenant Blakeney, I have every reason to be well satisfied with him as an officer of great zeal and activity. His exertions at the battle of Barossa obtained him the approbation of Lieutenant-General Graham, by whom he was recommended to the commander-in-chief for promotion.

" His conduct also in the late action with the enemy at Arroyo de Molinos was very conspicuous, and did not, I believe, pass unnoticed by Lieutenant-General Hill.

" I have the honour to be, etc., etc., etc.,

" ALEXANDER ABERCROMBIE,
" *Lieutenant-Colonel* 28th *Regiment.*

" COLONEL WILSON, ETC., ETC., ETC., *commanding the Brigade.*"

FROM THE RIGHT HONOURABLE GENERAL LORD HILL, G.C.B.

" PORTALEGRE, *November* 24th, 1811.

" MY LORD,—I had an opportunity of witnessing Lieutenant Blakeney's zeal and gallantry at the head of the light infantry which formed the advance guard of General Howard's column at Arroyo de Molinos on the 28th ultimo. I have therefore much pleasure in forwarding and recommending his memorial herewith enclosed.

" I have the honour to be, etc., etc., etc.,

" R. HILL,
" *Lieutenant-General.*

" LORD FITZROY SOMERSET, *Military Secretary.*"

FROM LIEUTENANT-COLONEL BROWNE, C.B., *late* 28th *Regiment, commanding* 56th *Regiment.*

" SHEERNESS, *October* 4th, 1814.

" MY DEAR BLAKENEY,—I have to acknowledge yours of the 28th ultimo, and am happy to bear testimony to your gallant conduct as an officer whenever an opportunity offered, which was conspicuous in the battle of Barossa, so much so that it

was the cause of my recommending you to the protection of
Sir Thomas Graham. And believe me, my dear Blakeney, your
ever sincere friend,

"T. F. BROWNE.

"CAPTAIN BLAKENEY, 36th *Regiment.*"

FROM LIEUTENANT-COLONEL CROSS, C.B.

"KILKENNY, *August 23rd,* 1814.

"SIR,—Understanding that Captain Blakeney is about
memorialising His Royal Highness the Commander-in-chief
for the rank of major in the army, founding his claims on his
services and wounds, I have great pleasure in bearing testimony
to the fact of his having twice volunteered to serve with this
battalion in the Peninsula before he was effective; and that
upon every occasion after his joining that the regiment was in
fire his conduct was highly meritorious, and his gallantry when
it was the proud lot of the battalion to charge and carry the
enemy's redoubt on the heights of Andaya on November 10th
was most conspicuous; and on this occasion it was his great
misfortune to receive the severe wound under which he is still
suffering, and I accordingly with great respect presume to
recommend his case to the favourable consideration of His Royal
Highness the Commander-in-chief.

"I have the honour to be,

"WILLIAM CROSS,

"*Lieutenant-Colonel* 36th *Regiment.*

"MAJOR-GENERAL TORRENS, *Military Secretary.*"

FROM MAJOR-GENERAL SIR CHARLES BELSON, K.C.B.

"FERMOY BARRACKS, *August 22nd,* 1814.

"SIR,—Captain Blakeney of the 36th Regiment (late of the
28th Regiment) having written to me for testimonials of his
services whilst under my command, to be submitted to you, I
have the honour of stating that he entered into the 28th
Regiment very young, and that he served with it until March
1812 in the campaign under the late Sir John Moore, on that
retreat and at the battle of Corunna. He was in the light

company, and distinguished himself particularly at the Bridge of Betanzos. His conduct was also conspicuous at Arroyo de Molinos, and was noticed by Lieutenant-General Lord Hill upon that occasion. I beg to add that he is an officer who will put himself forward and distinguish himself whenever he may be employed, and to recommend him for such reward or promotion as His Royal Highness the Commander-in-chief may be pleased to grant.

> "I have the honour to be, etc., etc., etc.,
>
> "C. Belson,
> "Lieutenant-Colonel, *commanding* 28th *Regiment*
> "Major-General Torrens, *Military Secretary.*"

The above letter, which was enclosed to me, was accompanied with a note containing the following few words :

> "My dear Blakeney,—I hope the enclosed will answer your purpose (and in justice I could say no less) to promote your wishes. I have not time to say more.
>
> "Your friend,
> "C. Belson.

> "P.S.—The first troops that leave this country will be your old friends, the 28th."

The above strong testimonials I never had an opportunity of presenting to the illustrious personage for whose perusal they were intended. The Duke of Kent did not survive to return to the capital. His Royal Highness expired at Sidmouth, the place from which he did me the honour of writing the letter quoted, the last perhaps which he ever either penned or dictated. Thus in the general calamity which afflicted the nation by the death of His Royal Highness, I was in common with the whole of my fellow subjects doomed to mourn a great national loss ; and for myself deplored the untimely fate of a royal and generous prince, who would have extended his protection to me, as his letter, I think, clearly demonstrated.

In the early part of the year 1820 a partial brevet took place to reward meritorious officers, whose names through oversight had been passed over. I presented myself to H.R.H. the Duke of York, and asked to be included. His Royal Highness replied that the partial promotion contemplated was intended as a reward for services performed in the field. I took the liberty of remarking that it was for services performed in the field I applied for promotion, adding that I should not value promotion otherwise obtained. The duke then said that in mentioning services overlooked, allusion was made to those officers whose names were mentioned in despatches. In reply I felt emboldened to remark that, although my name was not mentioned in despatches, yet, besides other strong testimonials, I was strongly recommended for distinguished conduct in two different actions by the generals who respectively commanded in each, than whom the British Army cannot boast more brilliant military characters— Lords Hill and Lynedoch. His Royal Highness was pleased to make a pencil note, and bowed. I retired ; and of the import of that note I remain to this day ignorant, as I never had further communication on the subject.

During my interview with the Commander-in-chief I presented the Duke of Kent's letter, which was returned next day without comment. Against the presentation of this letter I was strongly advised ; but guided by my own sentiments and feelings, I would not be dissuaded. I considered that whatever difference of opinion might have subsisted between the illustrious personages, all unfriendly feelings would cease in the breast of the survivor. Yet, though I felt chagrin at the little notice taken of His Royal Highness's letter, I consoled myself a little with the thought that the infant Princess Victoria, coming in

nature's course to the throne, might perhaps be pleased
to take into consideration that which her royal sire had
expressed so much anxiety to promote. But the royal
brothers now lie side by side in peace, and so close that

"The vet'ran's sigh, to gallant York that's sent,
   Glides trembling o'er the breast of virtuous Kent";

and the time has gone by for vexing either with my
claims.

CHAPTER XXXI.

I MAKE MY BOW.

DISAPPOINTED in all my well-founded hopes, for such I thought them, I departed to rejoin my regiment at Malta. Landing at Calais, I proceeded to Paris and thence continued my route to Marseilles. On the day we arrived at Avignon, where a large garrison was stationed, it happened that the commandant dined at the *table d'hôte*. I sat opposite to him, conversing with a young Spanish nobleman attached to the Spanish Embassy at the British Court, who took this route to return to Spain. Having met him in the diligence, I had soon discovered him to be a Spaniard, and in his language our discourse was maintained. During dinner the Peninsular campaigns became the topic of general conversation, in which I joined with the commandant, whom I soon recognised as an old opponent. He did not recognise me. Nine years had elapsed since our last meeting; he saw me walking lame into the room ; and I was in mailcoach trim. Having with apparent carelessness asked him if he knew the Prince Prosper d'Arenberg, he answered in the affirmative, and that they were particular friends. He added that they were both taken prisoners in the same action. He then asked if I had been in Spain during the period of the campaigns. I said yes, when he remarked that perhaps I was in the Spanish Service. I told him

that then, as well as now, I served in the British army.
He asked if I were an Englishman ; and when I said
yes, he remarked in that complimentary strain peculiar to
well-bred Frenchmen, that one rarely meets an individual
speaking the languages of three different nations and with
such exactness as to pass for a native of each. The Spanish
attaché, not to be second in courtesy, attested the justice
of the assertion so far as it related to Spanish, declaring
that until that moment he took me for his countryman.
The commandant then broke into the Spanish language,
which, to say the truth, he spoke far from well ; nor did
I ever meet a Frenchman who could speak it without
causing a smile from his auditors. Continuing his broken
and ill-pronounced Spanish, at which the *attaché* smiled
and looked at me, the commandant said that he spoke
in that language because he had taken me for a Spaniard,
on which I replied that for a similar reason I spoke to
him in French. He instantly fixed his eye on my
countenance ; he was beginning to recognise me. He then
quickly asked me if I knew Lord Hill ; and where I first
became acquainted with Prince Prosper. I told him that
I had the honour of knowing his lordship, and that my
first acquaintance with the prince was at Arroyo Molinos
in Spain. His eyes now opened wide and with apparent
emotion he asked if he might take the liberty of asking
my name, which I had no sooner mentioned than, starting
from his chair and striding round to where I sat, to the
no small astonishment of all present, he embraced me
warmly, saying that he would not kiss me, for he had not
forgotten Lisbon. He now presented me to the whole
company, which was numerous, as the British officer who
made him prisoner, and whom he had so often mentioned
as a "grand petit diable." He went on to tell how he

was made prisoner; but this I decline to repeat, as it was rather too florid in description and too flattering to me. I will put it briefly and in plainer words.

It may be remembered that in the action of Arroyo Molinos, on October 28th, 1811, I jumped over the wall, through a breach in which the head of the French column had passed and the rest were following. Before my leap I had noticed a martial figure nobly mounted, evidently the chief of a corps, leading on the French 40th Regiment of the line. He was not more than five or six paces from the breach, while I was from ten to twelve yards from it. Perceiving that he must pass through before I could come up, wild with excitement and conscious also that the commanding general was looking on, I rode at the wall, and having cleared it instantly turned round to the breach into which Colonel Voirol had just entered and was passing through. We met face to face and instantly commenced a martial duet. We were both superbly mounted, but the rocky nature of the ground was such that our horses were totally unmanageable. We soon fell, or rather dragged each other to the ground, when, true to the immutable laws of nature, I as the lighter and more trivial remained uppermost. On falling, I must instantly have been forked to death by the many Frenchmen around me; but all were too intent on flight to look to others, and immediately after Voirol and I came to the ground the most advanced soldiers of the 28th and 34th Light Companies charged through the opening in the wall, as I have before described. General Howard (now Lord Howard of Effingham) coming up, I said, "General, here is a colonel for you; take him in charge. I cannot stop; I must go on with the light bobs." In the encounter I had received a blow on the head, which knocked off my cap and set it rolling down the rocks. I pushed on bareheaded till I picked up a French foraging cap. After we returned in the evening from the pursuit of the fugitives, I found both my horse and cap. This was the scuffle which I mentioned in describing the battle ; and I now detail the circumstances, because my captive now supported my story, which critics might pronounce absurd, of an individual scuffling with a whole column.

The commandant, Colonel Voirol, was as fine, upright and soldierlike a person as could be seen, measuring upwards of six feet in height and proportionally well built in every respect. His antagonist of Arroyo Molinos, besides being of slight figure, was beneath the colonel in stature by some inches ; therefore it was perhaps that during his description of the manner in which he was made prisoner, he was scanned with dubious glance by all. The natives of France look with a very jealous eye upon any foreigner whose martial prowess is put in competition with that of the " Grande Nation Militaire." This feeling was still more apparent among the ladies, of whom there were many present ; for the women of France feel if possible more enthusiastic for military greatness than even the men ; and comparing battles with what they read of tournaments in romances, fancy that tall and robust figures must be invulnerable against any of slighter mould. But Voirol's gallantry was too well established in the French Army to suffer from the misconception of *table d'hôte* critics.

My gallant old friend cordially pressed me to remain with him for at least a few days ; but as I was travelling by diligence and my leave already expired, I felt compelled to decline his hospitality ; and I determined to depart after dinner, not having time even to visit the hallowed shrine where Petrarch mourned in pathetic numbers his incredible love for the wrinkled old wife of another. But poetry must have some object, real or ideal, in view to keep excitement continually on the stretch. The hour of departure being announced by the *conducteur*, the commandant accompanied me to the door of the diligence, and again cordially shaking hands I departed for Marseilles, where I embarked for that military hotbed, Malta.

Some time after my arrival I was visited by a most severe attack of ophthalmia. My right eye became more like a ball of fire than an organ of vision; the dreadful pain in my head entirely banished sleep for so long a period that I dread to mention it. I heard the clock of St. John's Church strike every hour and half hour, day and night, for a period of two months. I was bled, blistered and physicked to the last extremity, and bathed in warm baths until I often fainted from weakness; in addition to this, I had one hundred and ninety-five leeches applied inside and outside the eyelids. However, through a strong natural constitution I recovered; and by the unremitting care of Staff-surgeon Lindsay and Assistant Staff-surgeon Kennedy, who attended me, the ball of the eye was preserved, but its vision was lost. In consequence of this loss His Majesty was graciously pleased to grant me a pension.

In 1822 the regiment was removed to the Ionian Islands; having remained there until 1826 we were ordered home; and on arriving in England we moved into Lancashire. Soon after this the regiment was ordered to Ireland, and landed at Dublin, where we did garrison duty for some time.

At this time I was directed to appear before the General Medical Board, to have, as I supposed, the pension granted me for the loss of vision confirmed; but to my utter surprise it was discontinued, although the Medical Board,

as also the certificate of Doctor Guthrie, the medical
gentleman employed by Government in similar cases,
attested the loss of useful vision. Upon my waiting on
the Secretary of War, I was given to understand that the
Government had decided that no pensions should henceforth
be granted for the loss of limb or other injury, except
for actual wounds in the field. It is true that I had
received neither a bayonet wound nor musket-ball in the
eye; but as a proof of the correctness of Doctor Guthrie's
testimony, to this day (fourteen years since the injury took
place) I am obliged, to enable me to see clearly with the
left or sound eye, to close the defective one. But the
Secretary of War may have fallen into error in giving his
reasons for depriving me of the pension ; for persons were
indicated to me who continued to receive pensions for
injuries, though they were never wounded in their lives.
However, I would not quote names, lest in so doing, for
the purpose of strengthening my own claims, I might
endanger the interests of others.

The withdrawal of the pension disconcerted me much ;
for fully relying on the royal grant being as permanent
as the injury for which it was made, I had married a
Venetian lady of the famous family of Balbi. The
pension I had looked upon as some remuneration for my
long and arduous services.

Besides what I considered the injustice shown towards
me throughout, there were other considerations which
powerfully wrought on my feelings and rendered my position
extremely irksome. I mounted the castle guard in
Dublin as lieutenant in 1805 ; and now in 1828, after
three and twenty years, I mounted the same guard as
captain only. This was known and remarked by many
friends and acquaintances ; it was known too that in

the brilliant campaigns which took place in the interim
I had been present and serving in two distinguished corps ;
and I discovered, or fancied I discovered, something
bordering on doubt as to my military character in the
countenances of all who regarded me. To account for my
non-advancement, or remove the doubts consequently
entertained, was out of my power. Decorum prevented
my entering into detail of my own services. To speak
frankly, I was ashamed of my slender rank after such
a length of service ; yet in conscience I could not accuse
myself as the cause.

But my severest ordeal was yet to come ; and to support
this all my philosophy and long-tried patience were
insufficient. After remaining some time in Dublin the
regiment was ordered to Mullingar ; and here, as it would
appear, my second childhood commenced. I was compelled
to fall in with a squad composed of young officers, who
for the most part entered the Service many years after
H.R.H. the Commander-in-chief had noted my name for
a majority, and with soldiers who knew not yet how to
shoulder their firelocks. In this respectable company I
was condemned to be taught how to march—a branch
of military tuition from which I had considered myself
emancipated at least twenty years before. In this ordeal
I was chased through the barrack square by an ignorant
disciple of Euclid, commonly called a dress sergeant,
armed with a colossal pair of widely yawning compasses. This scrutiny of my steps after I had carried a
musket-ball in my leg for fourteen years ; after I had
marched as a boy in one of the most distinguished
regiments in the Service from Lisbon to Corunna, under
the best drill and strictest disciplinarian in the army, Sir
John Moore ; after I had crossed and re-crossed Spain

and Portugal in different directions without the mathematical precision of my paces having ever been found fault
with ;—after all this, and after twenty-four years' service,
to be brought up by a pair of compasses in the barrack
square of Mullingar was an indignity which I imagine
that human nature in its most subservient state could not,
nay, should not willingly submit to. Disgusted by this
Mullingar ordeal, which might be repeated again and again
for the good of the Service, I formed the determination
of immediately retiring from that Service. Add to this
contemptuous treatment of old officers the suppression of
the old-established institutions of the corps ; the celebration
of such martial *fêtes* as the anniversary of the battles of
Salamanca, Nivelle and Toulouse. Those were days upon
which it was the custom of the regiment that all the men
should wear the laurel, all the officers, whether married or
single, should dine at the mess-table and guests be invited,
thus giving an opportunity for those tales of war which
transmit a noble martial feeling into the glowing breast
of the aspiring young warrior who burns to prove the
temper of his steel. Sentiments such as these glowed in
the breasts of the young boys who joined the 28th Regiment
in 1803, 1804, and 1805, while with suppressed breathing
we rapturously listened to the old officers who lately
returned from Egypt told of the gallant feats of arms
they witnessed and shared, and so inspired us that our
heated imaginations pictured soldiers in fight as of more
than mortal size, and we longed "to follow to the field
some warlike chief" to lead the way to glory.

In the 28th Regiment the anniversaries of the battles
in which the corps had served were strictly observed as
days of jubilee and proud recollection. The month of
March in particular was one of revelry in commemorating

the battles fought in Egypt on the 8th, 13th and 21st. The
17th, the Feast of St. Patrick, was not forgotten; and to
these was subsequently added the 5th, the anniversary of
the celebrated battle of Barossa; so that in March we
had five days of celebration, which filled our hearts with
joy and on the following day our head with aches. The
inspiring war-cry, "Remember Egypt!" was after the
return from that country always used when leading into
action. The regiment may now use the names of many
other places wherein they fought and distinguished themselves; but I doubt if the mention of any subsequent
battle will act so powerfully on the minds of the men as
the soul-stirring words, "Remember Egypt!" and "The
backplates!"

Why this war against old officers and long-established
institutions? On the return of the victorious army from
the Peninsula and later from France, a crowd of Green
Park martinets rushed into the Service, who, looking upon
any distinction gained by others as a reflection on themselves, seemed to be stimulated by sentiments like those
of the Chinese emperor, who destroyed all existing records
in the hope that he might be considered as the first who
had reigned.

On the return of the regiment to Dublin, I, in pursuance
of my determination to retire, procured twelve months'
leave of absence to proceed to the Island of Corfu; but
previous to leaving England I made a last effort at the
Horse Guards. In an interview with Lord Hill, finding
there was no prospect of promotion, I took the liberty
of telling his lordship that it was not my intention ever
again to return to perform the duties of captain. His
lordship remarked that he did not see how that could
be, as officers on procuring leave of absence were required

to sign a declaration that they would neither exchange
nor resign before rejoining their regiments. I told his
lordship that I should find out a remedy; and on an
explanation being demanded, I said that I should forego
my year's leave and send in my resignation immediately.
Upon this, his lordship with that kindness and feeling
which endeared him to all, and which gained him the title
of "Our father" from every soldier in the 2nd Division
of Lord Wellington's army, a title more honourable than
all the well-earned brilliant stars which decorated his breast,
recommended me not to be too precipitate. I could not
avoid remarking that his lordship could hardly accuse me
of precipitancy when I had waited for promotion which
had been put off from time to time for fourteen years, and
at the expiration even of that extraordinary length of
time His Royal Highness's pledge still remained unredeemed.
Lord Hill declared that he could never pay the Duke of
York's legacies. I told his lordship that I resigned all
claim to the legacy, and rested my claims on their own
merits, upon which the General-in-chief desired me to
write to him, and he would see what he could do for me.
In consequence of this favourable omen I wrote to his
lordship, enclosing a copy of my memorial presented to
the Duke of York in 1814, together with the testimonials
which accompanied it. To this letter I received a renewal
of the old statement, that I was still noted for promotion
on a favourable opportunity; and so I became fully convinced of the truth that deep scars, fractured bones and the
strongest testimonials were of no avail unless bolstered
by other support. I hesitated no longer; and although
senior captain of my regiment I renounced my year's leave
of absence and immediately forwarded my resignation.

Thus the author of these Memoirs left the Army. He

served at the siege and capture of Copenhagen; he was
for twelve days in constant fight during Sir John Moore's
retreat to Corunna, and at the end of this campaign he
fought at the battle of Corunna in that division of the
army who drove the whole of the enemy's cavalry off
the field and turned his left wing ; he was for more than
twelve months at Tarifa continually engaged with the
enemy's |foraging detachments, and he was in both attacks
on the strong post of Casa Vieja ; he served in the
ever memorable battle of Barossa in that flank battalion
(to use the words of Lord Lynedoch) " which so greatly
distinguished itself in the action " ; he served in the
action of Arroyo Molinos, and he was present at the
siege and storming of Badajoz, where valour's self might
stand appalled ; he served through the Pyrenees as a
volunteer, where more continued hard fighting occurred
than elsewhere throughout the whole Peninsula campaigns,
and finally fought in the great battle of the Nivelle, in
which he had a leg shattered. Innumerable skirmishes in
which he was engaged and in which light companies are
so frequently employed need not be mentioned. Of his
conduct in these many actions the testimonials of commanding officers and colonels of regiments are a sufficient
witness. And yet after serving for a quarter of a century,
with feelings harassed by neglect and petty vexations, he
felt himself driven to retire, and that without the slightest
badge or mark of military service save those indelibly
imprinted by the searching weapons of the more considerate
foe. Whether he has been dealt with as might be expected
from a liberal, just and great nation is a question humbly
submitted to his Sovereign and his country.

INDEX.